DIES NON [NO WORK NO PAY] IN BANKING INDUSTRY

DIES NON [NO WORK NO PAY] IN BANKING INDUSTRY

C. Krishnamurthi

SERIALS PUBLICATIONS
NEW DELHI (INDIA)

First Published - 2009

ISBN: 978-81-8387-226-3

Published by

SERIALS PUBLICATIONS
4830/24, Prahlad Street, Ansari Road
Darya Ganj, New Delhi-110002 (India)
Phone : 23245225 Fax : 91-11-23272135
E-mail: serials@satyam.net.in

To

MY PARENTS

Contents

Justice
Prabha Sridevan

12-05-2008

Foreword

It is my privilege to write the foreword for this book, "Dies non in Banking Industry", by Mr. C. Krishnamurthi.

It is the outcome of a deep study of the complexities of industrial adjudication spanning several decades. Soon after independence, the Supreme Court gave the place of pride that social and economic justice deserve and the decisions of the Supreme Court and the High Court endeavour to adjust the rival claims of the employer and employees in a fair and a just manner.

I have gone through the book and I find that Mr. C. Krishnamurthi has quoted extensively from not only the important decision of the Supreme Court and High Court but also from the writers like Adam Smith, Huxley and others. The subject is dealt with under various headings, like Duties generally, Dies non, Strikes–justifiability, effects of strikes on contract of employment etc. Therefore, it helps the readers to immediately locate the point of law which the reader is looking for. I have no doubt that this book will be of great use to lawyers, Judges, academicians and also to the persons in the banking industry.

Mr. C. Krishnamurthi has traced the shift in judicial perspective echoing the contemporary socio-economic climate. Mr. C. Krishnamurthi has observed that while the question whether a strike is legal may be easy to answer, the question of justifiability which is purely judge made law is undergoing change and there is a fluidal process. He has also raised the question as to whether the associated issues like go-slows, work to rule warrant the application of *dies non* and that one should await future development in law to answer these questions.

When there is a discernible shift in the perspective of the industrial adjudicators, a book like this would definitely be of great use to maintain the fairness and justice is expected and to hold the balance equally between the workers and the Management.

I convey my best wishes to the writer and also wish that he would share his knowledge and practical experiences regarding labour management relations in banking industry, and there will be more books from his pen.

(Prabha Sridevan)

Preface

'No Work No Pay' was considered axiomatic amongst professional personnel men without taking into account the many intricacies and without considering the many situations in which the concept may come into play. All that it meant in the 1970 and 1980's was that if workmen struck work, the management will be entitled to deduct pro-rata wages for the period of the strike. Indeed in 1970 and 1971, dies non was a bold experiment. The union power was not only quite mature but was at its zenith as well in the banking industry and it was a bold management (or should we say the Chief Executive) who for the first time enforced the principle of no work no pay. It happened in the Union Bank Of India, Andra Bank and National and Grindlays Bank. From then on, one bank after the other enforced this dictum as and when the situation warranted.

The management actions were contested by the unions and employees and today we have a body of case laws on which to rely on and be guided by. To this body of knowledge often industries have also contributed in a large measure. This book attempts to bring these decisions and their implications with reference to the contract of employment in banking industry. This book will be useful for other industries as well, for every industry has its own parallel contract of employment.

C. Krishnamurthi

Preface

Acknowledgements

Acknowledging all those who influenced me in writing this book is indeed a difficult task. Soon after joining the Union Bank of India in 1971, I heard for the first time the then custodian Sri P. F. Gutta expounding on the concept of Dies Non in an Union-Management meeting. There was a 40 days strike and he enforced the principle of "no work no pay". He not only extended this principle to absence without leave but also to cases where on transfer employees refused to join duties in new place of posting. And then the 'icing on the cake' came. A union leader-a member of subordinate staff-refused to wear uniforms while on duty. The chairman consulted Sri R. Setlur of Crawford and Bayley and Company, solicitors, who counseler the chairman that the bank can apply the principle of dies non as the employee had not fulfilled his contract of employment. At about the same time, the Regional Director of National and Grindlays bank the late Sri Ken Warner and the late Sri Gopal Rao the Chairman of Andra Bank also enforced the principle of "no work no pay" against the striking employees. Indeed, in the face of union power at its zenith these Chief Executives of banks must have been very courageous in deciding to enforce the Dies Non principle. It was of strategic importance and deduction of wages for the strike period had the salutary effect of restoring parity in the collective bargaining process at individual bank's level and restraining employees from striking work at the slightest pretext. Enthused by the success, the Indian Bank Association issued an number of guidelines to banks on implementing the principle of "no work no pay". And sometimes in mid 1970 Sri C. Vijay the then Deputy Personnel Advisor of the Indian Banks Association authored a booklet (monogram) on the subject for the guidance of the industry. During the next 10 to 12 years the courts gave out a number of decisions on the subject which set the debate on "no work no pay" very contentious and emotional. In the mid 1980's the Late Sri M. N. Goipora the then Chairman Indian Bank Association issued directions at the industry level to modify slightly the implementation of the principle of "no work no pay" in as much as if any employee gave a letter to effect that he could not attend office because he was prevented by the striking employees in doing so, his wages were not to be deducted. The provocation for this decision was a complaint from the All India Bank Employee Association that their members due to fear of physical violence were in no position to attena office on days of strike called by the Bank Employees Federation of India even though the latter union was a minority union in Calcutta those days. Some personnel and legal experts, including the author, felt that that the decision of the apex body would water down the effect of 'no pay' principle and expressed it in as many words which was reported to have annoyed the Chairman of the Indian Banks Association. Be that as it may, the next major incident for me was to argue the principle of "no work no pay" before justice Khatri of the Central Government Industrial Tribunal, Bombay in a dispute regarding 100 days strike in ANZ Grindlays Bank. I did present the matter elaborately on behalf of the bank, the arguments lasting several days. Sri P. N. Subramanyan appeared for the employees. It is around that time while the preparing for the arguments that the desire to write a book on "Dies non in Banking Industry" arose. The actual writing itself had to wait for many more years due to paucity of time and other commitments. Now well into retired life, I found time enough to indulge in my pet subject. In this endeavor I cannot forget the help rendered by Sri R, Girees Kumar, Senior Manager, Industrial Relations Section, Canara Bank in updating me on the changes in special allowance attracting duties. My dear friend Ms. Feroza Sena of Union Bank of India was also of immense help.

My deep and heartfelt gratitude to Hon'ble Justice Smt. Prabha Sridevan who very kindly consented to write the forward. In fact not only did she write the forward but also suggested ways and means of making the book reader friendly. My grateful thanks to her. My indebtedness goes to Sri C. G. Anand, proprietor of MPP House, Law and General book supplier, publishers and distributors, for putting me in touch with the publishers of this book. Last but not the least.. Sri G. Somshekhar very willingly fed all the material to the computer and patiently went through the manuscript correcting mistakes. But for his help, the book would not have seen the light of the day.

C. Krishnamurthi

1

Dies Non-in Banking

Dies non or Dies non juridicus, according to Jowitts's dictionary of English law, means a day on which no legal business can be transacted, such as Sunday, Christmas day, Good Friday etc. In order to understand the term 'a day on which legal business can be done' it is necessary to understand the 'Business day'. The term Business day for the purpose of the English Bills of exchange Act, 1882 is any day other than:

(a) Saturday, Sunday, Good Friday, Christmas Day,

(b) a bank holiday,

(c) a day appointed by Royal Proclamation as a public fast or thanks-giving day,

(d) a day declared by order under section 2 of the Banking and Financial dealings Act,1971 to be a non-business day, is a business day[1]. In India, under the Negotiable Instruments Act,1881 the expression "Public Holiday" includes Sundays and any other day declared by the (Central Government) by notification in the official gazette, to be a public holiday. Thus, no Indian holiday can be public holiday, unless the Central Government declares it to be such in the official Gazette. The local governments do not have any power to declare a holiday under the Act. No other holiday is a public holiday for the purpose of the Act. Thus banks are expected to function on all days except when a holiday is declared under the Negotiable Instruments Act,1881.

In this back ground let us consider the word 'Dies non'. Dies non is said to mean as "no activity" in Oxford dictionary. Chambers 20th century dictionary states the word "dies" means "day". The Words "dies fasti" or "dies profesti" mean "days on which judgment could be pronounced, on which court could be held in ancient Rome or lawful days". "Dies "means "Lucky Day". "Dies non" is stated to mean "a day on which judges do not sit, or one on which normal business is not transacted "[2]"*Use of word dies non in settlement dated June 11,1992 therefore means that the said period is to be treated as without any business and therefore, non-existent by both i.e. employer and employees. Employees are therefore, not entitled to any remuneration for such period".*[3]

Notes

1. See Bills of Exchange Act, 1882-s.92; Banking and Financial Dealings Act, 1971-Sections 3(1),4(3),(4).
2. See All India Central Health Scheme Employee Association vs. Union of India, 2006, *I LLJ*, 798.
3. *Ibid.*

2

Bank-An Industry

Section 2(j) of the Industrial Dispute Act, 1947 defines the term "Industry". The definition of "Industry" has been subject-matter of review in series of cases by the Supreme Court and the matter is now finally decided by the Supreme Court in Bangalore Water Supply v. A Rajappa[1] where the court has held that 'Industry' as defined in Sec. 2(j) has a wide import. Where there is:

1. Systematic activity.
2. Organized by co-operation between employer and employee (the direct and substantial elements chimerical).
3. for the production and/or distribution of goods and service calculated to satisfy human wants and wishes (not spiritual or religious but inclusive of material things or services geared to celestial bliss, e.g. making, on a large scale, Prasad or food),prima facie, there is an 'industry' in that enterprise.

"Absence of profit motive or gainful objective is irrelevant, be the venture in public, joint, private or other sector. "The true focus is functional and the decisive test is the nature of the activity with special emphasis on the employer-employee relations. In the same judgment the concept of the expression "Industry" has undergone a revolutionary change. Industry has been put on a very wide canvas and those who contend that a particular establishment is not as industry should satisfy the court conclusively and indubitably that the said establishment falls outside the limits prescribed by the Supreme Court in the above decision. Though there are three separate judgments, the main judgment is by Justice Krishna Iyer. The sum and substance of the discussion, to put in one sentence, is that an establishment can be taken out of the pale of the industry only if it can be said to exercise sovereign or regal functions, or to use the expression of the learned Judge "Sovereign functions strictly understood". Simply because it is an establishment it cannot escape from the feature laid down by the Act. Establishments which even remotely engage themselves in economic adventure but which do not exercise solely sovereign and regal functions, have to fall within the expression "industry". Law of the land has thus been laid down by the judgment of the Supreme Court.

From the above decision, it is clear that the following criteria must be satisfied for any activity to fall within the definition of "Industry".

1. (a) There must be a systematic activity.
   (b) That activity must be organized by cooperation between the employer and employee.
   (c) It must be for the production of and/or distribution of goods and services for satisfying human wants and wishes.
2. Absence of profit motive is irrelevant
3. The activity mentioned at (1) above may be a venture by private, public or jointly by both or even by the government.
4. The true test is functional and what is decisive is the nature of activity. The emphasis here is on employer employee relations.
5. Even if philothrophy is behind running a trade or business, it will still be an industry.

The above decision of the Supreme Court came up for review[2] before that very court. The court, however, did not find any reason for reviewing the decision and hence, the decision of the Supreme Court in Bangalore Water Supply case holds the field.

In the above back ground if we were to analyze banking as an activity, one can say that it is nothing but a commercial activity and the primary motive is to earn return and profit. *"Since time immemorial such activities have been carried on by individuals generally. It is a private affair of the company though the case of the nationalized banks stands on a different footing. There may well be companies, in which majority of share capital may be contributed out of the state funds and in that view of the matter there may be more participation or dominant participation of the state in managing the affairs of the company. But in the present case we are concerned with a banking company which has its own resources to raise its funds without any contribution or share holding by the state".*[3]

Banking company" means a banking company as defined in section 5 of the Banking Companies Act, 1949, having branches or other establishments in more than one State, and includes the Industrial Bank of India, the Reserve Bank of India, the State Bank of India a corresponding new bank constituted under section 3 of the Banking Companies (Acquisition and Transfer of Undertaking) Act. 1969, and any subsidiary bank as defined in the State Bank of India (Subsidiary Banks) Act, 1959. The definition of the term "banking company" as mentioned above was inserted in the Act by Section 3 of the Industrial Disputes (Banking and Insurance Companies) Act LIV of 1949. This above clause as originally enacted in 1949 read as follows:

"(bb) 'banking company' means a banking company as defined in Section 5 of the Banking Companies Act, 1949 (X of 1949) having branches or other establishments in more than one State, and includes the State Bank of India and the Reserve Bank of India."

This clause (bb) was substituted by Section 64 and Schedule III, part II of the State Bank of India (subsidiary banks) Act of 1949 and read as follows:

"(bb)banking company means a banking company as defined in Section 5 of the Banking Companies Act, 1949, having branches or other establishments in more than one state, and includes the Reserve Bank of India and any subsidiary bank as defined in State Bank of India (subsidiary bank) Act, 1959."

Clause (bb) was again amended by the Industrial Development Banks of India Act, 18 of 1964 and after the words "and includes" the words "the Industrial Development Banks of India" were inserted. And what is the business of banking? Banking means the acceptance for the purpose of lending or investment of deposits of money from the public, repayable on demand or otherwise, and withdrawal by cheque, draft, order or otherwise. Sections 6 and 7 of the banking companies Act, 1949 deal with the forms of business which the banks may engage. And to achieve these business purposes, the bank as the employer has engaged employees and through their cooperation the banks carry on the systematic activity of their business. Today, the banking business includes such activities as credit card business, selling insurance, advising high network customers on investments, mutual fund business etc., and in all the activities employees (Workmen) have an important role to play. It is through their cooperation that the banks are able to carry-out their services. Therefore banks fall within the definition of the term "Industry" under the Industrial Disputes Act, 1947.[4] It cannot be disputed that land development banks are industry within the meaning of sec 2(j) of the I.D Act.[5]

Notes

1. Bangalore Water Supply vs. A. Rajappa. AIR 1978 S.C., p. 549, 1978, LIC, 467.
2. Coir Board, Ernakulan vs. Indira Devi P.S. 1999, I.L.L.J., 1109
3. See Federal Bank Ltd. vs. Sagar Thomas, 2004, I.L.L.J, 161. In this case the Supreme Court was examining whether a writ will lie against the bank.
4. See Dhar Jilla Sahakari Bhoomi Vikas Bank Maryadit, Dhar vs. Labour Court, 1996, ÈLLJ, 1065.
5. *Ibid.*

3

Contract of Employment

"Sastry Award as modified" sets the written down employment contract in banks. But then written down terms of contract are not complete in themselves in explaining the terms and conditions of the contract of employment. In the case of Hindustan Lever Ltd., the Supreme Court had an occasion to go through 3 letters written by the company and its union in which the management had stated that they will not contest issues about field force on the basis that they are not "workmen". The Supreme Court held that the letters constitute binding agreement between the parties since the parties did not repudiate the agreement (and swore by the agreement)[1]. It is settled law, as far as this country is concerned, the expression terms and conditions of employment would ordinarily include not only the contractual terms and conditions but also those terms which are understood and applied in practice or habitually by common consent without ever being incorporated in the contract. Being so, it is not the written down rules alone but all the understandings, practices, customs and usages also would constitute the terms and conditions of employment. "Sastry Award as modified"[2] in a sense, therefore, is not the complete contract of employment but the terms of the "award as modified" along with the practices, etc. and also such legal provisions which are super imposed on existing ones would constitute the terms and conditions of employment. As a matter of fact, the Supreme Court in the case Central Bank of

India vs. Sisir Kumar Shaw had made the following observation: "*In order to understand the point implied in this case it is not necessary to refer to the details of Sastry Award of 1953 or the Desai Award which ceased to apply in the year 1966*". This does not seems to be correct since under section 19(6) of the Industrial Disputes Act ,the award does not cease to be in force or cease to be binding on the parties, until the parties intimate to each other of their intention to do so through appropriate notice and even in that case the terms of the award will continue to be in force till they are replaced by a settlement or award etc.[3] All the bipartite settlements at industry level do mention that both the awards are binding on the parties as modified by the various settlements entered into through the process of collective bargaining at the industry-level. The service conditions have also been buttressed and modified by various practices which have emerged through the course of time.

A word about the working of the mind of adjudicator of those days. As far as the Tribunals and adjudication proceedings go, the mind of the adjudicator of those days can be understood from the Bank Award Commission's Report. Shri P.B. Gajendragadkar, in the introductory to the above report observed:

"*A judge who takes up such an assignment is never likely to over-rate his competence to discharge his duties in that connection. The decision of industrial disputes in a modern democratic welfare state does not rest merely on arithmetical considerations, nor even soley on considerations of economics. As the thesis developed by Mrs. Barbara Wotton eloquently indicates, the discovery that the determination of a wage structure in a modern industry involves, to some extent, ethical and social considerations had changed the complexion of industrial adjudication in the present age. In assessing the relative importance and validity of the cases placed before an Industrial Tribunal by the trade or industry and the employees, a judge must inevitably depend upon the technical advice which may be available to him and must patiently weigh the respective arguments which are urged before him. Usually, he is new to the subject of industrial disputes and must approach his task in the proper scientific spirit of enquiry. He may perhaps be able to claim that, by his experience at the Bar and on the Bench, he has been trained to consider problems presented before him for his decision in a detached and objective manner by weighing carefully the pros and cons urged before him by the parties in support of their respective contentions. It is obvious that the decisions of an Industrial Tribunal must be informed with wisdom and fairness. An attempt must always be made to reach conclusions expeditiously and with a faithful regard, not only to the interests of the contesting parties before the Tribunal, but also to those of the public weal. A judge must no doubt be able to respond to what Justice Holmes so aptly described as "the felt necessities of the times". But, nevertheless, this ultimate decision must not be influenced by any bias, even sub-consciously, and it must always rest on a logical and dispassionate consideration of the data placed before him."*

The observations were made at a time when there was uncertainty on the role of social justice in relation to industrial adjudication. In J.G. Yakheria vs. Regional Provident Fund Commissioner, Chief Justice Chagla took the view that in construing a social legislation the Court must "even if necessary strain the language of the Act in order to achieve the purpose which the legislature had in placing this legislation on the statue book."[4] In Prakash Cotton Mills case,[5] he further went on to say that no labour or social legislation can be considered without applying the principles of social justice in interpreting its provisions. "We must not forget that we are no longer living in the age of Laissez-faire and the relations between the employer and the employee are no longer solely governed by the principles of contract. Contractual rights and obligations are now subject to the principles of industrial law and also the principles of social justice." This was in the year 1957.

In the year 1958[6] the Supreme Court placed the concept of social justice in its proper perspective. "Social and economic justice have been given a place of pride in our constitution and one of the directive principles of state policy enshrined in Art 38 requires that the state shall strive to promote the welfare of the people by securing and protecting, as effectively as it may be, a social order in which justice, social, economic and political, shall inform all the institutions of natural life. Besides, Art. 43 enunciates another directive principle of providing that the State shall endeavor to secure, by suitable legislation or economic organization or in any other way, to all workers, agricultural industrial or otherwise, work, a long living wage, and conditions of work ensuring a decent standard of life. The concept of social and economic justice is a living concept of revolutionary import; it gives sustenance to the rule of law and meaning and significance to the ideal of welfare state.

In its attempt to do social justice, industrial adjudication has to adjust between the rival claims of the employer and workers in a fair and just manner, and this object can best be achieved by dealing with each problem as it arises on its own facts and circumstances.

Coming down a little from these lofty heights, in J.K. Cotton spg. and Weaving Mills Co. Ltd. and the Labour Appellate Tribunal, the Supreme Court emphasized the relevance, validity and significance of the doctrine of social justice.

"Indeed the concept of social justice has now become such an integral part of industrial law that it would be idle for any party to suggest that industrial adjudication can or should ignore the claims of social justice in dealing with industrial disputes. The concept of social justice is not narrow or one-sided or pedantic, and it is not confined to industrial adjudication alone. It is founded on the basic ideal of socio-economic equality and its aim is to assist the removal of socio-economic disparities and inequalities; nevertheless, in dealing with industrial matters, it does not adopt a doctrinaire approach and refuses to yield blindly to abstract notions, but adopts a realistic and pragmatic approach. It, therefore, endeavors to resolve the competing claims of employers and employees by finding a solution which is just and fair to both parties with the object of establishing harmony between capital and labour and good relationship. The ultimate object of industrial adjudication is to help the growth and progress of national economy, and it is with that ultimate object in view that industrial disputes are settled by industrial adjudication on principles of fairplay and justice. That is the reason why on several occasions industrial adjudication has thought it fit to make reasonable provision for leave in respect of the workmen who may not strictly fall within

the purview of Factories Act or the shops and Commercial Establishments Act."[7]

And all these cannot be brought about unless the Industrial Tribunals are vested with the jurisdiction to interfere with employer's liberty to set the contract of employment and also interfere with his management functions. What is the extent of this power to interfere? What are the preconditions necessary to satisfy in order to interfere? Are there any limitations for the exercise of this power? In other words, how to operationalise the concept of social justice. These questions have been answered by the Supreme Court in various decisions. The ratios set by these decisions have been ably stated in Soonawala's book on Supreme Court decision in Industrial Law.

"In industrial law employer's freedom of contract is not unlimited, and it is not open to him to claim that determination of the conditions of service in any industry is exclusively a management function with which the Industrial Tribunal has no power of interference in any case whatever. The employer's right to fix the terms of employment of his workmen is subject to the requirement of social justice, and in every case in which a dispute arises between the workmen and their employer as to any condition of service, it is the duty of the Tribunal to examine all the facts and circumstances of the case to see whether that condition of service is fair to the workmen and to revise it if it is found to be unreasonable or unfair to the workmen. Thus, in dealing with such matters the Tribunals are not fettered by the terms of the contract of employment or the Standing Orders, and they have a right to interfere and modify those terms when such interference is demanded in the interest of social justice and fairplay. In other words, the doctrine of freedom of contract has to yield place to the higher claims of social justice, whenever it becomes necessary for the promotion of industrial harmony.

However, the Tribunal would not be justified in interfering with the employer's freedom of contract lightly or only on abstract considerations. It must carefully weigh and balance the rival claims in the light of all the relevant factors in each case as it arises, and it is always a matter of making a reasonable adjustment between the conflicting claims of labour and industry. The process of making a reasonable adjustment is not easy and a heavy responsibility has always got to be discharged with care whenever the occasion arises, and it is the duty of the Tribunal to revise and modify a condition of service which is harsh and unfair so as to make it reasonable and fair to both the parties."

The conclusion that seems to be fair therefore is that the notions of social justice may, to a certain extent, be taken into consideration while dealing with contractual obligations and in matters relating to employment contracts. The aforesaid stated principle has not remained static, it has also been evolving keeping with the changes in societal thinking and keeping in with the changing role of the judiciary. It was thought that the whole gamut of our labour legislation was to check, control and circumscribe uncontrolled managerial exercise of power with a view to eschew the inherent arbitrariness in the exercise of such functions. Traveling beyond this, a section of judicial authorities felt that the judges have a duty to state law where the statute itself remained silent. "It would certainly save the judges trouble if Acts of Parliament were drafted with divine prescience and perfect clarity. In the absence of it when a defect appears, a judge cannot simply fold his hands and blame the draftsman. He must set to work on the constructive task of finding the intention of parliament, and must do this not only from language of the statute, but also from a consideration of the social conditions which gave rise to it and to the mischief which it was passed to remedy, and then he must supplement the written word so as to give 'force and life' to the intention of the legislature."[8]

In Avon Services Case, the appropriate government refused to refer a dispute for adjudication in the first instance regarding the termination of services of 2 employees. At a later date, the dispute was referred for adjudication. The contention of the counsel that the government having declined to make a reference under Sec. 10(i) of the Industrial Disputes Act, was not competent or had no authority to make the reference at a later date unless the government comes up with some fresh or additional material which must be disclosed or must appear on the face of the later reference was negatived.[9] Obviously the judiciary was traversing beyond the stated position in law.

And this was being done perhaps in the belief that it will help bring about social engineering. The employers, however, felt that labour is not only being considered as weaker side, but the legal machineries are a wee bit, to state it mildly, tilting towards the labour.

Justice Krishna Iyer in Gujarat Steel Tubes case said:

"Prefatory to this discussion is the appreciation of the constitutional consciousness with regard to Labour Law. The Constitution of India is not a non-aligned parchment but a partisan of social justice with a direction and destination which it sets in the preamble and Art. 38, and so, when we read the evidence, the rulings, the statute and the rival pleas we must be guided by the value set by the Constitution. We not only appraise Industrial Law from this perspective in the disputes before us but also realize that ours is a mixed economy with capitalist mores, only slowly wobbling towards a socialist order, notwithstanding Sri Garg's thoughts. And, after all ideals apart, "law can never be higher than the economic order and the cultural development of society brought to pass by that economic order". The new jurisprudence in industrial relations must prudently be tuned to the wavelength in our constitutional values whose emphatic expression is found in a passage quoted by Chief Justice Rajamanner of the Madras High Court. The learned Judge observed:

"The doctrine of 'laissez faire', which held away in the world since the time of the Adam Smith has practically given place to a doctrine which emphasizes the duty of the state to interfere in the affairs of individuals in the interests of the social well being of the entire community. As Julian Huxley remarks in his essay on "Economic Man and Social Man: Many of our old ideas must be retranslated, so to speak, into a new language. The democratic idea of freedom, for instance, must lose its nineteenth century meaning of individual liberty in the economic sphere, and become adjusted to new conception of social duties and responsibilities. When a big employer talks about his democratic rights to individual freedom, meaning thereby to claim to socially irresponsible control over a huge industrial concern and over the lives of tens of thousands of human beings whom it happens to employ, he is talking in a dying language."

46. Homo economies can no longer wary the social order. Even so the Constitution is ambitiously called socialist but realists will agree that a socialist transformation of the law of labour relations is a slow though steady judicial desideratum. Until specific legislative man dates emerge from Parliament the Court may mould the old but not make the new law "Interstitially, from the molar to the molecular" is the limited legislative role of the court as Justice Holmes said and Mr. Justice Mathew quoted (See (1976) 2 S,C,C. at p. 343."[10]

But then things changed with the first attempts at globalization. Perhaps the judicial views also changed. There was a fresh breeze-so to say-and the pendulum swung back that wee-bit to correct the imbalance. In the case of Syndicate Bank vs. Umesh Nayak the Supreme Court observed: "*With the emergence of the organized labour, particularly in public undertakings and public utility services, the old balance of economic power between the management and the workmen has undergone a qualitative change in such undertakings. Today, the organized labour in these institutions has acquired even the power of holding the society at large to ransom, by withholding labour and thereby compelling the management to give in on their demands, whether reasonable or unreasonable. What is forgotten many times is that as against the employment and the service conditions available to the organized labour in these undertakings, there are millions who are either unemployed, underemployed or employed on less than statutory minimum remuneration. The employment that workmen get and the profits that the employers earn are both generated by the utilization of the resources of the society in one form or the other, whether it is land, water, electricity or money which flows either as share capital, loans from financial institutions or subsidies and exemptions from the Governments. The resources are to be used for the well-being of all by generating more employment and production and ensuring equitable distribution. They are not meant to be used for providing employment, better service conditions and profits for only some in this task, both the capital and labour are to act as the trustees of the said resources on behalf of the society and use them as such. They are not to be wasted or frittered by away by strike and lock-out. Every dispute between the employer and the employee has, therefore, to take into consideration the third dimension, viz., the interests of the society as a whole, particularly the interest of those who are deprived of their legitimate basic economic rights and are more unfortunate than those in employment and management. The justness or otherwise of the action of the employer or the employee has, therefore, to be examined also on the anvil of the interests of the society which such action tends to affect. This is true of the action in both public and private sector. The management in the public sector is not a capitalist and the labour an exploited lot. Both are paid employees and owe their existence to the direct investment of public funds. Both are expected to represent public interests directly and have to promote them."*[11] Therefore, in course of time a judicial view that industries are institutions held by magnates in trust for public good is a view that is distinctly possible in this country. Labour and management will then have to function within the frame-work of discharging that trust for public good.

The other function which has influenced the employment contract is the collective bargaining process. The banks are represented by the Indian Banks Association and the employees are represented by the All India Bank Employees Association and the National Federation of Bank Employees. There are two more unions viz., the Indian National Bank Employee's Congress and National Organization of Bank workmen, which are also signatories to the industry level settlements. This collective bargaining process has laid low many principles enunciated judicially and in their place new ones have emerged. Take for example, house rent allowance: the rationale for house rent allowance was that though it was an item to be taken into account while fixing basic wage and dearness allowance structures, the judicial authorities thought that in big cities where housing accommodation is scarce and rents abnormally high, it is necessary to provide for house rent allowance. Through collective bargaining, the employees in the banking industry have come to enjoy the benefit of house rent allowance in all the places in the country.

The principles of relating house rent allowance to scarce housing accommodation and abnormally high rents has been flexed to include house rent allowance as a term and condition of service of employees in all places. The principle in its pristine legal glory has given way to accommodation due to bargaining power. There have been more such instances where legal principles as enunciated has yielded place or have been replaced by rules evolved through collective bargaining. In future, there will be more instances. In this emerging trend, as Prof. Otto Khan-Freund pointed out, "There is everywhere a constant need for finding a judicium finium regundrom between collective bargaining and legislation of all kinds as instruments for the regulation of conditions of employment wages and hours, holidays, pensions, health safety and welfare, and even, increasingly, social security". This need is likely to be felt the most in banking industry.

Yet another factor which has set the employment contract is practices, customs and usages. What are practices, customs and usages? For our purpose, habitual action is called "practice". It is the same thing as habit or custom. Custom is also called as immemorial usage. It is unwritten law. Custom is used in the sense of a rule. According to Stroud's Judicial Dictionary, "Custom" may be defined to be a law or right not written, which, being established by long use and the consent of our ancestors, hath bin and daily is put in practice. "Custom" is something that has the effect of local law.[12] A custom to be valid, must be certain, reasonable in itself and of immemorial origin. Law Lexicon defines custom as "a rule of conduct, obligatory on those within its scope, established by long usage. A valid custom has the force of law". "Custom is to society what law is to state"[13]. Further the law Lexicon states: "A valid custom must be of immemorial antiquity, certain and reasonable, obligatory, not repugnant to statute law, though it may derogate from the common law. The important thing to note is that this custom can be changed by an enactment. And this is precisely what happened in State Bank's case[14] where from the time of Imperial Bank of India (which later on become the State Bank of India) the employees had a customary right to receive bonus at the rate of one month's wages for every half year of service.

"The award of the Industrial Tribunal dated December 10, 1983 had upheld the claim made by the employees that they have a customary right to receive bonus at the rate of one month's wages for every half year of service. As the Payment of Bonus Act, 1965 had not abrogated, the right of employees to claim bonus on the basis of custom that Award which was in accordance with law then in force, had not been interfered with by this Court. The fact that such an award had been made, however, does not by itself without anything more have the effect of preventing Parliament for all time to come from amending the law on basis of which that award was made, subject to the amendment being within the legislative competence of Parliament, and not being inconsistent with the provisions of part-III of the Constitution.

The right of the Bank's employees to receive bonus on the basis of custom is a right available to them only so long as past custom affords a legal basis for grant of bonus. The fact that an Award had been made under the Industrial Dispute Act, declaring that right in the employees, does not preclude Parliament from legislating that no bonus on basis of custom shall be payable to the employees of public sector Banks, and that only the bonus payable in accordance with the Payment of Bonus Act shall be payable only to those eligible under that Act. Had the law at the time the award was made, been what it is after the impugned amendment the Tribunal could not have made the award.

The impugned Act is not one which merely declares that the judicial verdict of the Industrial Tribunal invalid. The act does not show that Parliament was seeking to exercise appellate powers over the Tribunal or this Court by enacting the amending Act. What this Act does is to prohibit the grant of bonus to the employees of public sector Banks except in accordance with the Payment of Bonus Act, and to limit that payment only to those eligible under that Act. The law so enacted is to have effect notwithstanding anything contained in any other law including the Industrial Disputes Act, and notwithstanding anything contained in any judgment, decree or order of any Court or Tribunal. The award of the Tribunal has become unenforceable, not because of a fiat of Parliament that it shall not be enforced, but because the law on basis of which the award was made has been altered and the enforcement of the award would be inconsistent with the amended law.

The power to enact law, which includes the power to amend the laws in force, and to modify or abrogate law based on custom is a plenary power of Parliament within the fields allotted to it under the Constitution, subject to the limitation contained in Part-III, and subject such law being consistent with the basic structure of the Constitution."

And finally in paragraphs 36 and 37 of the judgment the Court held: "It was open to Parliament to legislate on the subject of payment of bonus based on custom, notwithstanding the award that had been made by Tribunal holding that there was custom in the Bank to pay one month 's wages every half year, to all its employees. Parliament having legislated that bonus to the employee of public sector Banks shall be payable only in accordance with, and to those eligible under the Payment of Bonus Act, it is no longer open to the employees to claim bonus on basis of custom. The award directing payment of bonus on that basis cannot be regarded as having resulted in a special law which overrides the law to be enacted by Parliament.

37. The impugned enactment has not interfered with the judicial function and Parliament by enacting that law has not encroached into the judicial domain. It has acted within the field of its legislative competence."

Now the term "Usage" will include what people are now or recently in the habit of doing in a particular place. It may be that this particular habit is only of recent origin or it may be one which has existed for a long time. According to Stroud's Judicial Dictionary, usage is that which is known as a recurring modern practice in a locality or business and does not require a prescription as a custom does. In Butterworth's Words and Phrases usage is defined as follows:

"Usage may be broadly defined as a particular course of dealing or line of conduct generally adopted by persons engaged in a particular department of business life, or more fully as a particular course of dealing or line of conduct which has acquired such notoriety, that where persons enter into contractual relationships, in matters respecting the particular branch of business life where the usage is alleged to exist, those persons must be taken to have intended to follow that course of dealing or line of conduct, unless they have expressly or impliedly stipulated to the contrary; that is to say that rule of conduct amounts to a usage, if so generally known in the particular department of business life in which the case occurs, that, unless expressly or impliedly excluded, it must be considered as forming part of the contract. Usage in this sense must be distinguished from user or enjoyment in relation to incorporeal rights, and from the course of conduct of the persons interested under a particular ancient charter or other ancient document. In this last sense it is limited to the conduct of persons actually affected by the document in question, and may be referred to only for the purpose of showing the meaning of expressions which by reason of their antiquity have become obscure (И Halsbury Laws (3rd Edn.) I82).

"Usage" means any practice or method of dealing which reasonable persons in the same situation as the parties usually consider to be applicable to the formation of their contract (Uniform Laws on International Sales Act 1967, Sched. 2).

"There may be a usage in one place varying from that which prevails in another. Where the usage is general, and prevails to such an extent that a party contracting with a wharfinger must be supposed congnisant of it, then he will be bound by the terms of that usage. But then it should be generally known to prevail at that place." Holderness v. Collinson (1827), 7 B. & C. 212, per Bayley, J., at p. 216."

According to Jowitt's Dictionary of English law "Usage" is practice long continued. "Usage means a uniformity of conduct in respect to matters of common interest. Hence Coke says, in speaking of custom and prescription, 'as for usage, that is the efficient cause or rather the life of both; for custom and prescription lose their being, if usage fail.' Finally, the law Lexicon. According to it, in order to establish usage it was not necessary to require proof of its existence for any length of time. The word 'Usage' would include what the people are now or recently in the habit of doing in a particular place. It may be that this particular habit is only of a very recent origin, or it may be one which has existed for a long time. If it be one regularly and ordinarily practiced by inhabitants of the place where the tenure exists, there would be usage. "What is important to note here is the fact that usages also become part of the contract of employment. Thus the service conditions of workmen are either the creation of statutes, and/or of the contract of employment." What service conditions would be available to particular employees, whether they are liable to the varied, and to what extent, are matters governed either by statute or the terms of contract."[15]

Briefly speaking, this employment contract in banks covers 4 sections viz. the first dealing with wages and allowances and for working hours for performing work, the second with service conditions like leave, leave travel concessions, medical aid etc. which benefits flow out of the contract of employment, the third on the social security laws affecting banks and its employees and the fourth on disciplinary action for misconducts if any committed by employees.

This is only one part. In Common Law, the relationship between an employer and employee is a matter of contract and hence there must be an offer and acceptance. This offer and acceptance may be by deed or by written down words. The offer must be "absolute" and the acceptance must be unqualified.

Generally, the employment offer letter does not specify all the terms in their detail. The letter merely mentions salary and place of reporting and a few terms. The letter implies that all other terms as are necessary to give effect to employer-employee relationship are binding on the parties. For our purpose, it is important to understand that for an employment contract to come into existence there must be a consideration for employment. In other words, there must be an obligation on the part of the employer and an obligation on the part of the employee, which should bind then reciprocally. In normal cases, this can be seen from the duties rendered by the employee and the wages paid by the employer. When the appointment letter mentions that all rules and regulations will be applicable and the rules provided for executing an agreement on a specific form containing termination clause, then even if no agreement was executed the service conditions will be impliedly applicable.[16]

Notes

1. See Workmen of Hinustan Lever vs. Hindustan Lever Ltd., 1984 LIC, p. 1573 at 1576.
2. Sastry award and Desai award continue to be in force. See Bank of India vs. Presiding Officer, 2002, ILLJ, 232.
3. South Indian Bank vs. A.R. Chacko, 1964, ILLJ, 19.
4. J.G. Vakharia vs. Regional Provident Fund Commissioner, 1957, ILLJ, 448 at 451.
5. Prakash Cotton Mills Ltd. vs. State of Bombay, 1957, II LLJ, p. 490 at 494.
6. See State of Mysore vs. Workers of Gold Mines, AIR 1958, S.C. 923.
7. 1963, II LLJ, 436.
8. Principles of Administrative Law by Griffity and Streat 4th Edition at pp. 98-99.
9. Avon Services (Production Agencies) Pvt. Ltd as Industrial Tribunal, 1979, I LLJ, p. 1.
10. Gujarat Steel Tubes vs. Workmen 1980, I LLJ, p. 131.
11. See 1994, II LLJ, p. 836.
12. Per Cleasly B., Hall vs. Nothingham, I Ex. D 3.
13. Salmond's Jurisprudence.
14. State Bank Staff Union vs. Union of India, 2001, ILLJ, 846.
15. H.R. Adyanthaya vs. Sandoz (I) Ltd. 1995, I LLJ, 303.
16. Dowlatram Lekhraj Rupchandani vs. Western Railway, 1958, I LLJ, 456.

4

Duties Generally

Now let us see how the organized activity in banks takes place through the cooperation of the employees.

The foundation of any company depends on the duties performed by the employees. In banking industry, there are 2 cadres of workmen staff viz. the clerical cadre and the subordinate cadre. The necessity for the employees to perform the jobs entrusted to them is quite obvious. It may be pointed out that in banks it is not possible to fix the minimum quantum of work to be done in a day. "Even though a minimum may not be prescribed, the conditions of service must require that during the time that the employee is in the service of his employer he must at least give to the employer what he is entitled to viz. the minimum of his ability and of his skill and of his time."[1] For this the employee has to present himself at the time and place of work as required. Let us first deal with the duties that the clerical and subordinate staffs have to perform. Before coming back to the issue of time and place of work, scales of pay and other allowances have been laid down by settlements arrived at between the management and the unions (at the industry level) for "doing ordinary duties as such." Thus the bipartite settlements have created duties binding on the employees. The ordinary routine duties of clerks include writing, typing, duplicating, machine calculating, punching cards or tapes, operating computer terminals etc. The ordinary clerical work is therefore, the work pertaining to a clerk. Like the clerical work, the work of subordinate staff has also not been defined anywhere in the settlements and awards applicable to workmen. Hence, the designation of sub-staff member may denote his duties. For example, a hamal or cleaner will be expected to dust and clean furniture and fittings etc. Duties of a packer will not include maintaining cash book, sales register, stock book etc.[2] However, in the absence of any definition, duties which pertain to particular designations may stand modified to meet the individual needs of the banks. It is important to remember that if a person is appointed in a particular cadre, he is expected to perform all the duties which can normally be characterized as the duties of that class. An employee has those duties without which his services would not have been required. For e.g.. it is axiomatic that a computer terminal operator, has to work on the terminal. A watchman has to stop a thief.[3] The most frequent way in which it is determined whether a particular type of work is within the scope of employees duties is by past practice either in a particular office/bank or in the industry. A long standing practice may impose a duty on the employee. So then, what is duty? According to dictionary meaning it is "obligatory tasks, conduct, service or functions that arise from one's position, assigned service or obligation. According to Jowitt's dictionary of English Law 'Duty' is the correlative of right." In practice however, 'Duty' is usually applied to those acts which a person is bound to do by virtue of an office held by him e.g. as trustee, executor, director etc."

It is common knowledge that at the industry-level computerisation was introduced in 1984 consequent on the settlement dated 8th September 1983. Over the years, this has lead to changes in the duties of the clerical and subordinate cadre. In this regard Justice Walton's observation in Creswell Vs. Board of Inland Revenue is note-worthy," It is not correct to say that employees have a vested right to preserve their working obligations completely unchanged as from the moment they first began their work. An employee is expected to adopt himself to new methods and techniques introduced in the course his employment. Of course, the employer must provide the necessary training and retraining."[4]

Now let us turn our alteration to the current special allowance attracting duties which a bank may assign to a workman.

Those special allowance attracting duties are as follows:

Clerical Staff	*Subordinate Staff*
Telephone Operator	Liftman
Audit Clerks- Category 'A'	Cash Peon
Category 'B'	
Agricultural Assistant	Watchman
Teller	Armed Guard
Stenographer	Daftary
Asst. Head Cashier	Head Peon
Head Cashier-I	Electrician/AC Plant Helper
Head Cashier-II	Driver
Special Assistant	Head Messenger in IOB
Computer Operator-A	
Computer Operator-B (with passing powers)	

Note:

1. In the case of Special Assistant, the Special Pay payable for the period 1st November 2002 to the date of the Settlement shall be Rs. 1400/- p.m. and thereafter Rs. 1,600/-p.m.
2. Erstwhile Teller Category 'B', Assistant Head Cashier-Units of 5 and above, Head Cashier Category 'D' and Head Cashier Category 'E' shall now be termed/named as Teller, Assistant Head Cashier, Head Cashier-I and Head Cashier-II respectively.

The industry-wide bipartite settlements have specified the duties to be performed by the special allowance attracting jobs as also the quanta of special allowance. Details of such duties are given in appendix I. Apart from these; duties may be created by providing an employee with a tool or an object. Supplying uniform will surely create a duty on the part of members of sub-staff to wear them while on duty. That duty to wear uniforms becomes a part and parcel of the contract of employment.[5] Similarly at the Branch level, following the instructions of the customers will become part of the duty of the employee. In this context, a duty can arise when the employee perceives one in a given situation. What are such situations? One can be the very employment of the employee presumes certain duties on his part. A typist owes it to his employer to type out correspondence given to him.

A sorter in a bank has to sort out the mail. A clerk has to write neatly on the ledgers. One employee cannot disturb another employee who is at work. Grounds for suspicion that something is wrong imposes a corresponding duty to check more carefully.[6] A special Asst whose work is to "check", has to do this checking himself. Those situations can create duties. Power of attorney surely indicates nature of functions of the power of attorney holder.[7]

The second part of the issue on duties relates to the time (i.e. hours of work) and place factor. As far as the time factor is concerned, chapter 13 of the Bipartite settlement dated 19.10.1966 provides for the details. Let us look at those rules which are important from the point of view of the topic under discussion.

Provision

Rule # 1[8]

"Subject to the provisions of clause 2 and 11 below, the actual hours of work of full time workmen, exclusive of recess period, shall be as specified below:

	Week days (Excluding Saturday)	*Saturdays*
	(Hours per day)	
(a) Workmen other than Members of the subordinate Staff (Excluding category b) Below	6.1/2	4
(b) members of the sub-ordinate staff other than Drivers and Watch and Ward Staff	7	4.1/2
(c) Drivers	7.1/2	5

Discussion

Sub-clause (d) to Clause I speaks of all bank's Drivers including cash van drivers and drivers engaged to drive cars of executives, etc. The weekly hours of work of a Subordinate Staff who is appointed as a Peon-Cum-Driver are as under:

1. The hours of work of a driver during the period he is required to work exclusively as a driver would be that of the driver, viz., 7.1/2 hours during weekdays and 5 hours during Saturdays.
2. The hours of work of a driver during the period he is required to work for part of the day as Peon will be that of the driver, viz., 7.1/2 hours during weekdays and 5 hours during Saturdays.
3. The hours of work of a driver during the period he is required to work exclusively as Peon will be of a Peon, viz., and 7 hours during weekdays and 4.1/2 hours during Saturdays.

Provision

(a) The hours of work of a member of the Watch and Ward Staff shall be 8 hours in a period of 24 hours PROVIDED that the hours of work of a "Watch-man-cum-Peon" for the period during which he works as a peon, as also of a peon, for the period during which he is required to work as a 'watchman' or 'Armed Guard', shall be the same as those laid down in clause 14.2(c) above.[9]

Discussion

It is common knowledge that some banks employ workmen belonging to the Subordinate Staff who are designated as Watchmen-cum-Peons. Their conditions of service relating to hours of work and over time wages are as mentioned above. According to the above clause, the hours of work of a member of the watch and ward staff shall be eight in a period of twenty-four hours provided that the hours of work of Watchmen-cum-Peon for the period during which he works as a Peon as also of a Peon for the period during which he is required to work as a Watchman or Armed Guard shall be 7 hours on week days (excluding Saturdays) and 4.1/2 hours on Saturdays.

What would be the appropriate hours of work of a watchman-cum-peon while he is posted on watchman's duty is a normal question, which frequently comes up for consideration. As stated earlier, for members of the Subordinate Staff including Peons (but excluding watch and ward staff) their hours of work will be seven hours on weekdays and 4 ½ hours on Saturdays and that the hours of work of a member of the Watch and Ward Staff shall be 8 hours in a period of 24 hours. It has been held that the hours of work of a Watchman-cum-Peon when he as a Watchman is 8 hours and when he works as a Peon is 7 hours.

It is clear that a special provision relating to the work of Watchman-cum-Peon is made in clause 4.3(c) and it provides that the hours of work of a Watchman-cum-Peon for the period during which he works as a Peon as also a Peon for the period he is required to work as a Watchman or an 'Armed Guard', shall be the same as those laid down in clause No. 14.2(c) above. This clearly shows that a workman who is substantively appointed as a peon but is required to work as a Watchman on exceptional occasions shall be required to work even as a Watchman only for a period of seven hours on week days and four and half hours on Saturdays. In other words, such a peon will have to be paid overtime wages for any work done by him in excess of seven hours on week days (other than Saturdays).[10] Clause 14.2(2)(c) does not appear to lay down clearly what the hours of work of a Watchman-cum-Peon will be on the days such workman is required to work as a Watchman. Nevertheless, by necessary implication, it may be said that the hours of work relating to Watchman in clause 14.2(b) will apply to the hours of work of Watchman-cum-Peon during the period he works as a Watchman. In other words, a Watchman-cum-Peon will be a member of the Subordinate Staff on the days on which he works as a peon and a Watchman-cum-peon will be a member of the Watch and Ward Staff on the day on which he works as a Watchman for the purpose of their respective hours of work. This is clear from the fact that a specific provision in respect of the hours of work of the Watch and Ward Staff is made in clause 14.3(c) and it is provided therein that the hours of work of the member of the watch and ward staff shall be 8 in a period of 24 hours. It has been held that the hours of a watchman cum peon when he works as a watchman is 8 hours and when he works as a peon is 7 hours.[11] *"Now it has to be seen whether if a watchman-cum-Peon works as a Watchman he should work for 7 hours as contended by the petitioner or for 8 hours as contended by the respondent. If it was the intention of the parties that whenever a person is designated as Watchman-cum-Peon he should work only for 7 hours whether he works as a Peon or as a Watchman then in clause 14.2(c) itself it would have been made clear by stating that members of the subordinate staff "including watchman-cum-Peon". But the very fact that the Watchman-cum-Peon is not specifically mentioned in Section 14.2(c) and in view of the fact that the reference made to the working hours of the watchman-cum-peon under the proviso to clause 14.3(c) it is clear that the intention of the parties was that whenever the Watchman-cum-Peon worked as a peon his working hours should be as per clause 14.2(c) and so the proviso of the Clause 14.3(c) has been added. Clause 14.3(c) also shows that the watchman has been included under the watch-and-ward staff and that is the reason why so far as the person who works as watchman-cum-peon is concerned, in order to make it clear that when such a person works as a peon his working hours would be only as per clause 14.2(c) the proviso to clause 14.3(c) has been added. It is also now seen that for the purpose of extracting the work of a peon or a watchman from a person during the absence of a peon or watchman same persons have been designated as watchman-cum-peon so that their services may be requisitioned and posted as watchman or as peons as the case may be. So whenever such a person works as a peon he has necessarily to work for 7 hours only on week days excluding Saturdays and 41/2 hours on Saturdays as provided under Clause 14.2(c) and that whenever he works as a watchman he should work for 8 hours as provided in Clause 14.3(c) for a member of the watch-and-ward staff. So the proviso to clause 14.3(c) makes it clear that he can be asked to work for 7 hours only if he works as a peon and not otherwise. So I agree with the contentions of the respondent that so far as the petitioner is concerned he has to work for 8 hours whenever he is posted as a watchman and that he has to work for 7 hours only when he is posted as peon."*

What do these provisions mean? The management can insist that the concerned employee should be punctual in his attendance. In a case, while considering the hardships of the employee, the employer had earlier decided to take a lenient view for late attendance of employees by condoning, the lapse on their part in attending office over a long stretch of time, it cannot be contended that the practice has been transformed into a customary concession or privilege, having the force of a conditions of service. A unilateral decision of the employer in exercise of his prerogative to take a lenient view and to condone some lapses does not constitute a change in service condition and unpunctuality still remains a misconduct. An action which is a misconduct of an employee does not constitute a privilege of the employee authorizing him to resort to the misconduct even when the employer does not intend to condone such misconduct. In such case, no notice of change under Section 9A read with the Fourth Schedule is required to enforce punctuality.[12] The hours of work also indicate that the employee has to devote his entire time in working diligently for the employer so as to advance the undertaking of the employer. He should not remain idle. "*If he is unable to utilize his time for the* benefit and advantage of the employer at that for which he is employed, he may, without becoming *liable to account for benefits so acquired, make other use of it not inconsistent with the discharge of his duties to his employer which he has undertaken.*" It is expected that the servant should work sincerely[13] and he should not absent himself without leave.[14]

Provision

3. There shall be a recess for lunch which shall not be less than half an hour and not more than one hour on week days (excluding Saturdays) subject, however, to the requirements of any statutory provisions like the Shops and Commercial Establishments Act.[15]

Discussion

It is the statutory provision which will determine the length of lunch recess. Subject to this, the actual recess can vary between half an hour to one hour. Though in Calcutta and Kerala, the Shops and Establishments Act provides for one hour's lunch recess, the employees in most of the banks avail of lunch recess only for half an hour and thereby leave the office early in the evening for going home. The availing of lunch recess for half an hour is clearly contrary to the Shops and Establishments Act provisions in these States.

Provision

4. Primarily it will be for the workmen to decide the actual length of recess within the limit fixed as aforesaid and the majority decision of the workmen in any branch or establishment shall be adopted in case of difference of opinion with the Management. Where, by arrangement with the Bank, recess is availed of by any workman or workmen on Saturdays, such recess shall be duly marked in the Attendance Register.[16]

Discussion

In certain states the Shops and Establishments Act provides for half an hour lunch recess. Here the employees can ask for a lunch recess not exceeding one hour. The majority decision will prevail here. Where, however, the Shops and Establishments Act provides for one hour lunch recess the employees cannot ask for half an hour's lunch recess under this provision. In other words, subject to the provisions of the Shops and Establishments Act, the workmen can decide the actual length of lunch recess. It is, however, note-worthy that this clause only speaks of the "length" of lunch recess and not the actual timing thereof. In the absence of any prohibition it is for the Management to decide, the actual time when the employees shall avail of the lunch recess and this decision cannot be questioned.

Provision

5. The banks will be at liberty to fix at their discretion the actual timings of work, provided the maximum numbers of hours applicable are being observed. It is agreed that any change made by the bank in the actual timings of work of any workman

for staggering purposes as also any change in the weekly holiday of any workman consequent upon a change made by the bank in the weekly holiday of a branch/office will not require a notice of change under Section 9A of the Industrial Disputes Act, 1947. Sufficient advance intimation of such change in actual timings of work will, however, be given to the workmen concerned.[17]

Discussion

The Banks can fix the actual timings of work provided there is no violation of the Shops and Establishments Act provisions regarding opening and closing hours, lunch recess, etc., and provided further the working hours of the Staff conform to the provisions of the Bipartite Settlement. Such timings can be fixed differently for different departments. The Management has also been given the right to fix the timings of individual workmen, if necessary, by staggering their hours of work. Normally under Schedule IV read with Section 9A of the Industrial Disputes Act, 1947, notice of change is required to be given for staggering the working hours of the workmen. Where such change is affected in terms of a Settlement, notice of change need not be given. This clause provides for staggering and also specifically states that no notice of change need be given. Under this clause all that is required is to give sufficient advance intimation of the change in actual timings of work to the workmen concerned. It is better to give such intimation in writing to avoid controversies, though the clause itself does not prescribe for 'written' intimation to be given. The power to stagger the hours of work is an important weapon in the hands of the Management in effective utilization of staff. Such staggering can be resorted to even for curtailing overtime work and this cannot be questioned by the workmen. While on the subject, it is worth recalling the observations contained in paragraph 308 of the Sastry Award.

"The banks contended before us that they should have the liberty to fix at their direction the actual timing of work provided the maximum numbers of hours fixed by us are observed. The workmen stoutly opposed this proposal and vehemently contended that there

should be no staggering of working house. In our opinion, the banks must have the liberty of action claimed by them. Many types of work in a bank cannot be arrived within a system of fixed hours say between 9 a.m. and 5 p.m. For instance, the work of cash book writer, day book writers, supplementary book writers, internal audit, pass book writing, etc. can be conveniently attended only at different times. Dispatchers will have to take up work in connection with posting of letters only after they are signed by officers, sweeping and cleaning of bank premises or opening and locking of safe vaults may have to be done even before or after such prescribed working hours. Workmen in charge of safe vaults may have to remain beyond such hours to suit the convenience of the customers. Go-down deliveries may have to be made outside such hours even as desired by borrowers. To lay down a general rule fixing the actual timing of office hours as distinct from the total number of hours for a day's work would be to ignore the realities of the situation and the exigencies of bank work of various types. It is, therefore, necessary to recognize the right of the bank managements, to relax the rigidity in the observation of the usual hours of work wherever it is necessary or convenient or desirable to do so. The claim of the workmen, therefore, cannot be sustained."

Sometimes a question may arise as to whether it would be in order to stagger duty hours of some of the workmen staff for a few specified days in each month depending upon the work load at irregular intervals with prior notice to the workmen concerned?

It is felt that it would be in order to stagger duty hours of some of the workmen staff for a few specified days in each month depending upon the workload with prior notice to the workmen concerned.

Consequent upon the introduction of MICR clearing system by Reserve Bank of India, banks are required to change the duty hours of the staff handling the clearing work, and accordingly duty hours of some of them have been staggered. The concerned employees have been demanding payment of conveyance allowance, discomfort allowance, inconvenience allowance, breakfast allowance, etc. It would not be in order to pay any out-of-pocket expenses to the employees whose duty hours may have to be staggered in connection with clearing of MICR cheques, or for any other purpose. The payment of conveyance allowance or any other allowance of this nature is outside the provisions of the Bipartite Settlements. It may neither be feasible nor desirable to formulate a scheme for reimbursement of conveyance expenses without linking these to actuals in performance of duty. If there is a practice followed by some banks of paying a lump sum amount to the clearing representative far in excess of the expenses which are reasonably and legitimately incurred, the same is not a desirable practice.

Provision

6. The bank can require a workman, without his consent, to work beyond the aforesaid hours of work prescribed for him (called overtime work for the purposes of the settlement) subject, and however, that such overtime work shall not exceed 175 hours in any calendar year. As far as possible, prior intimation for overtime work will be given to the workman concerned before overtime work is to begin.[18]

Discussion

In the absence of any rules to the contrary requiring workmen to perform overtime work when called upon to do so, the workmen can refuse to perform such work[19]. In the banking industry since power is vested in the management to require a person to work over time without his consent, an employee cannot refuse to work over time without inviting disciplinary action against him. Deliberate refusal to work over time with the object of harassing the employer is misconduct.[20] It was the practice of the company to get the overtime work done without issuing any notice for such overtime work according to standing orders. The workman refused to put in overtime work on the plea that no notice was given to them. The learned tribunal held that no notice was necessary for overtime work.[21]

It should remembered that the limit of overtime hours is 175.The provision is honoured more in breach. The West Bengal Shops and Establishments Act prescribes a limit of 120 hours per annum on overtime hours and banks, in that State, are not permitted to require their workmen to work overtime beyond 120 hours. It should be noted that an employee deputed to attend a local court on behalf of the bank will have to be paid overtime wages if the court work necessitates his presence beyond his normal hours of work. On the basis of the same principles, if employees working in a mobile bank are required to work beyond their normal hours of work, they will be entitled to overtime wage. The claim of employees concerned for overtime wages on the day on which they were on polling duty during general elections is not tenable and should not be considered. If a public holiday has been declared or changed at a late stage, no overtime would be payable. Overtime would, however, be payable only if the notification is issued in advance and the employees are required to work after receipt of the intimation of change.

Provision

7. To regulate the proper distribution of such overtime work, the Management may in their discretion, prescribe from time to time, within aforesaid overall annual limit of 175 hours, a monthly or quarterly limit beyond which a workman shall not be required to do overtime work. No bank shall pay to any workman overtime allowance in excess of 175 hours.[22]

Discussion

This clause gives the right to the management to regulate overtime working. For this purpose the management can even distribute the number of hours of overtime each month.

No workman has a vested right on overtime wages. Therefore, the workman cannot demand overtime work. It is entirely up to the management to give such work or not.

Provision

8. Normally, the total period of work including overtime shall not, on any day, exceed in the case of workman other than members of the subordinate Staff, 8.1/2 hours and in the case of the members of the Subordinate Staff 9 hours, excluding the period of recess. In the case, however, of an emergency, of

which a responsible officer of the bank concerned shall be the sole judge, or when in the case of Subsidiaries of the State Bank of India the exigencies of government work at the close of the financial year so require, a workman can be required to work in excess of the aforesaid hours. The provisions herein shall be subject to the provisions of any law relating to the ceiling on the hours of work or overtime applicable to the establishment concerned.

This clause[23] provides for a limit, over and above the normal 6 1/2 hours work, of 2 hours of over time work per day on clerical staff. It will be recalled that the working hours of go-down keepers are 8 hours and their timing are decided by the time the customers take for storing or taking out their goods. Is it that they can be asked to work only for half an hour overtime is a legitimate question that may arise. The word 'normally' can be interpreted flexibly to mean that this is an extra-ordinary situation and that they can be required to work more than half an hour's over time. The word 'normally' excludes emergency situation. In such instances a workman can be required to stay on beyond his working hours. The test applied almost universally is whether the employer can require a workman to stay on in a given situation will be judged by the reasonableness of the employer's orders. Where stopping work at the end of the working day will play havoc with the employer's business, the workmen can legitimately be expected to stay on. In one of the dispute, the Madras High Court observed: "if (counsel) were right, the moment the clock shows that the end of the normal working day has arrived, the workers would be entitled to walk away from the site of their work and the contractor or other employer cannot require them stay on even for a half an hour. Apparently the person entrusted with the execution of the work when the clock strike and he must have other employees on hand ready to take the place of individuals who have completed their normal working day. More often than not, this requirement will be found to be impracticable if not impossible."[24] The clause also clarifies that ceilings prescribed are further subject to any other legal provisions on the subject. Naturally, the provisions relating to ceilings on overtime under the various Shops and Establishments Act will prevail.

Provision

9. Any day declared as holidays under the Negotiable Instruments Act. 1881, for half-yearly and yearly closing of accounts, shall be deemed to be normal working days for all workmen employed in all banks.[25]

On the days declared as holiday under the Negotiable Instruments Act for half-yearly and annual closing all employees must attend to their normal work including the closing work. Workmen will be entitled to overtime wages, if any, only where they are required to perform work either before or after their normal working hours. The Sastry Tribunal in paragraph 183 of its Award observed: "*No case has been made out by the workmen for any special allowance. Overtime on those days, if any be paid at the rates and under conditions prescribed by us.*"

Provision

10. For the first one quarter of an hour of overetime work (hereafter called the cushioning period) on any working day, there shall be no payment for the workmen other than members of the Subordinate Staff. If, however, the overtime extends beyond the cushioning period, overtime payment shall be made for the whole period of overtime work including the cushioning period. There will be no such cushioning period for the work done on Sundays and holidays. There will be no such cushioning period for members of the Subordinate Staff.[26]

Discussion

The cushioning period was originally awarded by Sastry Award. Paragraph 301 of the Sastry Award is relevant for understanding the reason for introduction of the Cushioning Period. "*.... The provision for overtime payment which we propose to make should not result in workmen going slow and prolonging their work for the purpose of earning overtime payment. This is best done by providing for a short interval of time immediately after the close of the normal day's work for which period there is to be no* *overtime payment. The cushioning effect of such interval will obviate the dangers apprehended. This principle is in accord with the trend of recent awards by Industrial Tribunals.*[27] *The award went on to provide for a cushioning period as under: "for the first half an hour of Overtime work there shall be no payment and for every completed 15 minutes work thereafter the workmen will be paid at the rates to be laid down by us."* According to the above direction, for every completed 15 minutes work done over and above the half an hour cushioning period, the members of the Clerical Staff had to be paid overtime wages. Before the Desai Tribunal it was urged on behalf of the workmen that the effect of this provision was that for 44 minutes of work done beyond the usual working hours, no payment was being made by the banks. The result of the provision was that not merely the cushioning period of 30 minutes did not attract any extra remuneration but even the further 14 minutes beyond the cushioning period do not attract any extra remuneration if no further work beyond these 44 minutes was required to be done. The Tribunal concluded, *"In my view. If the workmen other than the members of the subordinate staff are required to put in work beyond the cushioning period of half an hour it is but fair that they should be paid. Therefore. I am giving a direction that for calculating overtime, any work done for less than one quarter hour should be counted as if the work had been done for one quarter hour."*

This cushioning period of half an hour was reduced to 15 minutes under the Bipartite Settlement dated 19.10.1966 and whereas no payment was to be made for the cushioning period under the Awards, the Settlement dated 19.10.1966 provided for overtime wage payment for the period of overtime including the cushioning period, where overtime work extended beyond the cushioning period.

It is important to note that there is no cushioning period on Sundays and holidays. This is a very fair provision for the cushioning period was visualized as the period during which, by sitting at his work the employees will be able to complete the day's work. In the case of Sundays and holidays since no work is to be done normally, the question of cushioning period does not arise. In view of the fact that some of the banks have started Sunday banking, it will be necessary to substitute the word 'Sunday' by the words 'weekly off' to reflect the correct meaning.

For the Subordinate Staff members there is no cushioning period. It is difficult to appreciate the rationale behind this exclusion. Surely, the principle of spill over work, which can be completed in a few minutes time, is applicable for work in all cadres of employment and, therefore, there is no justification for excluding Subordinate Staff from the application of this provision. It follows that if overtime wages is paid for any period including the cushioning period, then the cushioning period of 15 minutes will also be taken in to account for the purpose of the annual limit of 175 hours or such lesser hours as prescribed by the relevant Shops and Establishments Act.

A collective reading of the above provisions would lead to the conclusion that there is a place and time for employment and the employer has to provide the tools for work and the employee is bound to act work by virtue of the fact that he holds the office of a clerk or of a Sub-Staff. Having done that on the part of the employer, the employee is duty bound to obey all lawful orders of the employer.[28] These orders, of course, must be within the scope of work of the employee. Depending on the nature of his duties, the concerned employee should be present at his place of employment during his working hours. Thus a clerk should be present at the branch/office where he is posted during his hours of work. The need to work sincerely during the hours of work has been pointed out earlier. Such work should be rendered faithfully as well. In other words, the servant is duty bound to act with fidelity and honestly and should not place himself in such a position in which his interests may conflict with the bank's interests. Similarly an employee must discharge his duties in good faith. The manner with which he should conduct himself or function in the job has also been prescribed in the joint declaration by the union and management. The copy of the joint declaration is at appendix II. Briefly stated the joint declaration provides that:

1. Management should distribute work equitably so that every employee has a full days work.
2. Workmen should carry out all reasonable orders of the management.
3. Employees should not fix any arbitrary ceiling on the quantum of work.
4. Employees with dual designation will have to perform both the duties if required.
5. Go-down keepers working in branches can be asked to perform clerical duties.
6. Cash transactions may be attended to outside office hours on special occasions.
7. Clerical work will include drafting of letters, dealing with correspondence etc.
8. Balancing of ledger etc. should be done within office hours.

These are only general things. The more telling points in the joint declaration are reproduced here below:

"2 (1)every workman shall take all possible steps to ensure and protect the interest of the bank and discharge his duties with utmost integrity, honesty, devotion and diligence.

(2) Every workman shall be at his place of work, commence the allotted work at the time fixed and notified, work for full prescribed hour of work and give maximum output.

The one thing that is discernible in the above declaration is that apart from delivering maximum output the workmen have a duty to take care of the interest of the bank. The standard of care that is expected here is what a reasonable man will do under the given circumstances. Such a duty stands established by the 1st part of the declaration in 2(1). The other contents are understandable and in fact are implied even if not so stated in a contract of employment. What happens if the manager issues orders contrary to instructions contained in bank's circulars? If the manager issues any directions (in violation of the banks circulars) to the cashier regarding functioning of the cash department, then the cashier cannot be found fault with if he refuses to comply with such direction of the manager.[29]

Before we part with this topic, let us look at the concept of ancillary duties. This is necessary because "It is impossible to define in writing all the duties of every individual"[30] in a company. There would be some related duties which it is necessary to perform and these duties are called as ancillary duties. These duties may be such as their performance will lead to completing the production of a good as in the case of a person measuring the cloth being asked to cut the cloth[31] or house-keeping work related to the main work like cleaning the type- writer by the typist. One can add minor additional duties and incidental duties (to these ancillary duties). The example of additional duty can be requiring a stenographer to type an extract from another sheet. The example of incidental duty could be getting some special task done for which it is not possible to employ an outsider as the time taken for doing the special task will be relatively very small and the employee is capable of completing that task. These deal with ordinary duties. To this, one can add emergency duties. Such duties depend on the emergency conditions. These should exhaust the cocept of 'duties generally'.

Notes

1. North Arcot Dist Motor Workers Union vs. Angalamman Transport. Fort St. George Gazette 27.5, 1959 Part-I, suppl. I page 1 [Madras Labour Court].
2. Gangadhar Mishra vs. Director, Text book production and marketing-2006 IV LLJ p.92, see also British India Corp Ltd vs. D.R. Dogra 2006 IV LLJ p. 158. [Note: Plaintiff was not below that of an Asst. Engineer who does not perform the duties of an electric labour or a mechanic].
3. Jawahar Mills vs. Rajamanikam-1954 II LLJ 733.
4. See 1985 I LLJ 392.

5. See ANZ Grindlays Bank vs. Grindlays bank employees Union Bombay [This matter was decided by the city Civil Court in Bombay and went up to the Supreme Court in the year 1993].
6. Karnataka Bank Ltd vs. Sunita B Vatsaraj- 2007 III LLJ 714.
7. Thakur P. Mahrotra vs. Central Bank of India. Gazette of India dt 19.8 1950 part 2 and 3 p.436
8. Clause 14.1 of the Bipartite settlement dated 19.10.1966.
9. Clause 14.3(c) of Bipartite settlement dated 19.10.1988.
10. See Punjab National Bank v/s Workmen-Gazette of India, Part-II, Sec. 3(11), dated 5.6.1976, p.1960.
11. See Bank of Baroda vs. Workmen-Gazette of India, Part 11, Sec. 3(11) dated 17.5.1972 p. 228.
12. Gurudas Chatterjee and another v/s. State Bank of India and Others, 1983 I, I LLN 822, Publishing Co. vs. Harkins-9 Ont.L.R.504, at 508.
13. Fillient vs. Armstrong-(1837) 7.A.D and E.L. 557.
14. Thomas vs. Vivian (1872) 37 J.P. 228.
15. Clause 14.3 of the Bipartite Settlement dated 19.10.1966.
16. Clause 14.4 of Bipartite Settlement dated 19.10.1966.
17. Clause 14.5 of Bipartite Settlement dated 19.10.1966 as amended by Bipartite Settlement dated 17.9.1984.
18. Clause 14.6 of the Bipartite Settlement dated 19.10.1966.
19. See Jaihind Motor Service vs. Workmen-1958, II LLJ, 530.
20. Employees of BCB Ind. vs. BCB Ind and Printers Ltd. 1954, LAC 254.
21. Babcok and Wilcox of India Ltd vs. Their Workmen–1956, II FJR 82 at p. 90. See also Sridharan Motor Service, Attur vs. Ind. Tribunal- 1959, I LLJ, 381.
22. Clause 14.7 of Bipartite Settlement dated 19.10.1966.
23. Clause 14.8 of Bipartite Settlement dated 19.10.1966.
24. See Sridharan Motor Servicee vs. Ind. Tribunal-1959, I LLJ, 380.
25. Para 14.9-1st Bipartite Settlement, 19.10.1966.
26. Clause 14.10 of Bipartite Settlement dated 19.10.1966.

27. See Caltex Ltd. vs. their employees-1952, II LLJ, 183 at 189, and Associated Cement Cos. Ltd. V/s Their Workmen-1951 II LLJ 387 at pages 399 and 400.
28. T. Ramanujam vs. Corporation of Madras AIR 1955 Mad. 366.
29. Bank of India vs. Tapan Kumar Sil 2007 III LLJ 934. In the instant case the branch manager asked the cashier to use the cash key and open the cash vault and safe of the branch for the purpose of taking out the cash box with the help of an out side coolie. Needless to say the cashier refused to comply with the order of the manager.
30. Express News Paper Ltd. vs. Industrial Tribunal-1960, I MLJ, 96
31. Kushilal vs. Hukamchand Mills 1960-II LLJ, 626.

5

Wages

Section 2(rr) of the Industrial Disputes Act, 1947 defines wages. "Wages" means all remuneration capable of being expressed in terms of money, which would, if the terms of employment, expressed or implied, were fulfilled, be payable to a workman in respect of his employment or of work done in such employment, and includes:

I. Such allowance (including dearness allowance) as the workman is for the time being entitled to:

II. The value of any house accommodation, or of supply of light, water, medical attendance or other amenity or of any service or of any concessional supply of food grains or other articles:

III. Any traveling concession:

But does not include–

(a) Any bonus

(b) Any contribution paid or payable by the employer to any pension fund or provident fund or for the benefit of the workman under any law for the time being in force.

(c) Any gratuity payable on the termination of his service.

Wages Means

I. It is remuneration (capable of being expressed in terms of money).

II. It includes all allowances (like dearness allowance) to which a workman is entitled to and excludes bonus, employers contribution to pension/provident fund and gratuity.

III. It is payable if terms of employment (expressed or implied) were fulfilled in respect of his employment.

Or

IV. For work done in such employment.

Wages means "Remuneration". The Dictionary meaning of the term "remuneration" is reward or pay for services rendered. Therefore the money becomes due and payable for services rendered. According to Stroud's Judicial dictionary, "Remuneration" is a wider term than "Salary". "Remuneration" is a quid proquo. "Whatever consideration a person gets for giving his services, seems to me a 'Remuneration' for him. Consequently, if a person was in receipt of a payment or percentage, or any kind of payment which would not be an actual payment, the amount he would receive annually in respect of this would be remuneration." (per Blackburn J.R.V. Postmaster-General. I QBD 663,664 Cp. Emolument).

The second thing we say is "wages" includes all allowances, like dearness allowance, city compensatory allowance, house rent allowance, other allowances, special allowances etc.

The 3rd factor is that these allowances are payable:

I. If the terms of employment [expressed or implied] are fulfilled in respect of his employment.

Or

II. For work done in such employment.

The "terms of employment" of any person refer to all matters covered by the contract of employment, either express or implied.[1]. "*.... (it) may include not only the contractual terms and conditions but those terms which are understood and applied by the parties in practice, or habitually, or any common consent without even being incorporated in the contract.*"[2] Terms of employment will surely include all the service conditions prescribed by "Sastry Award as modified." For example, the conditions prescribe for privilege leave for an employee. Then the wages of the employee is payable for the period of the privilege leave even though he does not work during that period. This privilege leave should be earned by the workman.[3] This is a term of employment.[4] Going down further we said that remuneration is payable for work done in such employment. What is employment? The word "employment" means occupation or act of employing or state of being employed. The term covers a much larger field. Therefore, looking at the expression employment both in its ordinary meaning as also from the meaning derived from the language in which it is used in the settlements pertaining to banking industry, it would be right to construe it as meaning the state of being employed or as referring to the existence of employer and employee relation.[5] Even so, for another light on the subject, let us look at Law Lexicon. According to Law Lexicon the words "employment" means "occupation or act of employing" or "state of being employed" and therefore, unless there is an indication to the contrary the normal meaning of termination of employment is the one namely the cessation of the relationship between the employer and the employee. The use of the expression "employment" must be construed as deliberately made. If rule 55B of the Central Services Rules, 1957, was meant to cover a wide a field, that is to say, it was to cover termination of every character it would have used the word "appointment" instead of the word "employment" because in that case all appointments whether initial or on promotion would then be covered. It is not as if the expression "appointment" was unknown to the legislating authority. The word "employment" covers a much larger field in matter of conditions of service, the right to promotion, etc., than the word "appointment". The expression "employment" both in its ordinary meaning and the meaning as derived from the language used in other rules it would be right to construe it as meaning the state of being employed or as referring to the existence of employer and employee relationships- [Shanti Kusum Das Gupta V. Oil and Natural Gas Commission. Dehra Dun, U.P, A. I. R 1970, Guj. 149 at pp. 154-55.].

The real test for deciding whether the contract was one of employment was to find out whether the agreement was for the personal labour of the person engaged, and that if that was so, the contract was one of employment, whether the work was time-work or piecework, or whether the employee did the whole of the work himself or whether he obtained the assistance of other persons also for the work-[Harish Chandra Bajpai vs. Triloki Singh. 12 E. L. R. 461 at pp. 487-488 (S. C)].

The word "employment" said Lord Finlay in Davidson and Co vs. M'Robb, (1913) A. C. 315 must mean the same thing when in apposition with "in the course of" as it means when in apposition with "out of". Employment was held to mean the discharge of the duties of the workman. This was understood to point to the specific work he was employed to do. In this context, therefore, remuneration is payable only if the specific work allotted to the workman is done in the manner prescribed by the employer.

Notes

1. See Bradan Dunne Ltd. vs. Fitzpatrick- 1958 I R. 29(37).
2. British Broadcasting Corporation vs. Hearb 1978 A.E.R. (118) (C.A).
3. Andra Bank vs. P. Balkrishna, 2005, III LLJ 892. ["...... and the workman has to render active service and thereby earn privilege leave to his credit].
4. Patna Electric Supply Co. Ltd. vs. Workmen, 1957 II LLJ 575 at 578.
5. See Shanti Kusum Das Gupta vs. Natural Gas Commission U.P. 1970 AIR (Guj), 149 at 155 [see For e.g. clause 19.5(m) inserted by Settlement dated 17.9.1984].

6

Dies Non-I

The principle of no work no pay has been a subject matter of controversy in the banking industry. Hence in the following analysis, we try to find out the correct legal position on the matter.

The question that comes up for discussion often is that whether a bank would be justified in withholding wages during a workman's absence from his place of work without permission from his superiors. If so, what is the scope of this right? Will this principle of no work no pay apply to a case in which the employee is physically present, but does not perform any work? Will it apply to a case in which an employee is physically present and works but does not perform the work he is required to perform or performs only some of the duties allotted him? Can we apply the principle of 'no work no pay' to a situation of go-slow? Are there any formalities which should be observed by the employer prior to the exercise of the right to deduct the wages for the period of no work?

The issue involved in all the questions raised above centers around the contract of employment and its implications. According to the contract of employment the employee is under an obligation to work during the entire working hours, as part of the employer's organization, at a fixed place of work, with equipment provided by the employer, and he is under the supervision (arranged by the employer) over his method of working. In addition to the above, the Courts may, in any class of contract, imply a term in order to fully reflect any intrinsic failure of expression.[1] The employee is also expected to be ready to work when called upon and thus the employer has a right to give orders and the employee is duty bound to obey the orders within the general scope of his contract of employment. An employee who fails without a reasonable cause to serve or refuses to serve the employer breaks his contract. If, however, he is unable to work for reasons beyond his control, he will not commit a breach of contract.[2]

At this point it is worth noting that the essence of a contract of employment is service for wages. This is inherent in the definition of wages under the Industrial Disputes Act, 1947.

It is absolutely essential for an employee to be present at the time and place of his work. This has been acknowledged by the joint declaration in as many words. In place of the work really means the place of duty of the employee. The converse of the above proposition would imply that it is also a vital part of the contract of employment that an employee is under obligation not to absent himself from work without good cause during the time he is required to be at work by the terms of his contract of employment. It is the duty of employees to be available for work and do the work, if offered by the employer, in a reasonable manner. Under the general law, the performance of service in accordance with the contract of employment is a condition precedent for earning remuneration or salary. Therefore, absence for a day or part of it without reasonable cause will be, in a given case, a good ground for deduction of wages. "If the petitioners deliberately and in a concerted move merely attended the site or place of work during the periods in dispute and did not work at all to coerce the respondent to agree to their demands, they were not entitled to salaries for those periods as they were guilty of breach of contract. The petitioners did not earn their salaries for the said periods as there was complete non-performance by them of their duties."[3] The standing orders provided that "any workman who after registering his attendance.......... is found absent from his place (of work) during working hours without permission, shall be treated as absent from the time of his absence and his wages shall be subject to deduction in accordance with the provisions of the payment of wages Act,1936......" The High Court held that "...... *it is clear that the management is entitled to deduct wages of an employee for his absence from duty in accordance with payment of wages Act. The provision basically provides that wages shall be payable when an employee works. If he is absent, his wages shall be deducted."*

If that be the position i.e. wages can be deducted for absence from work, then the authority entrusted with an enquiry on the subject issue under the payment of wages Act will not have the jurisdiction to see whether the absence was justified. The authority under the payment of wages Act, cannot sit in appeal over the decision of the employer to charge-sheet the employee for his absence. Once the authority finds that the employee was absent and deduction was made for his absence from duty, his jurisdiction to further enquire into the matter comes to an end.[4] Such deduction of wages for the period of absence need not await the out-come of any adjudication proceedings. [5] "*It is only after deduction is made that the adjudicatory authority gets jurisdiction to adjudicate the dispute."*[6]. In other words, the management is free to deduct wages for the period of absence while paying wages for the month/week (as the case may be), in which the absence took place. Same is true in the case of willful absence. Wages will not be payable for the period of willful absence.[7]

Now if under the payment of wages Act,1936, there is a provision to deduct 8 days wages for a day's absence. What is the legal position if an employer wants to avail of the provision under that Act?

In Orient Paper Mills Sramik Congress Vs. Orient Paper Mills the action of the management in deducting the wages under S. 9(2) of the Act had come up for examination.[8] *Though this Court was not directly concerned with the proviso to S. 9(2), yet it applied its mind to the said proviso and it observed in Para 6 that though the principles of natural justice would not be attracted in the case of normal or ordinary deduction as contemplated under S. 9(2) whereas in case of penal or further deduction under the proviso to S. 9(2) the said principles must be followed. "This conclusion was arrived at by this Court referring interalia, to S. 26(3)(g) of the act, which has provided that rules may be prescribing conditions subject to which deduction may be made under the proviso to S. 9(2). A reference to rule 16(2)(c) of the Payment of Wages (Mines) Rules, 1956 (shortly stated, the rules) shows that no deduction under the aforenoted proviso can be made from the wages of any employed unless at least one week before such deduction is made a notice has been displayed outside the office of the mine and which must fulfill the other conditions mentioned in the rule. On the face of these statutory provisions, we are satisfied that a notice has to be issued before deduction can be made under the proviso to S. 9(2) of the Act.*

Should the notice be a special one to each workman or, a general notice of the type visualized by rule 16(2)(c) of the rules would do? "According to Sri Ratho appearing for the management, a general notice is sufficient in this regard. In support of his contention, he has referred to Section 9: Deduction for absence from duty–

I. *Deductions may be made under CI.(b) of sub-sec(2) of S.7 only on account of the absence of an employed person from the place or places where, by the terms of his employment, he is required to work, such absence being for the whole or any part of the period during which he is so required to work.*

II. *The amount of such deduction shall in no case bear to the wages payable to the employed person in respect of the wage period for which the deduction is made a larger proportion than the period for which he was absent bears to the total period, within such wages period, during which by the terms of his employment, he was required to work;*

Provided that subject to any rules made in this behalf by the State Government, if ten or more employed persons acting in concert absent themselves without due notice (that is to say without giving the notice which is required under the terms of their contracts of employment) and without reasonable cause, such deduction from any such persons may include such amount not exceeding his wages for eight days as may by any such terms be due to the employer in lieu of due notice.

Explanation. For the purposes of this section, an employed person shall be deemed to be absent from the place where he is required to work if, although present in such place, he refuses, in pursuance of a stay-in-strike or for any other cause which is not reasonable in the circumstances to carry out his work.

[I. Managing Director, Mining and Allied Machinery Corporation Ltd. vs R.K. Bhatacharya 1971, LIC 1339; and

II. Balaiah (D) Vs Indian Detonators Ltd., Kukatpalli 1976- II LLN 50].

From what has been stated in the aforesaid two decisions and the provisions finding place in the rules, we are satisfied that a general notice of the type given in the case at hand would meet the requirement of law; and as such, it cannot be held that the deduction in the present case was in violation of the principles of natural justice. In taking this view, we have also borne in mind the provision of S.10(IA) of the Act which requires a notice on the employed person where deduction has been made under CIs.(c),(m),(n) or (o) of subsection(2) of S.7 of the Act, whereas in the present case the deduction is under CI.(b) of S. 7(2)."[9]

From the above discussion, it will be clear that an employee is entitled to his salary for the work done and there cannot be an exception to this rule.[10] And what happens if an employee is prevented from working. Absence from duty by an employee must be of his own volition and it cannot cover his absence when he is forced by circumstances created by the employer from carrying out his duty. This issue was considered by the Gawahati High Court in the French Motor Car Co. Ltd's case.[11] In that case the workmen reported for duty but they were asked to execute a guarantee bond before they could be allowed to resume duties by the management. In the bond it was stated that after resumption of duty the employees would not resort to strike of any sort. This the court felt is an unfair labour practice. "So the employees were justified in refusing to give this undertaking." An employer can deduct wages under section 7(2) of the act for absence from duty. Absence from duty by an employee must be of his own volition and it cannot cover his absence when he is forced by circumstances created by the employer from carrying out his duty. In the case in hand as the absence of the employees was not voluntary, in as much as they were not allowed to resume their work without signing the guarantee bond, no deduction can be made under the Act." In this case, there was no issue of illegality of strike.

In Bhingare D.M. Vs. C.T.R Manufacturing Industries Ltd, the Bombay High Court had considered the issue of an undertaking from a single workman. This workman was giving production according to a 1984 settlement. The management insisted that he should give production under a 1989 settlement. Since the workman did not oblige the management, he was not allowed to report for duty. The workman filed a complaint under the Maharastra Recognition of Trade Unions and prevention of unfair Labour Practices Act, 1971. The Industrial Court directed the employer to allow the workman resume his duties. The workman reported for work but the company did not allot any duties to him. The company meanwhile requested the court to review the interim order which the court did. The company was permitted to take an undertaking from the petitioner to the effect that he would carry out the work allotted to him and as done by him earlier. Again the company did not assign any work to him. Under the circumstances the Bombay High Court observed.[12]

"In the present case, there are no allegation against the Petitioner that he had resorted to any indiscipline resulting in violence or a strike, gherao, go-slow, etc. An undertaking was sought only because the workman had failed to achieve the norms of production. This may amount to a misconduct for which action can be taken under the Model Standing Orders. However, by insisting upon a bond or undertaking, the employer in this case has committed an unfair labour practice. This is because neither under the appointment letter, nor under the Model Standing Orders, was the petitioner expected to furnish an undertaking. By directing the petitioner to give such an undertaking the company sought to incorporate a term in the contract of service, unilaterally which was impermissible. The submission that

there is no prohibition on the employer insisting on such an innocuous undertaking cannot be countenanced as that would give the employer liberty to seek an undertaking at his own whims and fancies. The facts and circumstances of this case amply prove that an employer could opt for an easy way out to take action against a workman, under the guise of an undertaking, rather than taking any disciplinary action in accordance with the Model Standard Order or Rules applicable.

When admittedly the norms of production were not fixed in 1984 for the drilling machine and shearing machine, the Company would not have insisted upon these norms. There is no dispute that the workman was willing to give production in accordance upon an undertaking that he would give production as was being given by other employees which he was achieving earlier is in my opinion, incorrect. The production levels sought were on the basis of the 1989 Settlement. These norms were fixed in the 1989 Settlement without consultation with the workmen who were actually working on these machines. The petitioner was all along working in the Fabrication Department and not on either the drilling machine or shearing machine. Therefore, to insist upon norms which were fixed in the 1989 Settlement for the drilling machine and shearing machine is an unfair labour practice.

The investigating officer has also found that the workman was not given work despite interim orders of the Industrial Court. Therefore, the Industrial Court ought to have considered all these factors and held that the company had committed unfair labour practice. But in an illegal strike situation or where there is violence in the factory, the situation can be different. Unfair labour practice consists of insisting on a bond from the workmen who are on a legal strike. The underlying object in treating it as unfair labour practice appears to be to extent protection to workmen against possible humiliation or victimization for their legitimate trade union activities. This clause has no reference where the bond is insisted in a situation de hors of and unconnected with any such strike. There is no nexus between the reasons for such bond and the strike of the workmen. No such question of humiliation or victimization can arise when ill advised workmen are found to be bent on indulging in act of assaults and violence, intimidation, go-slow tactics and other illegal activities in defiance of legal provisions, standing orders and rules of conduct implicit in accepting jobs by them."[13] In cases pertaining to Engineering Mazdoor Sabha and Motipur Sugar Factory, the courts had held earlier that the employers were driven to ask for such bond in view of the continued "go-slow" and obstruction to production. The court could not find any fault with the employers. Consequently refusal to take employees on work was upheld by the courts. Thus the employer was justified on insisting on the bond.[14]

Thus in an illegal strike situation or where there is violence in the factory, or where union and employees indulged in improper activities, abused the staff members on duty and did not respond to the call of the management to rejoin work, the view could be different. In pride Hotel's case the employees went on an illegal strike. And this is what the court had to say:

"It is not disputed that Hotel Executive Ashoka is Five Star Hotel. It is also not disputed that it has provided uniform to the employees of the hotel which is to be used by them during working hours. If some of the staff members use red-bands on their heads over such uniform, could it be called as a decent thing or proper thing? Neither the customers nor the management would like it. Uniforms are meant for maintaining the uniformity amongst the members of industry or organization as a matter of discipline and decency. Anybody who attempts to demolish it would be liable to be called as a person committing an in-disciplined act or at least an improper act which would be tarnishing the discipline code of the work of an institution or organization or the company. Apart from that, it would be causing serious damage to the commercial reputation and goodwill of the said institution, organization or company. It is a matter of experience that in hotel business, one needs tidy things and discipline in work, and uniform as well as good service and other services rendered, satisfactory tune in it is of utmost importance. On that count, mainly the hotel industry grows and earns the business as well as goodwill. Whether the management is entitled to protect its business, goodwill and discipline? The answer considered from all corners would in unequivocal terms would be in the affirmative.

When the strike is not legal as the petitioner union did not follow the legal formalities before going on a legal strike and when the act on the part of the respondents hotel management is not "lock out", as held by the judgment of Division Bench of this Court, the Management, employer is entitled to ask for a bond and undertaking of good behavior in writing from such workmen. The Management is entitled to ask them to write such undertaking and bond in a particular form provided for protecting its interest. As a natural corollary, it goes without saying that it is legally entitled not to allow such workmen to enter the premises till he furnishes such undertaking or bond of good behavior.

Besides that, in the present case the members of the petitioner union indulged in improper activities like making false complaints to police, abusing staff members on duty and not responding to the call of the respondent to resume work. They also restrained other workers who were intending to resume duty, used the red-bands over the uniform provided by the hotel management and tried to tarnish the image of the establishment. These acts are indecent and improper. They are detrimental to the interest of the respondents hotel, because by such activities their prospective customers would be reluctant in coming to the said hotel either for lodging, boarding or for eating eatables in the restaurant. Who from the decent lot of the society would like to engage themselves in such indecent and improper atmosphere where some of the staff members are shouting slogans, following violence and presenting themselves in bad or shabby dress? In other institutions these acts may appear to be less dangerous in shade or shades but in hotel industry, which has back bone of decency, cleanliness, tidiness and charming presentation, it would be definitely dangerous to the interest of the said hotel business. When the strike is not legal and there is no lock out and when such employees are only writing letters and informing hotel management that they are ready to resume duty but not signing the undertaking and bond as required by the management for protecting its interest and security, the management would be justified in not allowing such employees to enter into the premises and to resume the work. Why should the management incur further expenses in security in permitting such employees to enter the premises for causing damages to the property as well as goodwill by their indecent and improper acts? Apart from that without following due course of law as record shows, the members of petitioner union intended to follow "go-slow policy". If such persons are permitted to make entry in the hotel premises and resume the work-duty, the person who would suffer more would be the customers because those who come to the said hotel would be waiting for the food to be served or services to be rendered and would be disappointed by the "go-slow" policy of the employees. The larger interest of the society is to be also protected by not permitting such employees to go for indisciplined activities.

The ratio of this judgment gets in tune with ratio of judgment cited above which show that such employer or employers are entitled to demand undertaking and the bond of good behavior executed from such employees for the purpose of maintaining discipline for internal business. They are entitled to get such undertaking and bond from such employees for protecting their property. This code goes further ahead by observing that such employer or employees are entitled to get such undertaking and bonds executed from them for the purpose of protecting likelihood of the loss in business and irreparable loss in goodwill. This court goes further in observing that such employer and employees are entitled to get such undertaking and bonds executed from such employee/employees for protecting the class of the society which comes to the hotel as its customers.

After careful examination of the record and the judgment and award passed by the industrial court, this court comes to the conclusion that the learned judge has carefully examined each and every relevant facet of the matter. He has considered the observation of the legal precedent submitted before it and after appreciating the evidence on record and adverting its judicial attention to the facts and circumstances has come to correct conclusion and passed the judgment dismissing the complaint of the petitioner. Therefore, this Court finds no necessity to issue a writ of certiorari as the said judgment is correct, proper and legal."[15]

This judgment, in fact, opens up several aspects of the contract of employment and non-payment of wages. For example if the Subordinate Staff do not wear uniform at all or do not wear the uniforms as prescribed, will the employer or bank be justified in marking them as absent and hence not pay them the wages for the days the Subordinate Staff did not wear the uniform. The answer is a resounding "yes". In fact the Bombay High Court is dispute between ANZ Grindlays, bank and its Bombay Union held that no wages would be payable to the members of Sub Staff.[16] This also brings an important aspects viz, the workman have a right to enter the place of work only for working during the working hours. If they do not have the intention to carry on their normal duties they have no right to enter the work premises. In the case of Bombay Dyeing company it was held that even assuming that the workmen had not indulged in violence, still the employer has a right to tell the workmen not to enter work premises in case workmen had made it clear that they have no intention to carry out their duties.[17] Lest we forget, we are dealing with issue that absence of the employee must be on his own volition to disentitle him for wages. Thus if the employee is illegally deprived of work, the principle of 'no work no pay' will not apply.[18] And this illegal deprivation came about because of the employee's dismissal from service which could not stand legal scrutiny. But then there are various shades to the issue of reinstatement and payment of wages on the principle of "no work no pay". At the other extreme end was this claim for wages against a bank. The Bank had terminated the services of the employee because the employee was convicted of an offence. On appeal by the employee, the conviction was set aside and the bank reinstated the employee. In such an instance would back wages be payable?[19]

A case involving a government servant in a similar case was considered by the Supreme Court. The employee was suspended from service pursuant to criminal proceedings launched against him and he was paid subsistence allowance. He was convicted by the trial court and was dismissed from service. On appeal he was acquitted and hence he was reinstated in service with full wages from the date of acquittal to the date of reinstatement. The question of payment of wages came up for consideration from the date of conviction to the date of acquittal. The government paid him 3/4th of the salary for the period on the ground that he was not fully exonerated. The Supreme Court held:[20] "*Keeping in view the facts of the case that the appellant was never hauled up for departmental enquiry, that he was prosecuted and ultimately acquitted, and on being acquitted he was reinstated and was paid full salary for the period commencing from his acquittal, and further that even for the period in question the concerned authority has not held that the suspension was wholly justified because 3/4th of the salary is ordered to be paid, we are of the opinion that the approach of the trial court was unassailable. The learned trial judge on appreciation of facts found that this is a case in which full salary should have been paid to the appellant on his reinstatement for the entire period. We accept that as the correct approach."* This judgment was given by a bench of 3 judges. This issue was considered in State Bank of India's case. The Bank is statutorily bound to terminate the services of any of its employees who has been convicted of any offence involving moral turpitude, as per Section 10(1)(b)(i) of the Banking Regulation Act, 1949. For not paying wages the bank placed reliance on the decision of the Hon'ble Supreme Court in Ranchodji Chaturji Thakore's Superintendent Engineer, Gujarat Electricity Board, Himmatnagar (Gujarat) and Another, AIR 1997 SC 1802: 1996(11) SCC 603 where the Court observed as follows:

"The reinstatement of the petitioner into the service has already been ordered by the High Court. The only question is whether he is entitled to back wages. It was his conduct of involving himself in the crime that was taken into account for his not being in service of the respondent. Consequent upon his acquittal, he is entitled to reinstatement for the reason that his service was terminated on the basis of the conviction by operation of proviso to the statutory Rules applicable to the situation. The question of back wages would be considered only if the respondents have taken action by way of disciplinary proceedings and the action was found to be unsustainable in law and he was unlawfully prevented from discharging the duties. In that context, his conduct becomes relevant. Each case requires to be considered in its own backdrop. In this case, since the petitioner had involved himself in a crime, though he was later acquitted, he had disabled himself from rendering the service on account of conviction and incarceration in jail. Under these circumstances, the petitioner is not entitled to payment of back wages. The learned single Judge and the Division Bench have not committed any error of law warranting interference."

This judgment was from a bench of 2 Judges and the earlier decision of the Supreme Court was not brought to the attention of the judges. And in the case of another Government employee the Supreme Court once again agreed with above 2 judges judgment. The court held: "*If prosecution, which ultimately resulted in acquittal of the person concerned was at the behest of or by the department itself, perhaps different considerations may arise. On the other hand, if as a citizen the employee or a public servant got involved in a criminal case and if after initial conviction by the trial Court, he gets acquittal on appeal subsequently, the department cannot in any manner be found fault with for having kept him out of service, since the law obliges a person convicted of an offence to be so kept out and not to be retained in service. Consequently, the reasons given in the decision relied upon, for the appellants are not only convincing but are in consonance with reasonableness as well. Though exception taken to that part of the order directing reinstatement cannot be sustained and the respondent has to be reinstated in service, for the reason that the earlier discharge was on account of those criminal proceedings and conviction only, the appellants are well within their rights to deny back wages to the respondent for the period he was not in service. The appellants cannot be made liable to pay for the period for which they could not avail of the services of the respondent. The High Court, in our view, committed a grave error, in allowing back wages also, without adverting to all such relevant aspects and considerations. Consequently, the order of the High Court in so far as it directed payment of back wages is liable to be and is hereby set aside.*"[21]

And in yet another 2 judges bench, the Supreme Court placed the whole issue on the right perspective. Given the facts it will be easy to see why each individual case will have to be considered on its own merits. The Supreme Court[22] said: "*It is true that when a Government Servant is acquitted of offences, he would be entitled to reinstatement. But the question is whether he would be entitled to all consequential benefits including the pensionary benefits treating the suspension period as duty period, as contended by Mr. Ranjit Kumar? The object of sanction of law behind prosecution is to put an end to crime against the society and law thereby intends to restore social order and stability. The purpose of the prosecution of a public servant is to maintain discipline in service, integrity, honesty and truthful conduct in performance of public duty or for modulation of his conduct to further the efficiency in public service. The Constitution has given full faith and credit to public acts. Conduct of a public servant has to be an open book; corrupt would be known to everyone. Their reputation would gain notoriety. Though legal evidence may be insufficient to bring home the guilt beyond doubt or foolproof, the act of reinstatement sends ripples among the people in the office/locality and shows wrong signals for degeneration of morality, integrity and rightful conduct and efficient performance of public duty. The constitutional animation of public faith and credit given to public acts would be undermined. Every act or the conduct of a public servant should be to effectuate the public purpose and constitutional objective. Public servant renders himself accountable to the public. The very cause for suspension of the petitioner and taking punitive action against him was his conduct that led to his prosecution for the offences under the Indian Penal Code. If the conduct alleged is the foundation for prosecution, though it may end in acquittal on appreciation or lack of sufficient evidence, the question emerges whether the Government servant prosecuted for commission of defalcation of public funds and fabrication of the records, though culminated into acquittal, is entitled to be reinstated with consequential benefits? In our considered view this grant of consequential benefits with all back wages, etc, cannot be as a matter of course. We think that it would be deleterious to the maintenance of the discipline if a person suspended on valid considerations is given full back wages as a matter of course on his acquittal. Two courses are open to the disciplinary authority, viz. it may enquire into the misconduct unless, the self-same conduct was subject of charge and on trial the acquittal was recorded on a positive finding that the accused did not commit the offence at all; but acquittal is not on benefit of doubt given. Appropriate action may be taken thereon. Even otherwise, the authority may, on reinstatement after following the principle of natural justice, pass appropriate order including treating suspension period as period of not on duty (and on payment of subsistence allowance, etc,)........"*

Following the aforesaid Supreme Court decisions, the Madras High Court[23] in the case of a bank employee came to the conclusion that back wages are not payable. "*In the present case the petitioner was incarcerated under Section 498-A of the Indian Panel Code and it can be nobody's case that the bank had instigated this prosecution. In terminating the services of the petitioner the bank was only complying with the statutory provisions which mandated the termination of petitioner's services. On hearing of the petitioner's acquittal, the respondent bank has been quick to reinstate the petitioner. It has, therefore, not played any role in petitioner's abstention from work or cessation from duty. Why then should the bank be fastened with the liability to pay salary to the petitioner. Should the employer also be burdened with payment of compensation of the wife's malicious prosecution? The answer can only be emphatically in the negative.*" In relying on the judgment of the Supreme Court the High Court felt that there is no contradiction between the 3 judges bench and the 2 judges bench.

Leaving this issue let us now turn to retrenchment. In the case of an employee where retrenchment compensation was not paid the court ordered payment of 50% of back wages citing the principle of "no work no pay."[24] "*........ admittedly the workman concerned has since not worked from the date of termination, the award of the labour court so far as it directs the payment of full back wages to the workman concerned deserves to be modified on the basis of the principles of "no work no pay" and the award in question deserves to be quashed so far as it directs of payment of full back wages.*" The principle is obvious: if the employer did not take work from the employees, wages will have to be paid by the employer. In one of the cases, the employer got permission to close his factory from 18th July, 1994. He had in fact applied for permission to close his factory on 31st March, 1994 and had, in fact, closed the factory from that date. The court held that the date of closure of the factory has to be taken into account and i.e. from 18th July, 1994 and that the employer will be liable to pay wages from 31st March to 18th July, 1994.[25] While on "closure", let us see the effect of illegal closure. Sec. 25(0) provides that the workmen shall be entitled to all benefits under any law for the time being in force as if the undertaking had not been closed... Benefits obviously include wages"

Hence, the employees will be entitled to their wages.[26] On that analogy, a driver, who is kept away from work by the company, will have to be paid his wages.[27] But then what happens when an employee applies for casual leave and that leave is not granted by the management. If thereafter the employee remains absent, the management will be justified in deducting his wages for the day.[28] The Bipartite Settlements governing the service conditions of employees provides that extra ordinary leave can be availed off by an employee when no ordinary leave is due to him. The settlement also provides that no pay and allowances are admissible during the period of extra ordinary leave. In this back-ground of the employment contract, wages will not be payable for the period of extra-ordinary leave.[29] What about absence due to trade union work. In the present case, the management had given time-off to the workman for attending court cases. And this concession was confirmed by the company from time to time. Since the company felt that the employee was misusing this concession, the management withdrew the concession resulting in a deduction of wages for 13 hours and 5 minutes. Now the case of the union leader was such deduction was done without affording him an opportunity to explain. The Bombay High Court held: "*Hence the employer had deducted the wages on the ground that Shri Mankar remained unauthorized by absent misusing the time-off concession given to him. A show cause notice was duly issued to him and reply was called. The order of deduction was made only after considering the explanation given by Shri Mankar. Under these circumstances, the Industrial Tribunal clearly erred in holding that it was necessary for the management to have held a full-fledged enquiry before ordering deduction.*"[30] The Sastry award[+] has held that legitimate trade-union activity should be done outside the office-hours and without detriment to the bank's interest. On the face of this provision, if trade union or other activities not connected with bank's work is done during working hours, the logic of "no work no pay" will apply. But where an employee says that he was away from his place of work to attend to company's court case, before affecting the wage-cut, the employee should be heard and a correctness of his claim verified before affecting the wage-cut.[31] Transfer is a condition of service. If the employee does not obey the order of transfer then for the period he does not report to the place of transfer, he will not be entitled to be paid the wages for the period.[32]

Now the principle of employer preventing the employee from working will come into play in the matter of suspension pending enquiry and payment of subsistence allowance. Payment of subsistence allowance and/or wages during the period of suspension has been dealt with in the various provisions of the Bipartite Settlement dated 19.10.1966, as further amended by the settlement dated 8.9.1983, which reads as under:

1. Subsistence Allowance during the period of suspension should be granted on the following scale:
   a. Where the investigation is not entrusted to or taken up by an outside agency (i.e. police/CBI), subsistence allowance will be payable at the following rates:
      1. For the first 3 months 1/3 of pay and allowances which the workman would have got but for the suspension.
      2. Thereafter ½ of the pay and allowances. After one year, full pay and allowances if the enquiry is not delayed for reasons attributable to the concerned workman or any of his representatives. Where the investigation is done by an outside agency and the said agency has come to the conclusion not to prosecute the employee, full pay and allowances will be payable after 6 months from the date of zreceipt of report of such agency, or one year after suspension whichever is later and in the event the enquiry is not delayed for reasons attributable to the workman or any of his representatives.

[*Note:*1. Any increment due to an employee or a rise or fall in the rate of dearness allowance should be taken into account for calculation of the quantum of subsistence allowance for each month.

2. The subsistence allowance will be 1/3 or ½ as the case may be, of the total emoluments. Even house rent allowance will be payable at 1/3 or ½ rates, as the case may be, during the period of suspension]".

It is clear from the above that the directions contained in paragraph 17.4 of Desai Award on the subject matter of subsistence allowance during the period of suspension pending enquiry has been modified by the settlement dated 8th September, 1983.

The comparative provisions of the Desai Award and the above referred settlement are as under:

Desai Award	*Settlement of 8.9.1983*
1. For first three months 1/3 of pay and allowances	1. No change
2. Thereafter, ½ of pay and allowance	2. (a) Thereafter ½ of pay and allowances up to the end of first year from the date of suspension. (b) After one year full pay and allowances.
3. Where enquiry is by an outside agency 1/3 of pay and allowances from the date of suspension to the end of 6th month and ½ of the pay and allowances for succeeding months till enquiry is over.	3. Where the outside agency conducting the investigations has come to the conclusion not to prosecute the employee full pay and allowances will be payable after 6 months from the date of receipt of report of the agency or one year after suspension whichever is later.

Full pay and allowances will be payable to bank employees even if they continue to be under suspension in case it is decided not to launch any prosecution and a report is received from the outside agency to that effect. In that case full wages will be payable after 6 months from the date of receipt of the report or one year after suspension whichever is later. In other instances, full pay and allowances will be payable after one year from the date of suspension provided the enquiry is not delayed for reasons attributable to the employee.

"The very opening sentence of the said provision says that where the investigation is not entrusted to or taken up by an out-side agency (i.e. police/CBI), a subsistence allowance will be payable (i) for the first three months 1/3rd of the pay and allowance which the workmen would have got but for the suspension (ii) thereafter half of the pay and allowances irrespective of the fact that workman has been placed under suspension without formal initiation of a department enquiry. Clause (iii) however, deals with both the exigencies, where the enquiry is initiated and investigation is also being done by an outside agency. Under the said clause workman is entitled for full pay and allowances after one year of his suspension if the enquiry is not delayed for the reasons attributable to the concerned workman or any of his representatives. But, where the investigation is also being done by an outside agency and the said agency has come to the conclusion not to prosecute the employee, full pay and allowances are payable after six months from the date of receipt of the report of such agency, or one year after suspension whichever is later. This clearly shows that the payment of full pay and allowances are to be made after one year irrespective of pendency of the criminal case. Otherwise the words after six months from the date of receipt of report of such agency would become redundant. For example if on investigation the outside agency concludes not to prosecute the employee within one month of his suspension then as per the said provision full pay and allowances will become payable after six months from the date of receipt of the report, but at the same time as per the said provision full pay and allowances would be payable one year after suspension, in view of the expression 'whichever is later'. Thus, this Court finds it difficult to reconcile the two on accepting the submission of the learned counsel for the bank.

The said view also finds support from the reiteration made in the last sentence after the words 'whichever is later', according to which full pay and allowances becomes payable after one year of suspension in the event the enquiry is not delayed for reasons attributable to the workmen or any of his representatives. Thus, it is evident that in a case where the outside agency submits report not to prosecute the employee the full pay and allowances are payable after six months from the date of receipt of the report, but denial of full pay and allowances cannot exceed one year after suspension. Any other interpretation would make either earlier period of six months or later period of one year mentioned in the said clause redundant.

It is by now well settled that the court should read difference in (sic) provisions in a manner that no part thereof is held to be superfluous or surplus and that where the language of a statute leads to manifest contradiction, a construction may be put upon it which emphasizes the managing of the words and even the structures of the sentence. (See AIR 1955 Supreme Court 830). Thus, this court holds that the petitioner became entitled for full pay and allowances after expiry of one year of his suspension and accordingly directs the respondents to pay full pay and allowances to the petitioner in terms of Shastri Award having regard to the fact that he has remained under suspension for more than one year.

In the result, this writ petition is partly allowed. In the facts arid circumstances, however, there shall be no order as to costs."[33] *In the States of Kerala and West Bengal the State Governments have enacted Payment of Subsistence Allowance Acts. In these states the payment of subsistence allowance and the quantum thereof will be regulated by the provisions of the aforesaid enactments.*

Whether the rule of 'no work no pay' will be applicable to cases of promotion will depend on the facts and circumstances of the case. The ordinary and the general rule is 'no pay no work' and therefore an employee who has not worked on a particular promotional post will not be entitled to the pay and allowances of that post. "*On the basis of the notional promotion given, such incumbent, obviously, shall be entitled to re-fixation of his salary. This is done to ensure that his present salary will not be less than his juniors. In the peculiar facts and circumstances of the case, if the incumbent has been wrongly denied his lawful claim of promotion and is made to suffer on account of administratative reasons for which he was not responsible, the court in such case keeping in view peculiarity of facts and circumstances obtaining therein may order payment of arrears when the incumbent was given promotion as was done in Vasant Rao Raman's case. In the present case we find no special facts or circumstances which necessitates deviation from the principle of 'no work no pay'*[34] As against promotion, if we are to look into illegal termination of employee from service, the law says that it is as if the termination never took place and hence full wages are payable to the employee.[35]

In K.V. Janakiraman's case, the employee was facing disciplinary/criminal proceedings and the sealed cover procedure was adopted when he was due for promotion. In this background when the matter went before the Supreme Court, that court said that when the employee is completely exonerated and is not visited with penalty even of censure indicating thereby that he was blame worthy in the least, he should not be deprived of any benefits including the salary of promotional post. "*We are not much impressed by the contentions advanced on behalf of the authorities. The normal rule of 'no work no pay' is not applicable to cases such as the present one where the employee although he is willing to work is kept away from work by authorities for no fault of his. This is not a case where the employee remains away from work for his own reasons, although the work is offered to him.*"[36]

It will be recalled that in the discussions on contract of employment, a pertinent point was made to the effect that the existing custom etc, can be over-ruled by law. This leads to an interesting point that law itself can set new terms and conditions of employment. For example: section 17-B of the Industrial Disputes Act 1947 which reads as follows: "Where in any case, a labour court, Tribunal or National Tribunal by its award directs reinstatement of any workman and the employer prefers any proceedings against such award in a High Court or the Supreme Court, the employer shall be liable to pay such workman, during the pendency of such proceeding in the High Court or Supreme Court, full wages last drawn by him, inclusive of any maintenance allowance admissible to him under any rule if the workman had not been employed in any establishment during such period and an affidavit by such workman had been filed to that effect in such court: Provided that where it is proved to the satisfaction of the High Court or the Supreme Court that such workman had been employed and had been receiving adequate remuneration during such period or part thereof, the court shall order that no wages shall be payable under this section for such period or part, as the case may be."

"From a reading of Section 17-B, it becomes clear that the employer shall be liable to pay such workman 'during the pendency of proceedings in the High Court, full wages last drawn by him, inclusive of any maintenance allowances etc. as indicated in Section 17.B of the Act. No doubt, an affidavit by such workman is required to be filed that the workman had not been employed in any establishment during the period. In the instant case, affidavits have been field by both the workmen."[37] Workman is entitled to the benefit under Sec. 17.B even if the employer is ultimately held to be not an industry under the Industrial Disputes Act.[38]

Now this is as far as a section 17-B is concerned. The courts have traveled beyond the scope of Section 17-B. Thus, the High Court could even grant wages as interim relief on terms beyond the parameters of section 17-B. In the case of Food Craft Institute, and Rameshwar Sharma the High Court held that Sharma had established that the amount being paid to him was grossly insufficient and deserved to be enhanced. The wages notified under the Minimum Wages Act, 1948 was a reasonable index of wages which should be admissible to the workman. Consequently the High Court granted relief to the workman.[39]

The Delhi High Court[40] was of view that Sec. 17-B did not preclude the High Court from awarding to the workman the amount higher than the last drawn wages." *The power to award such higher amount was traceable to Article 226 of the Constitution of India*" It is interesting to note that Section 17-B itself only spoke about "full wages last drawn" by the employee. In Dena Bank vs. Kirti Kumar T. Patel[41] , the Supreme Court held that the term meant the wages "*actually paid and not the amount that would be payable.*" This amount is not recoverable from the employee should he lose his case in the court. This Sec. 17-B also does not preclude the High Court or the Supreme Court by exercising the powers under Act 226 and 136 of the

Constitution of India from granting such higher amount as is considered necessary in the interests of justice. Such a direction will be de hors Section 17-B of the Industrial Disputes Act, 1947.[42] The Supreme Court[43], however, held that it will be in the interest of justice to ensure, if the facts of the case so justify, that the payment of any amount over and above the amount payable under Sec 17-B is ordered to be paid on such terms and conditions as would enable the employer to recover the same. And "if the workman has no tangible security to offer (to cover the differential) a personal bond would do."[44]

Now in U.P. the provisions of Section 17-B of the Industrial Disputes Act, 1947 do no exist in the U.P. Industrial Disputes Act. Hence the issue of compliance of that Section by the employer does not arise at all.[45] The Supreme Court went on to hold[46] that this will not preclude the employee from making a fresh application for grant of interim relief in his favor in accordance with law. One notices here that the court has used a language of restraint when it said "in accordance with law."

This needs to be considered in the background of the 2 Dena bank decisions mentioned supra. It was noticed there in that section 17-B does not preclude the High Court in exercising the powers under Art. 226 for granting such higher amount as is considered necessary in the interest of justice. There is no doubt that relief under Sec. 17-B can be granted for that has a legal basis. If there is no Section 17-B, the employment relationship comes to an end (subject of course to decision of the court) and there can be no basis-either fundamental basis or ordinary or other legal right or even an enforceable contractual right by which any relief can be granted. This aspect needs to be considered elaborately[47]. Can a claim for money not based on any provision of a statute be entertained and a writ of a mandamus be issued? Further even assuming that such a monetory claim arises from a contract of employment can writ for such monetory claim be issued to enforce contractual obligation even if it is meant to correct manifest, injustice or to remedy a breach of contract? One will have to wait for the development of law in this area. This power to interfere de hors Section 17-B is a judge made law.

Like law, judge made law can also change or lay-down conditions of employment. Sec. 33(2)(b) of the Industrial Disputes Act, 1947 provides for applications where employer seeks the approval of the Industrial Tribunal for dismissing the workman. In such circumstances, the employer was considered to have the right to suspend without payment of wages, a workman found guilty of misconduct pending disposal by the Tribunal of his application under Sec. 33(2)(b) for approval to dismiss or discharge the workman. In Lakshmi Devi Sugar Mills Ltd Vs. Ram Sarup, the Supreme Court held that if permission was accorded, the workman would not be paid anything for such period of suspension because his misconduct is proved and he is liable to be dismissed from the date of the finding against him. Thus, when the employer suspends the workman pending the order of the tribunal on his application and the Tribunal grants the permission applied for, the workman is not entitled to any wages for the period of suspension. "*So far as the employer is concerned, he has done all that he could be to bring the contract of service to an end, and if section 33 had not been there, the contract would have come to an end immediately after the conclusion of the employer's enquiry, and the employee would not have been entitled to any further wages. It is unfair to expect the employer to continue to pay the employee even after he had come to the conclusion that the employee was guilty of misconduct and that he should be dismissed, simply because of the accidental circumstance that proceedings in a previous dispute are pending before a Tribunal.*"[48] Thus all that Section 33 did was to make a basic change in the ordinary law of master and servant by imposing a ban on master's right to dismiss a servant found guilty of misconduct and pending the approval or permission of the Tribunal, read an implied term giving a right to the employer to suspend the workman found guilty of misconduct." *It follows that if the Tribunal grants the permission applied for, the suspended contract would come to an end and there will be no obligation to pay any wages after the date of suspension.*"[49] This was the law as pronounced by the Supreme Court and it remained so till 1986. In 1983, the Supreme Court came up with a decision to the effect that a civil servant pending consideration of his appeal filed against his conviction until the appeal was disposed off finally would be entitled to subsistence allowance. And it was felt that non payment of subsistence allowance would result in denial of reasonable opportunity to the employee to defend himself in the approval/permission application proceedings. And the Supreme Court held: "...... *the workman does not cease to be a workman until the Tribunal grants permission to dismiss the workman and the management dismisses the workman pursuant to such permission. An order of suspension by itself does not put an end to the employment. The workman continues to be an employee during the period of suspension and it is for this reason ordinarily the various standing orders in force in several factories and industrial establishments provide for payment of subsistence allowance which is normally less than the usual salary and allowance that are paid to the workman concerned. An order of suspension no doubt prevents the employee from rendering his service but it does not put an end to the relationship of master and servant between the management and the workman. When an application is made under S.33(3) of the Act the workman is entitled to defend himself before the Tribunal. In those proceedings it is open to him to show that the domestic enquiry held against him was not in accordance with law and principles of natural justice and the action proposed to be taken against him by the management is unjust and should not be permitted. Sometimes it may be necessary for either of the parties to lead evidence even before the Tribunal. The proceedings before the Tribunal very often take a long time to come to an end. In this very case the proceedings were pending before the Tribunal for nearly six years. Most of the workman are not in a position to maintain themselves and the members of their families during the pendency of such proceedings. In addition to the cost of maintenance of his family the workman has to find money to meet the expenses that he has to incur in connection with the proceedings pending before the Tribunal. In this case the appellant was in receipt of salary and allowances till the end of the disciplinary enquiry. But from 13th August, 1979 he was not paid even the barest subsistence allowance till 5th August, 1985 when the Tribunal passed its order / award on the application of the management and the complaint of the appellant. It is true that in the instant case the Tribunal granted the application of the management and rejected the complaint of the appellant. It was also quite possible that the Tribunal could have rejected the application of the management and upheld the complaint of the appellant in which case the appellant would have been entitled to continue to be an employee under the management of the factory and the disciplinary enquiry held against him would have no effect at all. Because it is difficult to anticipate the result of the application made before the Tribunal it is reasonable to hold that the workman against whom the application is made should be paid some amount by way of subsistence allowance to enable him to maintain himself and the members of his family and also to meet the expenses of the litigation before the Tribunal. And if no amount is paid during the pendency of such an application it has to be held that the workman concerned has been denied a reasonable opportunity to defend himself in the proceedings before the Tribunal. Such denial leads to violation of principles of natural justice and consequently vitiates the proceedings before the tribunal and subsection (3) of S.33 of the Act and any decision given in those proceedings against the workman concerned. No material has been placed before us in this case to show that the appellant had sufficient means to defend himself before the Tribunal."*

The 2 earlier decisions of the Supreme Court were pointed out to the bench.

"But neither of above two decisions the Court considered the question from the angle from which we have approached the problem. In neither of them the Court had the occasion to consider the whether the denial of payment of subsistence allowance during the pendency of the proceedings under Section. 33(3) of the Act would amount to violation of principles of natural justice. They approached the question from the angle of the common law right of a master to keep a workman under suspension either during the pendency of a domestic enquiry into an act of misconduct alleged to have been committed by a workman or during the pendency of an application under Section 33 of the Act. These were perhaps halcyon days when such applications were being disposed of quickly. If the Court had realized that such applications would take nearly six years as it has happened in this case their view would have been different. An unscrupulous management may by all possible means delay the proceedings so that the workman may be driven to accept its terms instead of defending

himself in the proceedings under S. 33(3) of the Act. To expect an ordinary workman to wait for such a long time in these days is to expect some thing which is very unusual to happen. Denial of payment of at least a small amount by way of subsistence allowance would amount to gross unfairness."[50] It is necessary to recall here that the Hotel Imperial's Case the judgment was by a bench of three judges, where as in Fakir Bai's Case the bench consisted of two judges. Yet the law stands altered!! In Ram Lakhan's case[51], it was held that the nature of application under Sec. 33(2)(C) is similar to the application under Sec. 33(1) and 33(3) and in both the cases the jural relationship continued between the employer and the employee and it is not severed or snapped till the permission is granted or approval is accorded. In the case of Standard Chartered Grindlays Bank Ltd.[52] the bank had filed an approval application before the Industrial Tribunal. The employee while opposing the application applied for subsistence allowance. The claim for subsistence allowance was granted by the Tribunal. Relying on all the above judgments in Air India Ltd's case, a single bench of the Bombay High Court pointed out that in Jaipur Zila Shakari Bhumi Vikas Bank Ltd. [2002 I LLJ p. 834] the Supreme Court had held that till the approval application is granted by the Tribunal, the jural relationship of master and servant continued. The judge went on to hold that therefore, where the employee is ready and willing to work for the employer, but is prevented by the employer from doing the work he is entitled to monthly wages. The single bench also held that the judgment in Fakirbhai read with Jaipur Zila Sahakari Bhumi Vikas Bank Ltd, declares that all employees concerned with Sec. 33 of the Act shall be entitled to subsistence allowance. This decision of the Single bench was set aside by the Division Bench of the High Court.[53]

Let us consider one more aspect. Under the general law, performance of work in accordance with the contract of employment is a condition which has to be fulfilled for earning wages unless, of course, the employer prevents the employee from discharging his duties in which event he is liable to pay wages. Now if the employee promises to produce a definite piece of work or a definite period of completion of service, unless it done, no wages will be payable[54]. Such contracts are indivisible by nature. The employee may, however, be entitled to remuneration for the period he actually worked when there is a usage to that effect or where there is an implied agreement to that effect or where the contract has been frustrated or where it has been so altered by the employer that the employee is entitled to regard it as at an end.[55] At this juncture, we can with profit look at Halbury's Laws of England: "*Performance of duty is condition precedent to remuneration. When the contract of employment is an as the entire contract, providing for payment on the completion of a definite period of service or of a definite piece of work, it is a condition precedent to the recovery of any remuneration in respect of it that the service or duty shall be completely performed, unless*

1. *The employer so alters the contract as to entitle the employee to regard it as at an end, in which case the whole sum payable under the contract becomes due; or*
2. *There is a usage in that the employee is entitled to remuneration in proportion to the time actually served; or*
3. *It can be inferred from the circumstances that there has been a fresh agreement between the parties that payment shall be made for the service actually rendered under the original contract, or*
4. *The contract has been frustrated, in which case the employee is entitled to recover from his employer such sum not exceeding the value of the benefit to the employer of anything done by the employee as the court considers just.*

"*What amounts to a breach of contract-There is a breach of the contract of employment whenever the employee absents himself from work without just cause or excuse or leaves his employment without just cause or excuse before the expiration of the agreed term, or, when no term has been fixed for the duration of the contract, without giving due notice. There is also a breach where the employee wrongfully repudiates the contract, refusing to be bound by it in the future; it is immaterial whether his repudiation is express or implied from his conduct, provided his intention to repudiate it is clear.*

A refusal to obey a lawful order or a refusal to serve the employer faithfully, by 'working to rule' or interpreting lawful orders in an unreasonable way, both amount to breach of contract."[56]

Performance of duty by the employee being a condition precedent for earning remuneration, the remuneration does not become due if there is a substantial breach of the contract on the part of the employee. A breach of contract by the employee also entitles the employer to claim damages, but does not authorise him to forfeit remuneration which has already been earned, i.e. which has become due before the breach, unless there is an express term to that effect [see Halsbury's Laws of England, 4th edition, vol. 16, paragraphs 581 and 583]- The legal position that an employee forfeits remuneration not only when he absents from duty but also when he willfully does not discharge his duty, is clearly brought out from the decision of the Court of Appeal in Secretary of State Vs. ASLEF, [1972] to All E.R. 413. In that case the employees had resorted to "work to rule". In that context Lord Denning M.R., observed as follows."

"Now I quite agree that a man is not bound positively to do more for his employer than his contract requires. He can withdraw his goodwill if he pleases. But what he must not do is willfully to obstruct the employer as he goes about his business. That is plainly the case where a man is employed singly by a single employer. Take a homely instance, which I put in the course of argument. Suppose I employ a man to drive to the station. I know there is sufficient time, so that I do not tell him to hurry. He drives me at slower speed than he need, with the deliberate object of making me lose the train, and I do lose it. He may say that he has performed the letter of the contract; he has driven me to the station; but he has willfully made me lose the train, and that is a breach of contract beyond all doubt. And what is more, he is not entitled to be paid for the journey. He has broken the contract in a way that goes to the very root of the consideration; so he can recover nothing".

"So much for the case when a man is employed singly. It is equally the case when he is employed 'as one of many' to work in an undertaking which needs the service of all. If he, with the others, takes steps willfully to disrupt the undertaking, to produce chaos so

that it will not run as it should, then each one who is a party to those steps is guilty of breach of his contract. It is no answer for any one of them to say 'I am only obeying the rule book', or 'I am not bound to do more than a 40 hour week.' That would be all very well if done in good faith without any willful disruption of services; but what makes it wrong is the object with which it is done. There are many branches of our law when an act which would be otherwise lawful is rendered unlawful by the motive or object with which it is done. So here it is the willful disruption which is the breach. It means that the work of each man goes for naught. It is made of no effect. I ask : Is a man to be entitled to wages for his work when he with others, in doing his best to make it useless. Surely not. Wages are to be paid for services rendered, not for producing deliberate chaos."

Thus in a contract of employment the liability to pay wages arises when the employee works in terms of the contract of employment except when he is on leave in terms of the contract of employment or because of circumstances beyond his control such as non-opening of bank's branch, etc. Therefore, if an employee does not perform his work as undertaken by him in his offer of employment, he is not entitled to wages. For example, where putters in coal mines, remained idle on a particular day in view of a dispute about computation of wages, it was held that wages became due each day as they were earned and that for the four days when the workers did not work they were not entitled to wages. Yet in another case the employee was found absent from Monday to Wednesday. The Court found that the employment was on weekly basis and held that in that the employee was not entitled to wages for work done on Thursday and Friday. The contract of employment was thus considered indivisible.

"Where a contract consists of mutual promises, they may be dependent, independent or concurrent.........Where the promises are dependent due performance by one party of his promise is a condition precedent to the other party performing his promise and the non-performance of such a condition precedent releases the other party from his obligation to perform the contract." It is clear that[57] apart from statute, payment of wages or other remuneration is a matter of contract.[58]

Though the aforesaid view is the position under the English Law, in India the accepted position is that a contract of employment is on a monthly basis and that wages are generally payable monthly.

Thus though in manufacturing, industrial workers may be designated as "daily rated workmen" wages are paid only at the end of the month. This position is also statutorily embodied in section 4(2) of the Payment of Wages Act which lays down that "no wage period shall exceed one month."

Most of the High Courts also are of the view that the contract of employment is monthly. In Ralli Bros vs. Ambika[59] it was held that where salary was payable by the month and the employee leaves without notice, he is not entitled to the salary for the day's work i.e. the broken period of the month. In Dharma Behara vs. Seven Daks[60] it was held that a monthly paid employee wrongly leaving in the middle of the month would lose his salary only for that period he had not worked. This position was reiterated in A.M.Chokalingam Mudalier Vs. G.Mohammed Sherif Sahab[61]. In that case the employee was engaged from 1st April 1938 to 31st March 1939. The employee left without justification on 20th March 1939. His salary was Rs. 18/- per month payable in lump sum - Rs. 296/- at the end of the year. The learned judge in that case felt that to treat the contract as indivisible was inequitable.

However, in Arjun Vs. Homusjee Shapurjee Servai[62], Mcleod and Shah, it was held that wages were earned every day although they were not paid till the end of the month. It seems well settled that the contract of employment is presumed to be monthly and though wages are payable by month, for the purpose of deduction of wages, taking an equitable view of the matter, wages should be considered to be earned from day-to-day and the workman would be entitled to wage for the day's actual work.

In this background let us examine the contract of employment in Banks. Clause 13.2 of the Bipartite Settlement dated 19th October, 1966, lays down that an employee who desires to obtain leave of absence other than casual leave shall apply in writing to the Manager or any other officer appointed for that purpose. An employee, therefore, cannot remain absent without permission. Clause 13.7 of the aforesaid Bipartite Settlement reads as under:

"Gazetted holidays (that is Bank Holidays under the Negotiable Instruments Act) other than Sundays shall not be prefixed or suffixed to any leave without the sanction of the competent authority having been first obtained. An employee who overstays his leave (except under circumstances beyond his control for which he must tender a satisfactory explanation) shall not be paid his pay and allowances (other than house rent allowance based on pay, i.e. basic pay, officiating and special allowances, if any last drawn) for the period he overstays and shall further render himself liable to such disciplinary action as the management may think fit to impose."

In the chapter dealing with hours of work clause 14.2 specifies the actual hours of work of a full time workman exclusive of recess period. Clause 14.8 specifies the normal total period of work including overtime. The cumulative effect of these provisions is that an employee of the Bank is entitled to his wages for work done during the month during the stipulated hours of all working days. The contract thus entitles a workman to his wages when he has actually worked during the stipulated period every day of all the working days in the month. The employee, however, need not work if he is not given any work although he is willing to work. He cannot also be faulted if he does not work due to situations beyond his control such as illness, during times of civil commotion, etc. If the correct position is as stated above, a bank would be entitled to withhold wages during a workman's absence without permission/leave from his place of work. In one of the judgments of the Calcutta High Court[63] proceeded on the basis that the contract of employment is not a divisible one.

In that case, the Court considered the justification of wage deduction on 3 occasions viz.,

I. For varying periods from 2 hours to 25 and 30 minutes on 4 dates viz 3,4,6 and 17th June, 1975.

II On 30th June.1975 when employees abstained without prior santion of leave.

III Mass demonstration on 1st and 2nd July,1975 for half an hour.

On items (I) and (III) the Court held that the bank is not justified in deducting wages and on item (II) the Court held that the bank is entitled to refuse to pay the pay and allowances.

Now let us see item (I). In the words of the Court: "*The members of the Award staff are permanent employees of the Bank. Each of the employees is entitled to a monthly salary on the basis of his scale of pay under the terms and conditions of his employment. The monthly salary payable to each of the employees is a fixed sum. Under the contract of employment the employees are required to attend to their work, during fixed hours. Although the employees are required under the terms of employment to work during fixed hours, it cannot be said, in my opinion, that the employees are paid on the basis of number of hours put in by the employees in course of any month. The salary payable to an employee is a fixed sum. The number of working hours, however, is not a constant and fixed number and the numbers of working hours may vary from month to month some months consists of 31 days while some months consist of 30 days and the month of February usually consists of 28 days. Again, in a particular month their may be holidays and the number of holidays may again vary from month to month. The employees are also entitled to get leave with pay and such leave may be casual leave or earned leave. The number of hours of work put in by the employee must, therefore, necessarily vary from month to month. Although the number of hours of work may vary from month to month, the employees get and are entitled to get the same amount of salary to which the employees are entitled under the contract of employment every month. To my mind, it cannot, therefore, be said that the employees earn their salary in any particular month on the basis of the number of hours of work put in. As the employees do not earn their monthly salary by putting in any fixed number of hours of work in course of the month, it cannot be said, in my opinion, that the employees earn their salary from hour to hour. They become entitled to their salary under the contract of employment so long as the contract of employment subsists. The employees are undoubtedly required under the terms of employment to work during the fixed hours of work. An employer engages the employee for getting his services and in return employer agrees to pay the salary or wages to the employee for getting his services. The rights and obligations of the employer and of the employee are generally governed by the contract of employment between the parties, subject, however, to any statutory enactment which may have any bearing on the question. The hours of work fixed for an employee under the settlement constitute a term of the employment. If any employee commits any breach of the said term by not doing the work in accordance therewith, the employer may have a cause of action against the employee for breach of contract and may seek appropriate relief for the breach. If, however, the contract of employment is kept alive and is subsisting, the employer cannot refuse to pay to the employee the salary payable to him under the contract and cannot claim to deduct any part of the salary payable to the employee unless the contract of employment or any other law authorises the employer to do so. If the hours of work fixed under the settlement be treated as the consideration for the engagement of the employee, any failure or refusal on the part of an employee, to work during some part of the entire period of the working hours will result in a partial failure of the consideration. The employer for partial failure of the consideration by the refusal or failure on the part of the employee to do the work for the fixed hours in their entirety cannot deduct any portion of the salary payable to the employee under the contract if the contract of employment is kept alive and subsisting, unless the contract of employment is held to be a divisible contract and on the basis of the divisibility of the contract of employment recovery can be made on the basis of the partial failure of the consideration. It is well-settled that in such a case the right of the employer is to claim compensation.*

In the instant case, the contract of employment is not a divisible one. The consideration of payment of the salary to the employees is not related to any fixed period of work for any month. The consideration is one and indivisible and on the basis thereof, the monthly salary is payable. As the consideration is not divisible and is not entirely dependent on the particular hours of work put in and the consideration is one, the failure or refusal on the part of an employee to do the fixed period of work on any particular day results in a partial failure of the consideration in consequence whereof an employer may claim compensation against the employee; but the employer cannot claim the right to deduct any part of the salary on any pro rata basis or otherwise."

On the (iii) issue relating to mass demonstration, while dealing with Section 7 and 9 of the Payment of Wages Act, the court observed: *"….. or authority to make any deduction from the wages of an employee is conferred under these sections and not by definition given in S. 2(6) of the Act. The Payment of Wages Act has no application in the instant case. The Shops and Establishments Act which applies in the instant case contains no provisions similar to the provisions contained in Ss. 7 and 9 of the Payment of Wages Act authoring and empowering the employer to make any deduction from the wages of the employee for absence from duty.*

It has to be noted that the language used in Ss. 7 and 9 of the Act speaks of deduction from wages. In the notices or orders in question the language used is also deduction from salary. As it cannot be said that the employees have not earned their wages or salary for their refusal or failure to do the work during the period they indulged in mass demonstration, the notices or orders in substance and in effect direct deduction from salary payable to the employees. Unless the employer is empowered or authorized by any Act or under the terms and conditions of the employment to deduct any part of the salary from the salary payable to the employees, any such deduction will be unauthorized and in excess of the power of the employer and will, therefore, be illegal. Under the conditions of service contained in the two Awards and the settlement there is no provision authorizing the Bank to deduct any part of the salary on a pro rata basis for failure or refusal on the part of the employees to carry on their work during any part of the working hours after the employees have attended office and joined their duties. The settlement, to my mind indicates that provisions has been made for this kind of conduct on the part of the employees, should any occasion so arise. Under the settlement this kind of conduct on the part of the employees is considered to be misconduct and relevant provisions have been made for dealing with acts of misconduct of the employees. The specific provisions in the settlement relating to such conduct on the part of the employees also go to show that the Bank cannot be said to enjoy the power of such deduction by any necessary implication. Para 19.5 of the settlement, which defines gross misconduct inter alia, provides - 19.5. by the expression 'gross misconduct' shall be meant any of the following acts and omissions on the part of an employee:

(a) ....

(b) ....

(c) ....

Wilful damage or attempt to cause damage to the property of the bank or any of its customers;

(c) *Wilful insubordination or disobedience of any lawful and reasonable order of the management or of a superior;*

(f) ....

(g) *Wilful slowing down in performance of work;* (h)

(i)

(j) *Doing any act prejudicial to the interest of the bank or gross negligence or negligence involving or likely to involve the bank in serious loss.*

(k)

(l)

(m)

(d) *Para 19.7 which defines 'minor misconduct' inter alia provides-19.7. By the expression 'Minor misconduct' shall be meant any of the following acts and omissions on the part of an employee:*

(a) Absence without leave or overstaying sanctioned leave without sufficient grounds;

(b) Unpunctual or irregular attendance;

(c) Neglect of work, negligence in performing duties;

(d) Breach of any role of business of the Bank or instruction for the running of any department;

(e) ....

(f) ....

(g) ....

(h) Holding or attempting to hold or attending any meeting on the premises of the Bank without the previous permission of the management or except in accordance with the provisions of any rule or law for the time being in force;

(i) ....

(j) ....

(k) ....

Failure or refusal to carry on with the work during working hours may constitute neglect of work and may also in appropriate cases constitute an act prejudicial to the interest of the bank or gross negligence or negligence involving or likely to involve the bank in serious loss. Depending on the facts and circumstances, an act of refusal or failure on the part of employees to carry on with their work during working hours by holding mass demonstrations during working hours instead of engaging themselves in their work may constitute "gross" or "minor" misconduct and suitable disciplinary action may be taken against employees concerned in-accordance with the provisions contained in the settlement. Such an act on the part of the employee, though it may constitute misconduct and may be dealt with accordingly does not authorize or empower the bank to deduct any part of their salary. To enable the bank to make any deduction from the salary of the employees the bank must have that power either on the basis of the terms of employment or under any law. But any neglect of work during working hours, whether by the failure or refusal to carry on with the work during the fixed hours it cannot be said that the employee does not earn his salary for the period during which he has not so worked. As in the instant case neither the contract of employment nor any other law authorizes the bank of deduct any part of the salary from the salary payable to the employee on the ground of the employee's failure or refusal to do the work during the said period, the notices or orders directing deduction on a pro rata basis from the salary payable to the employees must be held to be without any lawful authority and in excess of the powers enjoyed by the bank.

With regards to item (ii), the court held it in Bank's favor. "On this day some of the employees did not attend office without obtaining any leave on the ground that on the basis of the practice prevailing in the Bank they were not required to attend office as they were not connected with the work of the closing of accounts. This is, therefore, a case of absence for a whole day and this case is not concerned with the question of any pro rata deduction from the salary for failure or refusal to carry on with the work during sometime of the fixed hours of duty. Unauthorized absence from office for a day necessarily amounts to leave without sanction or authority. This authorizes and enables the bank to make any deduction from the salary for absence of the employees on the 30th of June, 1975: The absence has to be unauthorized and the Bank must have necessary authority under the conditions of service or any other statute to make the necessary deduction. I have no doubt in the facts and circumstances of the instant case that the absence of the employees on the 30th of June on the plea of the practice set up by them is clearly unauthorized and without any justification. The case of the employees of the practice prevailing in the Bank requiring the employee connected with the closing of the work to attend and permitting other employees to enjoy a holiday is clearly untenable. According to petitioners this practice has been prevailing in the Bank for over 2 years. This practice must, therefore, have been in vogue and force at the time when the settlement was arrived at Para 14.9 of the settlement provides:

"Any days declared as holidays under the Negotiable Instruments Act.1881 for half yearly and yearly closing of accounts, shall be deemed to be normal working days for all workman employed in all Banks."

This particular provision in the settlement clearly indicates that 30th June would be deemed to be a normal working day for all workmen employed in all Banks. As employees in certain Banks must have claimed that it was not necessary for all employees to attend on the half yearly and yearly closing days and might have set up a kind of practice prevailing in any Bank and as the Banks must have insisted that all employees should attend on these two dates this provision in the settlement must have been incorporated to put an end to any kind of practice that might have prevailed in any particular Bank with regard to attendance of all the employees of the Bank on these two days. It has also to be noted that the settlement itself contains special provisions for some Banks in chapter 21 and in Para 21.6 of the settlement some special provisions of Bank of India have been made; but no special provision preserving or maintaining such practice if there was any of the Bank requiring only the employees connected with the closing of accounts to attend on these two days of closing of accounts and exempting the other employees from attending office on these two days has been made. The said settlement is binding on the parties. In view of the specific provision made in Para 14.9 of the settlement expressly stating that any days declared as holidays under the Negotiable Instrument Act the half yearly and yearly closing of accounts shall be deemed to be normal working days for all workmen employed in all Banks. No reliance can be placed on the case of the employees who absented themselves on the 30th of June on the plea of such practice and the said case must be rejected. It has to be further noted that before the 30th of June the Bank had been issuing a notice every year to the effect that the said day would be considered to be normal working day for all employees and all employees would be required to attend. It does not appear that any protests were made with regard to the issuing of such notices by the Bank by raising the plea of the prevailing practice. The fact that not withstanding the provisions contained in the Settlement and the notices issued by the Bank some employees had not attended on these days of closing of accounts and had been paid their salary in the past does not either established the practice or justify the claim and conduct of the petitioners. In view of the specific provision in the Settlement which is binding on the petitioners the absence of the employees who absented themselves on the 30th of June without any application for leave must necessarily be held to be unauthorized and unjustified.

The conditions of service, to my mind, postulate that in case of such unauthorized absence the Bank will be justified in deducing the salary of the employee for the day of such unauthorized absence. Chapter XII of the Settlement deals with various kinds of leave available to an employee of the Bank and makes provisions for necessary rules relating to such leave. Para 13.7 contained in the said Chapter. inter alia, provides "An employee who overstays his leave (except under circumstances beyond his control for which he must tender a satisfactory explanation) shall not be paid his pay and allowances (Other than house rent allowance based on pay, that is, basic pay, officiating and special allowance) if any, last drawn for the period he overstays and shall further render himself liable to such disciplinary action as the management may think fit to impose". Para 13.27 contained in the said Chapter lays down "Any absence from duty without satisfying the requisite conditions under which leave may be taken or obtaining such leave on false grounds would justify any Bank, after giving the employee an opportunity to explain, in not treating the employee as on casual leave but as being absent without leave on loss of pay and allowance." The aforesaid conditions read with the other conditions of service indicate, to my mind, that an unauthorized absence from duty for a day justifies the Bank in deducting the pay and allowance to the employees for that day from the pay and allowances payable to the employee. In my opinion, the conditions of service make this position sufficiently clear expressly, and if not expressly, in any event by necessary implication. In the view that I have taken, it does not appear to me necessary to consider and deal with the various authorities which have been citied from the Bar on this aspect. The decision of Sabyasachi Mukherji, J., dated the 13th November, 1975 in Matter No. 798 of 1973 (Sukumar Bandopadhyava and others v. State of West Bengal and others) is also of no assistance, as the said decision turns on a construction of the specific provisions contained in the Rules. The said authorities to my mind, do not have any direct bearing on the question involved and are not of any great assistance.

The conditions of service may authorize and empower the Bank not to pay the pay and allowance for unauthorized absence from duty to an employee who did not attend office on the half yearly closing day, that is the 30th of June, 1975 on the plea that he was not required to attend office on the basis of the practice, in the Bank. This refusal to pay the pay and allowance to the employee for that day will, however, amount to a deduction from the pay and allowance payable to the employee in terms of the contract of employment. Refusal to pay is proper and justified not on the ground that the employee did not earn his pay and salary by not attending to work but on the ground that the Bank under the terms of employment is entitled to refuse to pay the pay and allowances for that day for unauthorized absence on the part of the employee."

And in the particular instance the Court went on to hold that there has been no violation of the principles of natural justice.

Bankers surely were not happy with the judgment. Surely in such instances, the employers right is not for compensation. Fortunately for the bankers, soon enough the matter came up for consideration in another Banks case.[64] Some of the employees remained absent from their work, shouted slogans and squatted inside the Bank's premises without doing any work from 3 P.M. to 5.45 P.M. The Bank did not pay wages for the period of absence of the employees who filed a claim petition under Sec. 33(C)(2) of the Industrial Dispute Act 1947. The judge considered several decisions, including the above referred judgment in Manoj Kumar Kanti's case. He disagreed with the judgment in that case and held:"*In the instance case before the petitioner had employed the respondent No. 2 there was a promise of doing work by the respondent no-2 on certain terms and the terms enjoined that the respondent no-2 would perform the work for certain hours in a month.*

His right to get remuneration is calculated on monthly basis but upon the performance of his work during the working hours, as stipulated in the agreement. In this context good deal of controversy has been raised on the question whether the contract was entire or divisible in the sense whether the employee earned the right to get the wages for any particular hour of work. On behalf of the petitioner, stress has been laid on Chapter XIV of the settlement between the parties which indicated that over time wages had to be calculated on hourly basis. Therefore, the remuneration payable to the employee was based on hourly work. On the other hand the respondent no-2 has contended that respondent was not a workman getting his salary hourly. He was a workman employed whose salary was calculated monthly. His right to get the remuneration or his right to get the consideration for his work was not correlated with hourly work. He has further argued before me that if the basis upon which the overtime was calculated is applied for payment of his wages it would result in an incongruous situation for payment of his monthly salary.

I am of the opinion that the wages, as in the words of Lord Denning, are the payment for services rendered. I am inclined to think that it is not so much a question of whether the contract is divisible or entire but reciprocal promises as the consideration, that is to say, the employer provides the employment and pays the remuneration and the employee performs the work during the period he is supposed to do the work. Therefore, the right of the employee to get the remuneration depends upon the performance of his work during the period of employment. If there is any failure of that consideration then taking a strict view of the matter the employer is entitled to refuse any payment at all. But, as has been noticed in "The Contract of the "Employment" " by M.R.Freedland. referred to here in before, very often policy considerations enter and deduction on pro rata basis is made to avoid undue hardship in the employer employee relationship. It is true that the definition of the payment of the Wages under the Shops and Establishment Act, which is applicable to the instant case, and the deduction of which wage is made an offence under S.14 of the Shops and Establishments Act brings in the definition provided by the Payment of Wages Act and that definition in express terms as remuneration that would have been payable if the terms of employment were fulfilled and one of the main terms of employment is undoubtedly in the instance case that the employee would work for a specified period of work during the working hours. Therefore, if the employee does not work for a specified period of work then the remuneration would not be payable. But in the instant case, because of the next aspect of the matter which I shall presently discuss it is not necessary for me to rest my decision on this aspect of the matter. But I express the above view about the employer's right to deduct wages tentatively with great respect to A.N.Sen, J. " The learned judge held that wages were payments for services rendered and pro rata deduction there of for absence without notice resulting in failure of consideration was permissible.

In a case between Mr V.Ramachandran and Indian Bank[65] a Division Bench of the Madras High Court upheld the principle of "no work no pay". The Court held that an employee had to do his duty to earn his wages and absence from duty would deprive him of the remuneration for the time during which he was absent from duty. The Hon'ble High Court repelled the contention that the employer could under such circumstances sue for breach of contract and claim compensation and not unilaterally effect a deduction from the wages.

The Punjab High Court in a dispute between Dharam Singh Vs. Bank of India[66] held that since the hours of work of the bank had been fixed, the employees had a duty to work for the full working hours in order to earn wages and that any stoppage of work during working hours would virtually affect the work for a whole day and it would also paralyse the working of the bank. The Hon'ble Court also held that for the purpose of wages, working hours were to be divided as the working hours of each day and that the day could not be split further. Further, the Hon'ble Court went on to hold that where wages were paid on monthly basis, the month could be reasonably split up into a number of days during the month but that it could not be split into hours, minutes and seconds. It was further held that the employees could not have unrestricted discretion to report for work any time of the day and still be at liberty to claim remuneration for working for the remaining part of the day. Deduction of pay for full day for absence of a portion of the day was upheld in that case. The Madras High Court had an occasion to consider a similar case.[67] During the arguments on behalf of the employee it was contented that the bank would be entitled to deduct pro/rata wages of the employees for the period of absence from duty. But it was argued that the employer had no right to deduct the whole day's salary for partial day's absence. The banks contention that the employees would not be entitled even to claim the pro/rata wages was repelled by the court for the reason that the bank in that case had acquiesced the breach committed by the employees by allowing them to work for the rest of the hours during which they had not struck work. In yet another case[68] Justice Nainar Sundaram after considering various decisions referred to disagreed with a judgment in Manoj Kanti Basu and held:

"In the instant case, one significant aspect which cannot be omitted to be taken note of is the relevant clause in the bipartite settlement. Chapter 13 deals with leave rules. Clause 13.27 thereof reads as follows:

Any absence from duty without satisfying the requisite conditions under which leave may be taken or obtaining such leave on false grounds would justify any bank, after giving the employee an opportunity to explain, in not treating the employee as on casual leave but as being absent without leave on loss of pay and allowance.

When the petitioner and the other Award staff abstained from duty for 4 hours on 29-12-1977, the respondent-Bank did not acquiesce in the breach of the contract and chose to treat the contract of employment for the day as totally breached and declared that there will be no pay for the day in question. Hence, the aspect of acquiescence, which had very much weighed with Padmanabhan, J. in V. Ganesan V. State Bank of India,[1981-I LLJ 64] is significantly absent in present case. As stated earlier, it would be wholly iniquitous to compel the employer to pay the employee when he has not worked to earn his wages. I am in entire agreement with the view expressed by Sadasiva Aiyar, J, in the earliest pronouncement in Chokalinga Mudaliar Vs. Mohomede Sherif Saib, (1912) 23 M.L.J.680, that the Court should not be too strict in treating the contract of service for a certain period and for a certain wages as indivisible. After all, a man should work to earn his wages and when he has not worked, he cannot be permitted to claim wages by bringing in too technical a rule that the contract is indivisible and in the absence of statutory provisions and rules, the employer must pay out wages even though not earned by the employee by performance of actual work and the employer must seek his remedy only by claiming compensation else where. Clause 13.27 of the bipartite settlement, to a very great extent supports the stand of the respondent–Bank that absence from duty without satisfying the requisite conditions will be treated as absence without leave on loss of pay and allowances. It is not as if the employees in the present case were not put on notice about the proposed action. May be, it would be a good ground for disciplinary action. But the proposition "no work, no pay" has been declared and settled without any ambiguity in V. Ramachandran Vs. Indian Bank, [1979- I LLJ. 122], by the Division Bench of this Court. It cannot be stated that we expressed a view only on the basis that the provisions of the Tamil Nadu Shops and Establishment Act, 1947 applied to the facts of that case. We were more on the general law that should apply to the stated situation. Admittedly, the petitioner and other Award Staff did not render any service in any part of the day in question. For four hours they abstained from work, committing a breach of the contract of service, which must deem to contemplate service being rendered for the whole of the day. Rightly, the respondent–Bank treated them in breach, did not acquiesce in the same, and declined to permit them to work for the rest of the working hours. The result is there was no service rendered by the employees for the whole day in question. Hence the rule "no work, no pay" squarely applied. As the matter stands, I am bound by the above pronouncement of the Division Bench. Viewed from this angle, I could not say that the action taken by the respondent–Bank is wholly untenable and has got to be discountenanced."

A similar issue was considered in the case between Vikram Tamaskar Vs. Steel Authority of India Ltd. The Madhya Pradesh High Court held that under the general law, performance of service in accordance with the contract of employment is a condition precedent for earning the remuneration or salary. *"If the contract is indivisible providing for payment on the completion of a definite period of service or a definite piece of work then no part of the remuneration can be recovered unless the service is completely performed. If an employee absents from work without just cause or excuse, he commits breach of the terms of contract. A refusal to obey a lawful order or a refusal to serve the employer faithfully by "working to rule" or interpreting lawful orders in an unreasonable way, both amount to breach of contract. Where the employees deliberately and in a concerted move merely attends the place of work and does not work at all with a view to force the company to agree to their demands, they are not entitled to salary for those as they are guilty of breach of contract of service. In such a case it could not be said that the conduct of the employee in not working or slowing down the work amounted to misconduct and the management could have taken action against the employees. It is not correct to say that the rules disentitled the management to deduct wages for the periods during which the employees did not work. The rules relating to penalty have no bearing whatsoever on the employer's right to deduct salary for non-performance of duty:"*[69]

In a case between Prakash Chandra Johari and Indian Overseas Bank, the Rajasthan High Court categorically held[70] that an employee is supposed to carry out his duties during the working hours and in case, he for any reason refuses to work or absents himself during these working hours without permission of the authorities competent to permit, the bank will be justified in deducting wages for the period of his absence.

The Madras High Court had another occasion to consider a similar issue. In that case,[71] The Madras circle of State Bank of India had issued a circular dated 11th November 1983. on the strength of that circular the Branch Manager of the bank effected wage-cut on an employee for not completing the work allotted to him. The wage cut is challenged in this writ petition. The High Court held that the employees did turn up for work and they did not absent themselves during any part of the day and the charges leveled against them are that they did not complete the work allocated to them though they were present for duty. This could only be the subject matter of scrutiny in a disciplinary proceedings after satisfying the requisite formalities, including the affording of an opportunity to the employees to make their say in the matter, and passing ultimate orders thereafter and certainly there could not be straightaway cut of the wages on the ground that the employees did not complete the work allocated to them as has been done now.

The issue of no work no pay was tested on the basis of constitutionality of the directive issued in the case of New Bank of India.[72] It was felt that if the banks circular framed a conduct rule banning any type of demonstration or agitation or criticism of the authorities, it would be violative of Art. 19(1)(a) of the Constitution of India. The Court observed: *"In the instance case, however, no action is being taken merely for participation in a demonstration or agitation. Action is being taken merely for absence from work during working hours. One may have fundamental rights of doing many things, but does not follow that those things can be done by him during office hours for which payment is to be made to him. These decisions are clearly distinguishable as they do not deal with the right of the employer not to pay an employee for any period during which no work is done. What has been laid-down in the circular is that if normal working hours is spent in demonstration or agitation caused any absence or abstention from duty then wages may be deducted for absence. This provision does not violate any fundamental right."*

The limit of the right to demonstrate was re-emphasized in Engineering Projects (P) Ltd. Vs Engineering Projects (P) Ltd. Employees Union 1986 Lab. I.C. 1266 (Dell) in these words:

"According to Article 19, every freedom to assemble peacefully, citizens freedom of speech and freedom to form association or union there is a limit to the said fundamental rights and they cannot exercise those rights in whatever place they please. Those rights cannot be exercised on the premises belonging to or occupied by another.

Therefore, though the employees of a Company have right to hold demonstration, give speeches and shout slogans to get their grievances redressed they have no right to indulge in those activities on office premises of the Company and interfere in the working of the company". To this, we may add "during the working hours" and if they do so, the employers will have a right to deduct wages on the basis of the now well established doctrine of "no work, no pay".

And while every one in the banking industry thought that the rule of "no work no pay" has come to stay, in the famous T.S. Kelawalas case the Bombay High Court held that the bank will not be justified in deducting full days wages for part days strike and in this behalf struck down the administrative instructions issued by the bank. That judgment[73] when it was pronounced assumed considerable importance. The High Court in analyzing the arguments on behalf of the bank held:

"Also looked at another way, it is important that under the conditions of service, wages are paid not from day to day or hour to hour, but by fixed sum on a monthly basis. The contract between the Bank and the workers is not a divisible one. It is a monthly contract. It is not the day or the hour but the month which is the unit of the contract of employment. All months do not have the same number of days. Some months may have holidays/Sundays. Other months may

have holidays with varying number of holidays in different months. The employees are also entitled to leave with pay, casual leave and the earned leave. The number of days and hours of work put in would therefore vary from month to month. Yet (permissible deductions apart), the monthly wage does not vary from month to month. Being a monthly contract, the consideration is one and indivisible and on the basis thereof a monthly salary is payable. Of course they are required to work during fixed hours. That is for administrative and public convenience. Yet that does not change the unit of the contract of employment from monthly to daily or hourly. Non-observance may give the employer a cause of action for breach of the contract and right to take appropriate remedy for such breach. But if the monthly contract is kept alive and subsisting, deduction by the Bank of a days wage or even a 4-hour deduction would be arbitrary and impermissible. Failure or refusal on the part of the employee to work during the fixed hours on any particular day may result in a partial failure of consideration. In consequence thereof an employer may claim compensation against the employee, but not the right to deduct any part of the salary on any pro rata basis or otherwise. (V.Ganesan V State bank of India). (1981) I LLJ 64 (Mad.) supra and P.K.Bose v. Bank of India. (1977)2 LLJ 285 (Cal.). In the absence of a specific term in the regulations, awards and settlements, the bank could not, in the guise of an administrative circular, unilaterally reduce the monthly wage and give the employee a lesser monthly salary than the one contracted. Giving the employee a lesser pay packet at the end of the month cannot (in the words of the Supreme Court in Khanzodes case) be "incidental to the obligation to carry out the purpose for which the Bank was constituted" or "giving effect to the provisions of the Act. Looked at either way the impugned circular must be struck down." In-spite of the decision of the Bombay High Court looking into various decisions of the other High Courts it seemed that the position in law was very clear Viz., that the bank would be justified in deducting the days wages for stoppage of work for part of the day on the basis that the employees had not worked. If this be correct construction of the terms of contract of employment, then, if an employee is merely physically present in the office but does not perform any work he will not be entitled to wages for that day. As regards the question whether the employee will be justified in not performing the work the employer wants him to perform, it may depend upon the scope of the employees duties and the deviation that the employer wants to make from the scope of such duties. If the scope of work allotted by the employer is a part of the employees normal duties or is ancillary to his main duties, or is connected with his main duties, then it will not be open to the employee to refuse to perform the duties given by the employer. In such instances the employer will be justified in deducting pro-rata wages if the employee refuses to perform the allotted work.

The Madras High Court considered the question as to whether days wages could be deducted because the employee refused to attend the clearing house. The High Court answered the question in the negative.[74]

" The reason for the proposed deduction of the wages for the day 20 February 1981, was that the petitioner refused to attend the clearing house at local State Bank of India which was stated to be part of the petitioners routine work allotted to him as per office order No. 7/80 dated 8 October 1980. The petitioner was not proceeded with by way of disciplinary action for disobedience of the office order No. 7/80 dated 8 October 1980. It is not a case of the petitioner totally abstaining from duty on 20 February 1981. He did report for duty on that day. But since he would not obey the office order No. 7/80, dated 8 October 1980, he was denied further work for the rest of the day. In the counter-affidavit filed on behalf of the respondents, there is no averment that the petitioner did not do any work at all on 20 February1981. On the other hand, the averments in the counter-affidavit indicate that the petitioner performed part of his duties. In the said circumstances, it will not be proper to invoke the principle "no work-no pay" and straightway deny the petitioner the wages for 20 February 1981. As already noted, the respondents have not resorted to any disciplinary action for disobedience of the earlier office order, by the petitioner. In the said circumstance, I have to countenance the prayer in the writ petition. Accordingly, this writ petition is allowed. No costs. However, if there had been in fact disobedience of the office order No. 7/80, dated 8 October 1980, and on that ground the respondents want to proceed against the petitioner in disciplinary

action, they are at liberty to do so." But in case the duties allotted by the employer are not within the scope of the employees normal duties it will be very difficult for the bank to justify deduction of wages on the ground that the employee has refused to perform the work allotted to him. On the issue whether wages could be deducted for performance of only some of the duties allotted to the employee it will be difficult to indicate in what sense or in what proportion his wages can be deducted. In the instance where the employee does not have time to perform all the duties the management will not be able to justify any deduction of wages. In circumstances where the management wants the employee to complete his work by sitting late, if the employee refuses to sit late and do overtime work, the management will be justified in taking disciplinary action. The management, however, will not be justified in deducting the days wages because the employee has already completed his contract for the day. On this same reasoning, if the employees are on a go-slow then the management will not be justified in deducting full days wages for go-slow but the management will have to take appropriate disciplinary action against the employees concerned. In Apar India Limiteds case[75] the Bombay High Court had an occasion to consider the issue pertaining to wage deduction for the period of go-slow and the High Court held as under–

"...... *in the absence of a specific term in settlement or statutory provision an employer has no right to reduce the wages or the emoluments on the allegation that the workers had resorted to go-slow tactics or had not performed their part of the obligation in a settlement."*

This does not appear to be good law[76] any more in view of the judgment of the Supreme Court in S.U.Motors Private Ltds case. That case was clubbed with Bank of India's appeal against the Bombay High Court judgment on the issue of wage deduction. This entire issue was considered along with T.S. Kelawalas case, which went to the Supreme Court.

Now let us look at the facts of Bank of Indias case. It appears that some demands for wage revision was pending at the relevant time. The All India Bank Employees union called for a strike. The Bank issued a circular for deduction of wages of employees who would participate in the strike. The banks union gave a call to employees to strike work for 4 hours in the morning. The bank called this a breach of employees contract of service and informed them that they will not be entitled to salary for the day if they struck work for 4 hours and that the employees need not report for duty for the rest of the working hours on that day. The employees went on strike. The Bank deducted full days wages. The Bombay High Court, as stated earlier, had held that the banks action is wrong. The Supreme Court asked:[77] "*The principal question involved in this case, according to us, is, not withstanding the absence of a term in the contract of employment or of a provision in the service rules or regulations, whether an employer is entitled to deduct wages for the period that the employees refuse to work although the work is offered to them.*" Going down some discussions later the Court said: "*Hence, in cases such as the present one, the only question that has to be considered is whether, when admittedly the employees refuse to work by going on strike, the employer is entitled to deduct wages for the relevant period or not.*" And the Court Continued:

"*Since the admitted position is that the service rules do not provide for such a situation, the question as stated earlier which requires to be answered in the present case, is whether there exists an implied right in the employer- Bank to take action as it has done. There is no dispute that although the service regulations do not provide for a situation where employees on a mass scale resort to absence from duty for whole day or a part of the day whether during crucial hours or otherwise, they do provide for treating an absence from duty of an individual employee as a misconduct and for taking appropriate action against him for such absence. Since the High Court has indicated a disciplinary action under the said provision even in the present circumstances, we will also have to deal with that aspect. But before we do so, we may examine the relevant authorities cited at the Bar.*"

The Supreme Court examined several lengthy and earlier decisions. Reading the definition of wages and strike as provided in the Industrial Disputes Act, 1947 together the Court observed:

"...... it is clear that wages are payable only if the contract of employment is fulfilled and not otherwise. Hence, when the workers do not put in the allotted work or refuse to do it, they will not be entitled to the wages proportionately."

The concluding portion of the judgment is note-worthy for its wisdom and sagacity.

"The service conditions are not expected to visualize and provide for all situations. Hence, when they are silent on unexpected eventualities, the management should be deemed to have the requisite power to deal with them consistent with law and the other service conditions and to the extent it is reasonably necessary to do so. The pro rata deduction of wages is not an unreasonable exercise of power on such occasions. Whether on such occasions the wages are deductible at all and to what extent will, however, depend on the facts of each case. Although the employees may strike only for some hours but there is no work for the rest of the day as in the present case, the employer may be justified in deducting salary for the whole day. On the other hand, the employees may put in work after the strike hours and the employer may accept it or acquiesce in it. In that case the employermay not be entitled to deduct wages at all or be entitled to deduct them only for the hours of strike. If further statutes such as the payment of wages Act or the State enactments like the Shops and Establishments Act apply, the employer may be justified in deducting wages under their provisions. Even if they do not apply, nothing prevents the employer from taking guidance from the legislative wisdom contained in it to adopt measures on the lines outlined therein, when the contract of employment is silent on the subject.

It is, however, necessary to reiterate that even in cases such as the present one where action is resorted to on a mass scale, some employees may not be a party to the action and may have genuinely desired to discharge their duties but could not do so for failure of the management to give the necessary assistance or protection or on account of other circumstances. The management will not be justified in deducting wages of such employees without holding an inquiry. That, however, was not the grievance of any of the employees in the present case, as pointed out earlier."

Hence, we are unable to sustain the impugned decision which is untenable in law. The decision is accordingly set aside with no order as to costs.

Notes

1. Chesire and Fifoot's Law of Contract, 9th, pp. 132.
2. Cronin and Crime's introduction to Industrial Law, 1974 Ed. p. 21.
3. Vikram Tamaskar Vs. Steel Authority of India Ltd. 1982 II LLJ page 84.
4. See Union of India Vs. Chhaganlal, 1974 LIC 497: Project Manager vs Authority under Payment of Wages Act, 2000 III LLJ, 1199.
5. Taichar Coal Mines Employees Union Vs. Taicher Colliery, 1994, III LLJ, 747.
6. Taichar coal Mines Employees Union Vs. Taicher Colliery, 1994 III LLJ, 747.
7. State of Rajasthan Vs Mohammed Ayub Naz, 2006, I LLJ, 742.
8. See, 1988 II LLN, p. 132.
9. See Taichar Coal Mine Employees Union Vs. Taichar Colliery, 1994 III LLJ, p. 747.
10. See Chandeswar Mestar Vs. Vice Chancellor, 2003, IV LLJ, 830 [NOC].
11. French Motor Car Co Ltd workers union Vs. French Motor Car Co. Ltd. 1991 I LLJ, p. 107, [Note: In this case the workmen resorted to go-slow and resorted to 3 days strike on 13.14 and 15 May 1974. Strike day wages were deducted. Thereafter they reported for the day. The employer insisted on a guarantee bond which the workmen did not give and this resulted in non-payment of wages for 16 days].
12. 2005 IV LLJ, p. 45 at 48.
13. Industrial Tubes Manufacturing Co Ltd. Vs. S.R. Sawant 1980, II LLJ, 444.
14. Engineering Mazdoor Sabha Vs. S. Taki AIR 1970 (Bombay) 402; Workmen of Motipur Sugar Factory Vs. Motipur Sugar Factory 1965, II LLJ, 162.
15. Maharashtra Labour Union Vs. Pride Hotels Ltd., 2003, IV LLJ page 285.

16. This case has not been reported. The special leave to appeal was also rejected by the Supreme Court at the stage of admission.
17. Bombay Dyeing and Manufacturing Co. Vs. Mumbai Majdoor Sabha 1987 I LLJ 50. [The work premises are not to be used by the workmen as a matter of right even though the workmen had no intention to carry out the work].
18. A. M. Khan and Others Vs. State, 1992, II LLJ, p. 140 at 146. See also Union of India Vs. Raijada – 2004, II LLJ, 953 at 961.
19. Vinod Kumar Malik Vs. State Bank of India, 2005, II LLJ, 968.
20. Brahma Chandra Gupta Vs. Union of India, 1984, SCC p. 268.
21. Union of India Vs. Jaipal Singh, 2004, I LLJ, 431.
22. Krishnakant Raghunath Bibhavekar Vs. State of Maharastra and other- 1997 I LLJ 1190 at 1191.
23. Vinod Kumar Malik Vs. State Bank of India, 2005, II LLJ, 968
24. Krishi Utpandan Mandi Samiti Vs. Industrial Tribunal-2004, IV LLJ 116. [*Note:* The court followed the law laid down in Hindustan Motors Vs. Tapan Kumar-2002, II LLJ, 1156].
25. Clifton Electronix vs. Lt.Governor, Delhi, 1995, II LLJ, 894; S.C. Banwari Vs. M.P. Rajya Bhumi Vikas Nigam, 2004, II LLJ, 252.
26. Clifton Electronics Vs Lt. Governor, 1996, II LLJ, 1110.
27. 2001, I LLJ, 381.
28. Pandian Roadways, Corp, Ltd. vs. Principle District Judge, 1996, II LLJ, 1229; See also State of Rajasthan Vs. Mohamed Ayub Nag 2006, I LLJ, 742.
29. See clause 13.35 of Bipartite Settlement dated 19.10.1966, Shrikant S. Sheldekar Vs. Central Bank of India, 2000, II LLJ, 580.
30. Pest Control (India) Ltd. Vs. C.D. Konale, 2000, III LLJ, 588 1 Para + 471 of the Sastry Award.
31. D. Jayabalakrishnan Vs. Tamilnadu Water Service and Drainage Board- 1996 I LLJ 877; see also Bhagwan Shukla Vs. Union of India and Others, 1995, II LLJ, 726.
32. 2001, I LLJ, page 957.
33. See Bhagawan Singh Vs. Canara Bank 2001-II LLJ, 636; Vidya Bhusan Prasad Vs. Canara Bank-CWJC No. 11923 of 1995-(Judgment dated 16.1.1997); Amiruddin Vs. State Bank of India-1995(i) AK PLR 164.

34. Manohar Burde Vs. Union of India, 2003, II LLJ, 304; State of Mysore Vs. C.R. Seshadri-C.A. No-875 of 1968 (Judgment dated 18.1.1974), Vasant Rao Raman Vs. Union of India, C.A. No. 709 of 1993 (Judgement dated 4.3.1993).
35. Pravin Solanki Vs. State of U.P. 2003, II LLJ 507, R. K. Khare Vs. U.P. Coop. Sugar Factories Federation Ltd. 2003, II LLJ, p. 725 Para 729; 2003, IV LLJ 102.
36. Union of India Vs. K.V. Janakiraman, 1991, II LLJ 570.
37. See India Perfumary Co. Vs. Presiding Officer, 2004 II LLJ, 413; University Granth Nirman Board Vs. Ude Singh Togaji Solanki-2003 IV LLJ 950 Dena Bank Vs. Ghanshyam-2001 II LLJ 252, 2001 I LLJ 1411.
38. A.I.R. 1957 S.C. 82 [*Note:* In this case the application for permission was under Sec. 33(i) of the Act].
39. Secretary General, Family Planning Assn, Member and Others vs. Sunil Kumar Shrivastava, 2007, II LLJ, 1020.
40. 2007, II LLJ 350.
41. Rajgariha Vishram Sadan vs. Vijay Kate, 2007, II LLJ 555.
42. 1998, I LLJ 1.
43. Dena Bank vs. Kirti Kumar T. Patel (1998), I LLJ 1; Dena Bank 2001, II LLJ 252.
44. *Ibid.*
45. Rajgariha Vishram Sadan vs. Vijay Kate, 2007, II LLJ 555 at 560
46. u PSRT corporation vs. Surendra Singh, 2007 III LLJ 155.
47. The Arguments will apply to Article 136 as well.
48. Ranipur Colliery Vs. Bhuban Singh-AIR, 1959 Sc. 833.
49. Hotel Imperial Vs. Hotel Workers Union, 1959, II LLJ 544 at 551
50. Fakirbhai Fulabhai Solanki Vs. Presiding Officer, 1986 II LLJ, 124;
51. Ram Lakhan Vs. Presiding Officer, 2000, I LLJ, 1067.
52. Standard Chartered Grindlays Bank Ltd Vs. Govind Phople, 2002 III LLJ 1036.
53. Air India Ltd Vs. Libio Fransisco Colaco, 2004, I LLJ 850.
54. Vikram Tamaskar Vs. Steel Authority of India, 1982, II LLJ at p. 86.

55. [*Note:* We have seen that in banks employees are expected to give maximum out-put. See p.....]
56. See 4th Edition. Vol. 16, Halsbury's Laws of England.
57. See Halsbury Vol. 16, p. 350 4th Ed. Para 552.
58. See Halsbury Vol. 9, 4th Edn. P. 356, Para 515.
59. Ralli Bros. Vs. Ambika, ILR 35, AII 132.
60. Dhuma Behara Vs. Seven Daks, 1886 ILR 13 cal. 80.
61. A.M. Chokkalinga Muddallar vs. G. Mohmmad Sharif Sahab-23 ILJ 680.
62. See Arjun Vs. Hormusjee Shapurji Seervai, 1921, ILR 46. BOM. 44
63. Manoj Kanti Bose Vs. Bank of India, 1977, II LLJ, p. 285.
64. Algemene Bank Vs. Central Government Labour Court, 1978, II LLJ 117.
65. See V. Ramachandran Vs. Indian Bank, 1979, I LLJ P. 122 ["Absence from duty, undoubtedly would mean that the employee had not worked during the period of absence"].
66. Dharam Singh vs. Bank of India, 1979 LIC 1079.
67. See V. Ganesan Vs. State Bank of India, 1981, I LLJ, P. 64.
68. See R. Rajamanickem Vs. Indian Bank, 1981 II LLJ P.367
69. 1982, II LLJ, p. 86.
70. 1986, II LLN p. 222.
71. 1982, LIC 909; See also State Bank of India Vs. Sudarshan, 1986 II LLN 278.
72. U.P. Bank Employees Union Vs. New Bank of India 1986 LIC 754.
73. Bank of India vs. T. S. Kelawala, 1988, I CLR 382.
74. Sengamalam vs. Indian Bank, 1988, I LLN, 878
75. 1980, II LLJ 344.
76. For details see next chapter on Go-slow and Dies Non.
77. Bank of India Vs. T.S. Kelawala, 1990, II LLJ 39.

7

Go-slow and Dies Non

If wages are payable only for work done, what about the issue of go-slow?

The word willful connotes deliberation and calculation: it conveys an intention to prejudice the interest of the employer. It rules out any possibility of the act being accidental or unintentional.[1] Willful slowing down in performance of work is the same thing as adoption of go-slow tactics. Go-slow[2], it has been held, is a serious misconduct. In the words of the Supreme Court.

"Go-slow, which is a picturesque description of deliberate delaying of production by workman pretending to be engaged in the factory is one of the most pernicious practices that discontented or disgruntled workmen sometime resort to. It would not be far wrong to call this dishonest. For, while thus delaying production and thereby reducing output, the workmen claim to have remained employed and thus to be entitled to full wages. Apart from this also, go-slow is likely to be much more harmful than total cessation of work by strike. For, while during a strike much of the machinery can be fully turned off, during the go-slow the machinery is kept going on a reduced speed which is often extremely damaging to machinery parts. For all these reasons, go-slow has always been considered a serious type of misconduct".[3]

In Ashok Motors Ltd. case, the Court held that whether the workmen be piece-rated or otherwise, the management has the right to expect them to turn out the normal days work which ordinarily would be the average daily production of the past before any trouble started and if the workmen pursue the slow down policy deliberately it would amount to misconduct justifying dismissal. Further, negativing the contention that even if go-slow is found to be existing, the entire body of the workers in the department should not be penalized by a summary discharge without picking up the delinquent workmen and punishing them individually after framing charges and conducting enquires against each of them. It was held, that go-slow offence alleged and found was the common collective offence which could only be dealt with and prevented by punishing the offenders collectively and not individually. Besides this, in a large concern where work is done on each part of a unit by batches of men and in various sections, it is practically impossible to pick out and punish individual workers for general concerted go-slow methods adopted by all workers of all sections. In such cases the absence of formally drawn-up charge sheet would be only an immaterial irregularity.[4] In another case, however, it was held that any punishment imposed for go-slow without complying with the principles of natural justice cannot be justified.[5] The observations of Chief Justice Shri Chagla is noteworthy:

"............ *therefore, both in the case of a piece-rated worker and in the case of a time rated worker, during the time that the employee has to work the employer is entitled to expect from him average speed and normal skill. In the case of the petitioner, if he is paid according to the work done by him, it is rather an incentive to do more work than to do less work. .... It is perfectly true that a piece-rated worker may on occasions put into his work every ounce of energy that he possesses. He may reach higher heights which it is not possible to reach everyday, he may surpass himself on certain occasions and nobody suggests that if a piece-rated worker does not maintain the same standard throughout he could be guilty of slowing down. But without reaching those heights it is expected even of a piece-rated worker that during that time he is serving his employer he must at least use his normal skill and average speed. .... It is perfectly true that in this case no minimum is prescribed by the contract of service, but we refuse to accept the position that because no minimum is prescribed it is open to the employee to produce what he likes and to work, as he likes and to disregard the interest of the employer. Even though a minimum may not be prescribed, the conditions of service must require that during the time that the employee is in the service of his employer he must at least give to the employer what he is entitled to, viz., the minimum of his ability and his skill and his time. If he deliberately refuses to give that minimum, he is guilty of misconduct as he would have been if he did not come up to the minimum if such a minimum had been prescribed under the contract of service."*[6]

When this is the position in law in a departmental enquiry where the alleged misconduct is "go-slow", it is not sufficient to inform the employee in the charge sheet that he is willfully slowing down the performance of his work. That may convey nothing to the employee. He may not even know the day on which he slowed down, the norm the employer expects him to fulfill and how he has not achieved that norm. Charge-sheet, should, therefore, contain these details.[7]

It was generally the belief that for the period of "go-slow", wages cannot be deducted on the principle of "no work, no pay" for it was felt that during the period some work was carried out. This very question came up for consideration before a division bench of the Bombay High Court. The issues involved were:

(I) Whether the employer can unilaterally reduce the wages on the ground that the employees have adopted go-slow tactics in violation of subsisting settlement and

(II) Whether the employer in such circumstances, invoke the principle of "no work no pay".

The High Court went on to hold that in the absence of a specific term in the settlement or statutory provision an employer has no right to reduce the wages or emoluments on the allegation that the workers had resorted to go-slow tactics or had not performed their part of the obligation in the settlement. On the issue of "no work, no pay" the Court held that principle will have no application to the facts of the present case.[8]

Since the aforesaid decision, generally the belief was that for dealing with go-slow only disciplinary proceedings could be initiated as provided under the companys service rules. In that circumstance the ruling of the Supreme Court in C.A No. 855 of 1987 is noteworthy. That case also related to go-slow and the Court did consider the Apar (Pvt.) Ltds ruling. The issue in that case was whether the company was justified in denying to the workers full monthly wages for the month of July 1984. The Industrial Court had found that the workers had indulged in go-slow but did not award wage-deduction as justified because of the Bombay High Courts ruling. The Supreme Court[9] in considering this matter observed:

"There cannot be two opinions that go-slow is a serious misconduct being a covert and a more damaging breach of the contract of employment. It is an insidious method of undermining discipline and at the same time a crude device to defy the norms of work. It has been roundly condemned as an industrial action and has not been recognized as a legitimate weapon of the workmen to redress their grievances. In fact the model standing orders as well as the certified standing orders of most of the industrial establishments define it as a misconduct and provide for a disciplinary action for it. Hence, once it is proved, those guilty of it have to face the consequences which may include deduction of wages and even dismissal from service.

But by its very nature, the proof of go-slow, particularly when it is disputed, involves investigation into various aspects such as the nature of the process of production, the stages of production and their relative importance, the role of the workers engaged at each stage of production, the pre-production activities and the facilities for production and the activities of the workmen connected therewith and their effect on production, the factors bearing on the average, production etc. The go-slow further may be indulged in by an individual workman or only some workmen either in one section or different sections or in one shift or both shifts effecting the output in varying degrees and to different extent depending upon the nature of product and the productive process. Even where it is admitted, go-slow may in some case present difficulties in determining the actual or approximate loss, for it may have repercussions on production after the go-slow ceases which may be difficult to estimate. The deduction of wages for go-slow may, therefore, present difficulties which may not be easily resolvable. When, therefore, wages are sought to be deducted for breach of contract on account of go-slow, the quantum of deduction may become a bone of contention in most of the cases inevitably leading to an industrial dispute to be adjudicated by an independent machinery statutory or otherwise as the parties may resort to. It is necessary to emphasize this because unlike in the case of a strike where a simple measure of a pro rata deduction from wages may provide a just and fair remedy, the extent of deduction of wages on account of a go-slow action may in some case raise a complex question. The simplistic method of deducting uniform percentage of wages from the wages of all workmen calculated on the basis of the percentage fall in production compared to the normal or average production may not always be equitable. It is, therefore, necessary that in all cases where the factum of go-slow and/or the extent of the loss of production on account of it is disputed, there should be a proper inquiry on charges which furnish particulars of the go-slow and the loss of production on that account. The rules of natural justice require it, and whether they have been followed or not will depend on the facts of each case."

Having considered thus the Supreme Court concluded: "*As stated above, all that was challenged was the right of the employer to deduct wages even when admittedly there is a go-slow which question we have answered in favor of the employer earlier ... . While therefore allowing this appeal, we direct that the appellant will not deduct more than 5 percent of the wages of the workmen for the month of July, 1984.*"

This ruling[10] of the Supreme Court is of great significance. Regarding the formalities to be completed by the employer before imposing wage deduction for strikes, absence etc. it must be remembered that the right to deduct wages for failure to fulfill the contract of employment is not the same thing as imposing a punishment on the employee. Wages are payable only for work done. The natural corollary of this proposition is that wages would not be payable for no work and, therefore, deduction of wages is not the same as imposition of punishment on an employee but merely the enforcement of the expressed or implied terms of contract of employment. In this context in the case between R.N. Shenoy Vs. Central Bank of India the High Court held that in such situations principles of natural justice would have no application. In other words, there are no fixed formalities to be followed for deduction of wages arising on account of employees absence without leave. Therefore, there are no specific formalities which need to be observed before wage deductions for unauthorized absence.

The same issue came up for discussion in yet another case where the Court observed: "*An employee gets his salary for the days he attends to this work or is absent on authorized leave and not for the days on which he fails to work. Like-wise a college student gets credit for attendance on the days he attends his lectures and not for the days of absence. We do not think principle of audi alteram partam can be stretched even to marking an employee or a student absent although as an automatic consequence. The employee may loses his wages for the day or the student the credit for attendance to entitled him to appear at the final examination.*

If graver consequences intended then due opportunity will be given to those disputing their absence."[11]

Notes

1. Zarikh vs. Fire Stone Tyer and Rubber Company Ltd., 1954, I LLJ 281 at 283.
2. See Vasant Govind Madhav Rao vs. Gujarat Rubber Works Ltd., 1956, I LLJ 731.
3. See Bharat Sugar Mills Ltd. vs. Jal Singh & Ors., 1961, II LLJ, 664. Also see Sasa Musa Sugar Works Pvt. Ltd. Vs. Their Workmen-1959 II LLJ 338. [It should be made clear that go-slow is not a strike-See Bal Santok Bal and Fine Kniting Co. Ltd., 1959, I LLJ 409 LT.].
4. Ashok Motors Ltd vs. Their Workmen, 1953, II LLJ 793.
5. Chandna Bali and Others vs. Muir Mills, 1953, II LLJ 864.

6. See Zarikh vs. Firestone Tyre and Rubber Co. Limited, 1954 I LLJ 281 at 282-284, also see J.M. Isreal and Ors. vs. Saxby and Farmer (India) Ltd., 1956 I LLJ, 72.
7. *Note:* It will be necessary to issue a show cause notice prior to deduction of wages for go slow. Such show cause notice, naturally, should set-forth all the details.
8. See Apar (Pvt.) Ltd. vs. S.R. Samant, 1980, II LLJ, p. 344 at 350 & 351.
9. Bank of India vs. T. S. Kelawala, 1990, II LLJ, p. 39.
10. Bank of India vs. T.S. Kelawala, 1990, II LLJ, p. 39.
11. See UP Bank Employees Union vs. New Bank of India, 1986 LIC 754.

8

After Math [Dies Non-II]

The Supreme Court judgment ought to have laid all doubts at rest on the issue of dies-non. In the Madras High Court at about that time an interesting matter of wage deduction for the strike period came up. The State Bank of India signed a settlement with its employees federation. The settlement was not implemented as the bank wanted permission from Central Government for entering/implementing the settlement. Copies of the settlement that should be sent to various authorities under the Industrial dispute (Central) Rules were not so forwarded by the management. The union issued a notice of strike. The conciliation officer called for a meeting. The Bank issued a circular on 12.10.1989 for wage deduction if the strike took place on 16.10.1989. The strike took place. A single bench judge while referring to the Supreme Court in Bank of Indias case held the strike to be illegal as conciliation proceedings were pending and found that wage deduction was justified. The Division bench however termed the wage deduction illegal.[1]

The Bombay High Court at about the same time in GMV Nayaks case had other views. The Court felt that the Supreme Court decision applies when there is no rule, regulation or any other provision in the service code dealing with a situation of this type, namely abstention of work for a part of the day and the consequent deduction of salary for such abstention.[2]

"In chapter XIV of the service code there is rule 9 which provides for the consequences of an employee willfully abstaining or refusing to work, though present on the premises, is applicable to the facts of the present case. It provides that an employee shall be treated as absent without leave for the period of such abstention or refusal and not for the whole day. It is this rule which was noticed by the Labour Court while holding that the management could not deduct the salary for the whole day if the employee is absent for part of the day.

It is impossible to accept a contention that notice put up by the management be treated as notice under Section.9-A of I.D Act. In the first place notice does not say that it is a notice under Section 9-A. Secondly it has not been given in the prescribed manner. If a law requires that a thing shall be done in a prescribed manner, it has got to be done in that particular manner and in no other manner. This notice was not served on the respondent though it might have put on the notice board. Most important is that this notice does not say that it intends to bring about change in the conditions of service contained in the service code. It proceeds on the basis that it has already brought about a change in the conditions of service. No employer has a unilateral right to alter the conditions of service, especially those contained in the 4th Schedule of Industrial Disputes Act. One must thus proceed on the basis that the conditions of service in the service code and in particular in chapter XIV on conditions of service by which the parties are bound. On that basis, it must be held that the petitioner had no authority to deduct the whole days salary of the employees for their absence for part of the day. Then it remains to be seen whether the Judgment of the Supreme Court in the case of Bank of India V.T.S. Kelawala 1990 I C.L.R. 748 permits the deduction of whole days salary for absence for part of the day. The facts in Bank of Indias case are some what different from the facts of the present case. What has been stated by the Supreme Court in Bank of Indias case applies when there is no rule, regulation or any other provision in the Service Code dealing with a situation of this type namely, absent for a part of the day and the consequent deduction of salary for such abstention. In the light of the clear language of the Supreme Court in the law thus laid down, the petitioner could not have taken action otherwise than in accordance with Rule 9 of Chapter XIV of the

Service Code. The fact that more than one person or a group of persons are involved does not make any difference to the applicability of Rule 9. The view taken by the Central Labor Court in the instant case is not affected by the decision in Bank of Indias case." The principle of "no work no pay" came up for consideration of the Supreme Court once again.[3] This time it was the Madras High Courts decision in State Banks case. After the wage settlement was signed at the banking industry level on 10th April 1989, it will be recalled that, the, management of SBI and its employees entered into 3 settlements on 9th June, 1989 one of which related to wage revision. This settlement was an improvement on the settlement arrived at industry level. The State Bank Employees Federation insisted on implementation of the 9th June, 1989 settlement. The State Bank took the position that they needed governments approval for implementing the settlement. The union issued a notice on 1st October 1989 giving a call for strike on the 16th October 1989 and struck work on that day. The Bank issued a notice on 12th October 1989 intimating of wage deduction for the strike period. While dealing with the case, the Supreme Court referred to not only Kelawalas case (Two Judges Bench) but also to Charukulam Tea Estates case [1969 II LLJ 407.Three Judges Bench] and Crompton and Greaves case [1978- II LLJ p.80- Two Judges Bench]. The question for consideration was whether workmen who proceeded on strike- whether legal or illegal-are entitled to wages for the strike period? Kelawalas judgment, it will be recalled, took the view that whether strike is legal or illegal, the employees are not entitled to wages. In the Charakulan & Crompton Greaves cases, the Court had earlier decided that for employees to get wages, the strike has to be both legal and justified. Thus the issue of justifiability of strike and payment of wages therefore did not arise in Kelawalas case. But then there is no contradiction in the 3 rulings. In all cases of illegal strikes the employer is entitled to deduct wages for the strike period. To be entitled to strike day wages, the strike has to be both legal and justified. The Supreme Court did not decide on the merits, but directed the Central Government to refer the dispute to adjudication. In a recent decision, the High Court of Madhya Pradesh has held that workman will not be entitled to any relief in the case of an illegal strike.[4]

The Kelawalas case again came in for consideration in the case of an illegal lock-out. The lock-out declared by Nellimarla Jute Mills and non-payment of wages for the lock-out period was considered by the Andra Pradesh High Court. "In view of the clear position, the management of the company cannot take a rigid stand that workman are not entitled to pay because they did not work during the period of lock-out which has been declared as illegal. The principle of "no work no pay" would apply when the workmen strike work as clarified by the Supreme Court in Bank of India vs. T.S.Kelawala. [1990II LLJ P.39]. That principle is not attracted straightway in the case of a lock-out, especially when the lock-out has been declared illegal. At any rate that matter cannot be fore-closed by forcing the workmen to give up their claim for wages during the lock-out period at the same time continuing the lock-out indefinitely and refusing to lift it until the workman agree for it. That is militancy on the part of management."[5] Wages will be payable for the period of lock-out where the lock-out is unjustified.[6]

The question whether the lock-out is justified depends on whether the lock-out was legal in the first place. An illegal lock-out per se is unjustified. If the tribunal holds that a lock-out is illegal, then there is no question of adducing any other reasons in regard to the justification or other wise of the lock-out. "The justification, if any, for a lock-out can fall for consideration provided that lock-out is held to be legal."[7]

There was another interesting case of a closure. The employer wanted to close the factory from 31st March, 1993. On this issue, the employer wrote a letter to the Delhi administration on 1.1.1993. The administration wanted the employer to deposit 2 months wages payable to 44 employees. The employer filed a writ petition in the Delhi High Court. The High Court asked the company to deposit the said quantum of money with the labour commissioner, who in term was directed to disburse the sum to the workmen, which he did. The matter came up for final hearing when a letter annexed to the employers counter affidavit, on the employers request, was treated as an application under Sec. 25(0) of the Industrial Disputes Act, 1947 for closure. The High Court directed the Labour Commission to dispose of this request. The Labour Commissioner permitted the employer to close the establishment on 15th July, 1994. The workmen claimed wages for the months of may and June. The High Court correctly felt that the date of the closure of the factory is from 18th July,1994 and not 31st March, 1993 and that the workmen would be entitled to all the benefits including wages till 18th July, 1994.[8] It is most basic, though it may be implicit, term of agreement between an employer and his employee that the employee shall make himself available to do his work and that the employer shall pay employees wages for doing so. Failure to pay wages, when an employee has made himself available for work, is a breach of agreement between them. That the employer has no work for the employee to do does not cause a suspension of his obligation to pay wages to an employee.[9] [see Premier Automobiles Employees Union vs. Premier Automobile Ltd. 1995 III LLJ p. 840]. But then what happens in a case where a large mass of employees are retrenched and sent to economic death and the remaining workmen strike work. In this case, the tribunal asked the employer to pay 50% of the wages for the strike period and this was confirmed by a single bench. The High Court in appeal while not agreeing with the Tribunals decision did not, however, set aside the order. [see Rajasthan Trade Union Kendra vs. J.K. Synthetics Ltd. 1996 II LLJ p. 347].

In another case, the question for payment of wages during lay-off was considered. The Court held that where lay-off was not justified, the workmen would be entitled to their wages for the lay-off period.[10] The employee could not report for duty because of illness. The doctor had certified that the employee was ill. The Municipal Corporation did not pay wages to the employee for the period he had abstained himself. The High Court rightly held that the wages are payable to the employee.[11]

In an interesting case, the employee was falsely implicated in a case and in order to deny him wages for the period of suspension the punishment of "censure" was imposed on him without any justification. The Court held that the employee would be entitled to wages for the period of suspension as the findings of the Enquiry officer was arbitrary.[11]

In an individual misdemeanor, in Reserve Bank of India, the Supreme Court had to deal with the case of an employees absence due to his arrest on a criminal charge which had nothing to do with the Bank. Sub-regulation 46(1) of the R.B.I. stated that when an employee was absent from duty on account of arrest for debt or criminal charge or is detained in pursuance of any process of law, he may be considered as on suspension from the date of his arrest or his detention till such date as the competent authority may direct on that behalf. The employee in such cases would be entitled to subsistence allowance under the Banks rules. The regulations vested the power on the bank to decide the period of such suspension on duty or on leave or otherwise. *"The power thus vested cannot be challenged. During the period, the employee renders no work, he is absent for reasons of his involvement in the misconduct and the Bank is in no way responsible for keeping him away from duties. The bank, therefore, cannot be saddled with the liability to pay him his salary and allowances for the period. That will be against the principle of "no work no pay".*[12] In an interesting case, the Tribunal ordered reinstatement of an employee in the service of the company with back-wages. The employee deliberately delayed joining duties. In such a case, after the order of re-instatement by a court of law, if the workman deliberately abstains from joining duties, then the workmen concerned will not be entitled to back-wages on the principle of no work no pay.[13]

Relying on the above ruling of the Supreme Court, the High Court of Andra Pradesh held: *"The absence of the petitioner during the said period was for reasons of his own involvement. The petitioner had thereby disabled himself from rendering service and not for any reasons attributable to the respondent corporation. The petitioner cannot therefore as of right claim to be entitled to full pay and allowances ...."*[14] Even if the workmen go on illegal strike for one day, the employer cannot deduct 8 days wages under the payment of Wages Act unless there is sufficient compliance with the provisions of the Section 9(2) and rule 16 of the said act. Here workmen struck work for one day. The strike was illegal because of the pendency of the conciliation proceedings. The management deducted 8 days wages and refused to accept the workmans explanation given collectively stating that they went on strike at the behest of the union. The authority under the payment of Wages Act found that the management had not complied with the provisions of the act while deducting wages for 8 days though the strike was illegal. The appellate authority confirmed that decision. The Madras High Court held that wage deduction has to be made only in the manner contemplated by the act and the rules there-under and that non-issuance of individual notice in regard to wage deduction would render such deduction illegal.[15] But otherwise employer can deduct wages for the days of unauthorized absence of the employee.[16]

In the case of illegal closure, the management has to pay for the period of illegal closure. In such cases, the workmen shall be deemed to be in continuous service so long as the illegal closure lasts and obviously they are entitled to full wages and allowances.[17] Suspension of operation is lockout and sans appropriate notice amounts to illegal lock-out. Since the lock-out is illegal wages for the lockout period will be payable.[18] But even in case of a legal lock-out which turns out to be a guise for closure of the factory, the employer will have to pay wages for the period of the lock-out. In this case, the employer had given appropriate notice etc and had fulfilled all the legal requirements for locking out the premises. The Industrial Court was satisfied with the company having followed all the legal requirements and refused to go into the justifiability aspect. The High Court felt that the company is trying to close down in the garb of lockout. Hence the court ordered lifting of lock-out and payment of wages for the period of the lock-out.[19] Where the employer closed the company without obtaining prior permission of the government, he is liable to pay wages to the workmen.[20] In another case, the workman went on a strike against the dismissal and suspension of 2 workmen.

The strike was declared illegal under the Bombay Industrial Relations Act. The union, there upon, informed the management that the workman are withdrawing the illegal strike and are reporting to work. The management insisted on a letter of good conduct, which was given by 210 workmen. About 178 workmen refused to give the undertaking and the management prevented them from joining duties. The Bombay High Court held that this action of the management amounted to illegal lockout and that wages are payable for the period of lock-out.[21]

What happens when some of the employees do not attend office on the day of the Bandh? This question was answered by the High Court of Madras in Nagammal Mills Ltd case[22] on 19.7.1990, a bandh was initiated by the state Government. The management did not declare a holiday on that day. Most of the employees did not report for duty. The High Court held that as per the provisions of section 9(1) of the Payment of Wages Act, the employer is entitled to deduct the salary if the employee is absent from the place of work for the period during which he is required to work. Having said this the High Court went on to consider the impact of section 7 of the Act. "*In this case, the non-payment of salary for employees for not working on July 20,1990 cannot be said to be deduction of salary. But it has to be construed as a failure on the part of the employees to earn wages by fulfilling the conditions of employment and performing their work. So the action of the management in this case cannot be construed as a deduction, but it has to be construed as employees failure to earn wages. Thereafter the High Court referred to Binnys case. The learned counsel appearing for the respondents have relied on the decision in Madras Labour Union v. Binny Ltd.(1995-I LLJ-588)(Mad) and the order in Civil Appeal No.208 to211 of 1991, dated October 1.1996. In the said decision the facts are as follows:- On November 24, 1989 the election to the Tamil Nadu State Assembly was held. According to the letter dated November 6, 1989 of the Commissioner of Labour, a paid holiday to all the employees was suggested to be given on November 24, 1989.But the management did not declare that day as a holiday. But the employees remained absent as a matter of right. A notice was issued for deduction of 8 days wages in terms of clause 20 of the standing Order. That was challenged by the employees. The writ petition was dismissed as not maintainable. On appeal, the Bench took a view that deduction of three days wages should be sufficient. Aggrieved against the same the above said Civil Appeals were filed. The Supreme Court without interfering with the merits of the case and also the finding of the Division Bench, directed the management to deduct the wages for only half-a-day instead of larger period. So, from the above said decision, it is clear that the employees are not entitled for wages, if they remained absent from their work.*

In this case also, the act of the employees will amount to deliberate refusal to work. Participating in the bandh is not a matter of right. The Full Bench of Kerala High Court in the decision in Bharat Kumar K.Palicha v. State AIR 1997 Ker291 which has been approved by the Apex Court in the decision in Communist Party of India (M) v. Bharat Kumar AIR, 1996 S.C. 184, has held as follows:

"If this be the position and if the call for the bandh and the holding of it entails restriction on the fundamental freedoms of the citizen, it has to be held that no political party has the right to call for a bandh on the plea that it is part of its fundamental right of freedom of speech and expression. Moreover, nothing stands in the way of the political parties calling for a general strike or hartal unaccompanied by express or implied threat of violence to enforce it. It is not possible to accept that the calling of a bandh alone could demonstrate the protest of a political party to a given decision or in a given situation.

The contention that no relief can be granted against the political parties in these proceedings under Art. 226 of the Constitution cannot be accepted in its entirety. As indicated already, this Court has ample jurisdiction to grant a declaratory relief to the petitioners in the presence of the political party respondent. This is all the more so since the case of the petitioners is based on their fundamental rights guaranteed by the Constitution. The State has not taken any steps to control or regulate the bandhs. The stand adopted by the Advocate-General is that the Court cannot compel the State or the Legislature to issue orders or make law in that regard. As we find that organized bodies and Associations or registered political parties by their act of calling and holding bandhs trample upon the rights of the citizens of the country protected by the Constitution, we are of the view that this Court has sufficient jurisdiction to declare that the calling of bandh and the holding of it, is unconstitutional especially since, it is undoubted, that the holding of bandhs are not in the interests of the Nation, but tend to retard the progress of the Nation by leading to national loss of production. We cannot also ignore the destruction of public and private property when a bandh is enforced by the political parties of other organizations. We are inclined to the view that the political parties and the organizations which call for such bandh and enforce them are really liable to compensate the Government, the public and the private citizen for the loss suffered by them for such destruction. The State cannot shirk its responsibility of taking steps to recoup and of recouping the loss from the sponsors and organizers of such Bandhs. We think, these aspects justify our intervention under Article 226 of the Constitution".

While approving the said decision, the Apex Court has held that" *there cannot be any doubt that the fundamental rights of the people as a whole cannot be subservient to the claim of fundamental right of an individual or only a section of the people and that there cannot be any right to call or enforce bandh which interferes with the exercise of the fundamental freedoms of other citizens, in addition to causing national loss in many ways. No political party or organization can claim that it is entitled to paralyze the industry and commerce in the entire Country or Nation and is entitled to prevent the citizen not in sympathy with its view point from exercising their fundamental rights or from performing their duties for their own benefit or the benefit of the State or the Nation, which would be unreasonable and could not be accepted as a legitimate exercise of the fundamental right by a political party or those sponsoring it.*

From the above, it is very clear that if an employee wants to show his protest in issue either at the instance of any external force or by himself and thereby he is not attending the work, during which period he has to work according to the terms of the employment, he must be ready to forgo the wages for the said period. When holding Bandh itself is against the interest of the nation, can the Government or its authorities direct the employers to declare that day as holiday with wages. Even if it is so, as has been done in this case, such direction would be nothing but illegal. In this case the Government had also declared holiday in support of the bandh, which is nothing but supporting illegality and unconstitutional activities.

In this case, it is factually found, which are not in dispute, that only with a view to participating in the bandh, the respondents absented themselves from attending the work. So, they are not entitled for any salary. So any employer cannot be compelled to pay wages to such employees for such period. Giving such direction would be adding premium to the illegality and against the interest of the society."

The aforesaid case law has pointed out to the Supreme Court decision and has added a new dimension for the application of the principle of "no work no pay". If the aforesaid case was the case of a bandh, in Rajnagar Textile Mills case, the employer did not give work to badli workers in violation of the agreement to absorb them in the company for certain number of days. The Gujarat High Court held that wages would be payable to the badIi workmen.[23] But then what happens when a lock-out is found to be legal. Can the employer deduct wages for the period of lock-out which is found to be legal? The Bombay High Court held after considering Supreme Courts decision in Bank of Indias case that such lockout should be justified as well. "Therefore, in so far as both the issues of strike and lock-out are concerned, merely because strike is legal or lock-out is legal that would not mean that the workers are entitled to wages or that the company is bound to refuse payment of wages."[24]

The proposition seems to be well settled that there cannot be any controversy since the decisions[25] of the Supreme Court that a person is not entitled to salary or wages for the period when no service was rendered by him.[26]

That being so, in an interesting decision, reminiscent of the decision in V.Ganesan vs. State Bank of India,[27] the Madras High Court held:[28] *"The only question that I will have to decide is whether the wages can be cut (for 15 minutes absence) and if so whether it should be pro rata for duration of the absence or wages can be cut for the entire day. The Supreme Court was concerned with two incidents of strike for a short period and resort to "go-slow" attitude by way of protest. I will extract the relevant passages from the said judgment. The principles which emerge from the aforesaid authorities may now be stated. Where the contract, Standing Orders or the service rules/regulations are silent on the subject, the management has the power to deduct wages for absence from duty when the absence is a concerted action on the part of the employees and the absence is not disputed. Whether the deduction from wages will be pro rata for the period of absence only or will be for a longer period will depend upon the facts of each case such as whether there was any work to be done in the said period, whether the work was in fact done and whether it was accepted and acquiesced in, etc."*

It is not enough that the employees attend the place of work they must put in the work allotted to them. It is for the work and not for their mere attendance that the wages/salaries are paid. For the same reason, if the employees put in the allotted work but do not, for some reason-may be even as a protest-comply with the formalities such as signing the attendance register, no deduction can be effected from their wages. When there is a dispute as to whether the employees attended the place of work or put in the allotted work or not and if they have not, the reasons therefore etc, the dispute has to be investigated by holding an inquiry into the matter. In such cases, no deduction from the wages can be made without establishing the omission and/or commission on the part of the employees concerned.

When the contract Standing Orders, or the service rules/ regulations are silent, but enactment such as the Payment of Wages Act providing for wage-cuts for the absence from duty is applicable to the establishment concerned, the wages can be deducted even under the provisions of such enactment.

On the facts of this case, it is clear that the petitioners absented themselves only for a short duration and later on they resumed duty. Even though the management says that they did not call upon the petitioners to continue their work for the rest of the day, it is clear that the respondents have acquiesced in resumption of duties by the petitioners, after the unauthorized absence for 15 minutes. Therefore, having regard to the dictum of the Supreme Court, i am clearly of the opinion that full days wages cannot be cut. I am also clearly of the opinion that the petitioners have absented themselves as a group contrary to the circulars. The conduct of the petitioners definitely deserves punishment. Nothing prevented them from seeking permission of their respective superiors for going out for a cup of coffee. The petitioners had defied circulars of the superiors. Indiscipline in any manner can never be tolerated.

I therefore direct the respondents to deduct only pro rata wages for the duration of the absence of each of the petitioners. The writ petition is ordered in the above terms. There will be, however, no order as to costs."

While things look simple as yet, there was this decision of the Andra Pradesh State Road Corporation (APSRTC), which proposed to recover wages from the workmen on the ground that they absented themselves from work without any reasonable or justifiable cause. The company by a notice asked the workmen to explain within 7 days of the notices as to why a penal wage cut of 8 days in addition to the wage cut for the days of absence should not be recovered from their salaries. This notice, needless to state was issued under the payment of wages Act, 1936. The workers contented that the Act was not applicable to them. The Andra Pradesh High Court held that the company has no authority in law to act against employees who were outside the pale of the Act.[29] In another interesting case the union demanded that wages be paid for June 1978 as though they were employed from that month though the actual work was to commence from August 1978. The Union had advised the workers to defer joining duties till such time that the issue was settled. The Bombay High-Court held that the union was ill-advised and that the employees are not entitled to such wages when work had not commenced.[30] The above decision is logical. Normally, it is not enough if the employees attend the place of work in order to earn wages; they must put in the work allotted to them. It is for work and not for mere attendance that wages are paid. It is also clear that whether the strike is legal or illegal, the workers are liable to lose wages for the period of strike. Now take a case flowing from the case law where the Court held that the workmen are beyond the pale of the Payment of Wages Act, 1936 merely because they earn a salary of over Rs. 1600/- per month. Can it be said then that the employer has no right to deduct wages for the strike period on the principle of dies non? The answer is that: *"It cannot be inferred that once the Payment of Wages Act ceased to apply the employer has no powers to deduct wages."*[31] It is relevant to recall the judgment of the Supreme Court in T.S.Kelawalas case *"We therefore hold that the workers are nor entitled to wages for the strike period even if the strike is legal."*

As a matter of fact, the Supreme Court in Kelawals case[32] had referred to a string of decisions which took the view that it is not only permissible for the employer to deduct wages for the hours or the days for which the employees were absent for duty, but it was also permissible to deduct wages for the whole day even if the absence is only for a few hours. In that case[33] the Supreme Court summarized the legal position which is as follows:

"Where the contract, standing orders or the service rules/regulations are silent on the subject, the management has the power to deduct wages for the absence from duty when the absence is a concerted action on the part of the employees and the absence is not disputed. Whether the deduction from wages will be pro rata for the period of absence only or will be for a longer period will depend on the facts of each case such as whether there was any work to be done in the said period, whether the work was in fact done and whether it was accepted and acquised in, etc.

When the contract, standing orders or the service rules/regulations are silent, but enactment such as the Payment of Wages Act providing for wage cuts for absence from duty is applicable to the establishment concerned, the wages can be deducted even under the provisions of such enactment."

And then in paragraph 28 of the judgment, the Supreme Court further made the position clear by holding that whether wages are deductible at all and to what extent will, however, depend on facts of each case and that even if the employees may strike only for a few hours if there is no work for the rest of the day, the employer would be justified in deducting the salary for the whole day. On the other hand, the employees may put in work after the strike hours and the employer may accept it or acquiesce it. In that case, the employer may not be entitled to deduct wages in full or even the pro rata wages for the hours of strike. The Kerala High Court while following the decision of the Supreme Court held that the Reserve Bank of India will be justified in deducting full days wages for partial days strike especially when the bank had intimated the workmen that if employees working in the department dealing with the public, do not discharge their duties as a part of concerted action or otherwise during the business hours and thereby cause disruption in public service even for a part of business hours, such employees will not be paid wages for the whole day. [34]

Almost immediately on the heels of the Kerala High Court s decision, the Madras High Court in a dispute between Steel Employees Union and Tamil Nadu Steels Ltd gave a decision to the effect that the employers decision to deduct 8 days wages in accordance with the provisions of the Payment of Wages Act, 1936 for an illegal strike on the 3rd shift of 14th August 1990 was not wrong. *The judgment said: "I am of the clear view that the impugned order of the respondent deducting 8 days wages from the members of the petitioner union is in order and in accordance with law and that it has not violated any law or even the principles of natural justice."*[35]

In Canara Bank a number of special Assistants refused to perform clerical duties. The settlement binding on the workmen and the bank provided that a workman entrusted with duties attracting special allowance can be required to perform routine duties of his cadre. In tune with this settlement the ALPM/ AEAM operators whenever they were working were assigned with normal duties in the clerical cadre when there was no work to be performed as ALPM operators. The workmen are, therefore, working as clerks and they have been assigned the duties of ALPM operators and as per the prevailing working condition they are when bound to attend to the routine duties as and when they are not provided with special allowance duties. Being so, the Madras High Court-after taking into account various decisions including the Supreme Court decision in Syndicate Bank v. K.Umesh Nayak came to the conclusion that the Bank was justified in deducting the workmens salary on the principle of "no work no pay"[36].

It is to be understood that the question of justifiability of a strike/lock-out or stoppage of work etc. can be gone into by an Industrial Tribunal based on facts and circumstances. *"The employees are free to decide whether to seek a reference under section of the Industrial Disputes Act or to go under the MRTU & PULP Act. But justifiability can only be gone into in an industrial dispute under the I.D. Act. The apportionment of blame can be decided and the right to receive wages considered." This was a case of a lock-out held to be legal.*[37] *In the case of an illegal lock-out, though it was so at its commencement, the employer will necessarily have to pay the workmen the wages for the period of the lock-out.*[38]

In terms of a settlement arrived at between the unions and the employer, in order to off-set the cost consequent upon a revision of wages the union agreed to increase the contact time from 3.5 working hours per day to full 8 hours and 6 minutes on week days and 5 hours on Saturdays to achieve the targets set. The management alleged that the employees have not met the production targets and have not met the contact time and decide to deduct wages in accordance with T.S.Kelawalas case. The High Court observed:[39]

"I will therefore proceed to consider whether the decision of the Supreme Court in the case of Bank of India vs. T.S. Kelawala and Ors. (supra) applies to the fact of the present case.

In the aforesaid case of Bank of India (supra) the respondent Nos. 3 and 4 i.e. the employees Unions gave a call for 4 hours strike on December 29, 1977. Hence the Bank on December 27, 1977 issued an administrative circular warning the employees that they would be committing a breach of their contract of service if they participated in the strike and that they would not be entitled to draw salary for the full day if they did so and consequently they need not report for work for the rest of working hours on that day. Notwithstanding such notice the employees went on a 4 hours strike from the beginning of the working hours on December 29,1977 which included banking hours for the public. The employees however resumed work on that day after strike hours and the bank did not prevent them from doing so. On January 16, 1978 the bank issued circular directing its Manager and agents to deduct the full days salary of those employees who had participated in the strike. The respondents filed a writ petition in the High Court for quashing the circular. The petition was allowed. The Bank preferred a Letters Patent in High Court which also was dismissed. Hence the appeal before the Apex Court by the Bank. In the fact of such a case the Apex Court considered among other points the scope of Section 7(2) of the Payment of Wages of Act 1936 which authorized an employer to deduct wages if the employee was absent from duty. In the aforesaid context the Supreme the Supreme Court made the following observations in 1990 II LLJ 39 at pp. 49-50.

"The principles which emerge from the aforesaid authorities may now be stated. Where the contract, Standing Order or the service rules/ regulations are silent on the subject, the management has the power to deduct wages for absence from duty when the absence is a concerted action on the part of the employees and the absence is not disputed. Whether the deduction from wages will be pro rata for the period of absence only or will be for a longer period will depend upon the facts of each case such as whether there was any work to be done in the said period, whether the work was in fact done and whether it was accepted acquiesced in, etc. It is not enough the employees attend the place of work. They must put in the work allotted to them. It is for the work and not for their mere attendance that the wages/salaries are paid. For the same reason, if the employees put in the allotted work but do not for some reason-may be even as a protest-comply with the formalities such as signing the attendance register, no deduction can be effected from their wages. When there is a dispute as to whether the employees attended the place of work or put in the allotted work or not, and if they have not, the reasons therefore etc. the dispute has to be investigated by holding an inquiry into the matter. In such cases, no deduction from the wages can be made without establishing the omission and/or commission establish on the part of the employees concerned.

When the contract, Standing Orders, or the service rules/ regulations are silent, but enactment such as the Payment of Wages Act providing for wage cuts for the absence from duty is applicable to the establishment concerned, the wages can be deducted even under the provisions of such enactment.

Apart from the aforesaid ratio of the decisions and the provisions of the Payment of Wages Act and similar statutes on the subject, according to us, the relevant provisions of the major legislation governing the industrial disputes, viz., the Industrial Disputes Act,

1947 also lend their support to the view that the wages are payable pro rata for the work done and hence deductible for the work not done. Section 2(rr) of the said Act defines wages to mean all remuneration...... which would, if terms of employment, expressed or implied, were fulfilled, be payable to workman in respect of his employment....... While section 2(q) defines strike to mean cessation of work or refusal to continue to work or accept employment by workman. Reading the two definitions together, it is clear that wages are payable only if the contract of employment is fulfilled and not otherwise. Hence when the workers do not put in the allotted work or refuse to do it, they would not be entitled to the wages proportionately."

From the above observations of the Apex Court it is clear that in a given case if any agreement is arrived at between the parties as regards number of working hours or norms of production and if there is shortfall of such terms, the employer is entitled to deduct wages and such shortfall would bring the case within the purview of Section 7(2) of the Payment of Wages Act. In such a case, for the purpose of adjudicating whether there has been really any violation of such agreement, or whether the employees are responsible for such violation, an investigation of fact is necessary and under such circumstances Section 15 of the Payment of Wages Act lays down the detail and more efficacious inquiry. In my view, all these disputed questions of fact cannot be effectively adjudicated in this writ application and it is better that those disputes should be resolved under the aforesaid provision of the Payment of Wages Act after taking oral evidence if necessary.

Therefore, I find substance in the preliminary objection of Dr. Banerjee that this type of disputed question of fact should not be adjudicated in this writ application particularly when the Deputy Labour Commissioner, West Bengal has already issued notice upon the employer for conciliation of the aforesaid dispute raised by one of the Unions who is not party to the instant writ application. Apart from that, the petitioners are also entitled to raise dispute in terms of Section 15(2) of the Payment of Wages Act.

In view what has been stated above, I am not inclined to entertain this writ application. In view of existence of efficacious remedy mentioned above I thus reject this writ application on that ground alone. This case does not come within the exceptions indicated by the Supreme Court in the case of Whirlpool Corporation (supra). I make clear that I have not gone into the merit. In view of disposal of the main writ application, the application for grant of interim order has become infructuous and the same is disposed of accordingly."

Thus, it will be noticed that since the judgment in Kelawalas case the courts have traversed in many directions like strike, lock-out, go-slow, justifiability of lock-out and strike, Payment of Wages Act, consequences of not complying with the concept of contract of employment, work done etc. Law does not stop moving with times. In an unusual case, the Bank of Rajasthan refused to grant casual leave to an employee. The employee wanted to avail of the leave to participate in a day's strike. The employee pleaded that he had submitted the application for casual leave but that in the absence of any communication from the management, he presumed that his leave has been sanctioned. Negativing the employees contention, the Single Bench and the Division Bench of the Rajasthan High Court held that leave cannot be claimed as a matter of right and that the principle of no work no pay will be applicable.[40] In Goodlass Nerolac Paints case, the Bombay High Court had to deal with reference to T.S. Kelawalas case. In the short question was, whether the company can deduct wages (relying on the aforesaid case) for the reason that the workman has not performed his part of the contract by working although he was present on duty.[41] The workman had dispute the fact that he was required to do the job of filling containers and had made out a case that this work was to be done by a junior worker and not by a person of his seniority. This contention was established by him before the Industrial Court. In the circumstances, the High Court held that the company ought to have held an enquiry before effecting any deductions from the wages of the concerned workman.

In Blue Star Ltds case, the company suspended its operations from 1st June, 1984 and simultaneously gave a notice for lock-out from 18th June, 1984 as workmen were indulging in go-slow, periodic cessation of work during working hours etc. The Bombay High Court found that lock-out notice given by the company is legal. The employees, however, have been factually lock-out with effect from 1st June,1984 on the basis of suspension of work with immediate effect. The employees were ready and willing to work but they were prevented from joining their duties on and from 1st June 1984. The Court went on to hold[42] that the workmen are entitled to wages from 1st June to 17th June, 1984.

In Metal Rolling Works also there was a similar instance of suspension of operation followed by a lock-out. The union and the management could not reach an agreement on the charter of demands. The management proposed that the issues involved be jointly referred to adjudication. While this suggestion was under consideration, the employees joined another union called "Association of Engineering workers." This union raised a charter of demands and the workmen indulged in go-slow, blocking movement of goods in and out of the factory, shouting slogan etc. The Tribunal granted injunction against the union & 13 workmen restraining them from resorting to any coercive action. In spite of this order the workmen continued to misbehave and the employer became apprehensive of the safety of his executives and of his property. The employer suspended operations with effect from 30th December 1983 and simultaneously gave a notice of lock-out from 16th January 1984. The union complained stating that the lock-out was illegal. In this petition the Tribunal gave an interim order restraining the company from removing any goods etc., from the factory. On February16th 1985, the Government made a reference on the issue of the lock-out. The Govermentt. along with the reference prohibited continuance of the lock-out. The company had a grievance in as much as there was no reference to ensure peaceful working in case the lock-out was lifted. In the meantime, the workers joined General Labour Union. This new Union by letter dated. 25-2-1985 assured full cooperation on the part of the employees in ensuring smooth functioning of the factory. The issue of opening of the factory was discussed between the representatives of the company and the union and 117 workmen were asked to report on 4-3-1985 for oiling, cleaning etc., of the machinery and normal working was resumed from 9th March 1985. The Tribunal came to the conclusion that the lock-out from 16-1-1984 was legal and justified and the workmen are not entitled to wages. Having said that, the Tribunal also held that the employer was not reasonably justified in not taking prompt action from 16-1-1985 i.e., the date of Governments order till 28-2-1985 and directed the petitioner to pay the workmen compensation equivalent to 10 days wages. The employer contested this award to pay compensation citing several decisions including the decision of the Supreme Court in Syndicate Bank vs. K. Umesh Nayak.[43] The Bombay High Court held[44] that the company had rightly relied on the decision to contend that by applying the principle underlying the said judgment it would be open for the petitioner to argue that since the lock-out was legal and forced upon the petitioner, the company would not be liable to pay any compensation. The court further held: *"In my view, merely because the state government had issued on order on 16-2-1985 that by itself did not create any right in favour of the workmen to attend to their work unless and until they had fulfilled other terms of employment express or implied."*

Relying on the Supreme Court judgments in Kelawalas and Syndicate Banks cases, the Gujarat High Court[45] refused to strike down the Central Banks notice for wage deduction from the employees wages on the basis of the principle no work no pay for the day when the employees participated in a march to the Parliament House. The Court held: "..... the questions regarding legality[46] of the strike and the consequent deduction of wages on the principle of "no work no pay" can be suitably determined by the industrial adjudicator under the provisions of the Industrial Disputes Act and it is not for this Court to enter into that arena in exercise of its unit powers. All these petitions are therefore rejected." But then the position will change if the employees are unable to attend office due to all-India bandh. In the case of Hindustan Aeronautics Ltd, the company refused to grant to employees special casual leave on the day when there was an all-India bandh. As a matter of fact there was a circular from Govt. of India requesting employers to grant special casual leave for the day. The High Court held that even assuming that the said circular was not mandatory, yet the management could not escape the scrutiny of the high court in the matter of exercising its discretion where discretionary power is not exercised in the spirit and nature with which it has to be exercised.[47]

"The employees of the Karnataka Road Transport Corporation struck work on 11th March, 1992 against the alleged privatisation move of the employer and again on 24,25,26th September 1992 because their union leader was assaulted by the public and on 28th July and 9th September demanding that the employer implement a Memorandum of understating arrived with the employees. The corporation issued a show-cause notice on 27-3-1992 proposing 8 days wage-cut for each days strike. The union objected to the move of the corporation. Conciliation failed and the Industrial Tribunal relying on the judgment of the Supreme Court in Bank of Indias case [1990 II LLJ 39] took the view that it is permissible to deduct additional wages. The Tribunal, however, held that deduction of 4 days wages for each day of strike will be reasonable. The single Bench of the High Court concurred with the Tribunals views. The Division Bench observed:

The decision of the Supreme Court in the case of Kelawala (supra) as noticed by us earlier, was mainly dealing with the question when employees are absent from duty for a part of the day, whether it is permissible for the employer to deduct wages for the entire day. That was also considered in the backdrop of absence of any regulations governing the said situation; that is not the situation here. Therefore, we are of the view that the principle laid down by the Supreme Court in the case of Kelawala (supra), strongly relied upon by Sri Rao cannot be considered as a binding precedent to take the view that it was permissible for the Corporation to deduct additional wages for the period of absence in addition to deduction of wages for each days absence. It is true that while considering the observation made by a high judicial authority like the Supreme Court, care must be taken to relate the observation of the Court to the precise issues before the Court and to confine such observation even though expressed in broad terms in general compass of the question before the Court. The decision of the Courts should not be followed generally like a statute irrespective of their particular fact situation; and in order to understand and appreciate the binding force of the decision, it is always necessary to see what were the facts of the case in which the decision was rendered and what was the point which was decided. It is well settled that the decision is an authority only for what it actually decides and not for what may logically follow from it. Every judgment must be read as applicable to the particular facts proved since generality of the expressions which may be found there are not intended to be expositions of whole law but governed or modified by the particular facts of the case in which such expressions are to be found. In the case of A-one Granites (supra) while considering the question as to whether the applicability of Rule 72 of the Uttar Pradesh Minor Mineral (Concession) Rules, 1963 was concluded by the earlier decision of the Supreme Court rendered in the case of Prem Nath Sharma vs. State of U.P. reported in AIR 1997 SC 2252: 1997(4) SCC 552, the supreme Court took the view that the question as to whether Rule 72 was applicable or not was never canvassed before the Court in the case of Prem Nath Sharma (supra) and the only question which was considered was whether there was violation of the said Rule and therefore, the earlier decision was not binding.

Having taken the view that the judgment of the Supreme Court in the case of Kelawala (supra) is of no assistance to support the contention of Sri Rao, we find it is desirable to independently examine whether the provisions contained in proviso given to sub-section (2) of Section 9 of the Payment of Wages Act can be applied to the facts of the present case. The Corporation in exercise of the power conferred on it under Sections 14 and 45 of the Road Transport Corporation Act with the previous sanction of the Sate Government has framed the Regulations known as the Karnataka State Road Transport Corporation Servants (conduct and discipline) Regulations. 1971. The said Regulations provides for initiation of disciplinary proceedings and imposition of penalty. Part-III of the Regulations provides for initiation of disciplinary proceedings. Regulation provides for imposition of both minor and major penalties. Clause(v) of Regulation 18-A which provides for levy of minor penalty reads as follows:

"18-A(v)Recovery from his wages or salary of the whole or part of any pecuniary loss caused by him to the Corporation by negligence or breach of orders or unauthorized absence from duty."

Further, it is also necessary to point out that Section 26 of the Industrial Disputes Act provides for imposition of punishment on any workman who commences, continues or otherwise acts in furtherance of, a strike which is illegal under the Act. The Tribunal as well as the learned single Judge have found that the strike resorted to by the workmen was illegal. Therefore, when a penalty is provided under Section 26 of the Act for illegal strike, it appears to us that it is not permissible for the Corporation to deduct additional eight days wages for each days absence in addition to the deduction of wages for each days absence. When the Regulations framed by the Corporation which provides for disciplinary proceedings and imposition of punishment and also Section 26 of the Industrial Disputes Act provides for imposition of punishment for illegal strike, it is not permissible to apply the proviso in Section 9 of the Wages Act to deduct additional wages for each days absence, however, one may disapprove of the concerted action of the workmen resorting to strike. In our view, we are also supported by the decision of the Andra Pradesh High Court in the case of G.Y.N. Chainulu vs. Depot Manager, A.P.S.R.T.C., Amalapuram reported in 1989-II LLJ 81.In the said decision, while considering the similar question after referring to the decision of the Supreme Court in the case of Rohtas Industries vs. Rohtas Industries Staff Union, AIR 1976 SC 425" 1976(2) SCC 82: 1976-I-LLJ 274, the court observed as follows 1989 II LLJ 81 at p. 84:

"4...... Therefore once a strike was declared to be illegal by operation of notification issued under Section 3 of the Essential Services Maintenance Act, then it is not a due notice, thereby the first limb of proviso to sub-section (2) of Section 9 is not satisfied. Then the question is whether the management is entitled to deduct 3 days wages, as ordered in this case. In this case the right to deduct wages is the only right the employer has against the employees for their absence from duty without due notice and without reasonable cause. But such absence from duty was declared to be an offence or penal, by operation of Section 4 of the aforesaid Act. Section 4 provides penalty for such absence from duty with imprisonment or with penalty or with both. Therefore, it creates penal consequences. The right to deduct wages for the same offence is created under the proviso to Section 9(2) of the Act. Thereby, since the right given under section

9(2) is inconsistent with the penalty or the liability created under Section 4 of the Essential Services Maintenance Act Section 8 of the aforesaid Act prevails over Section 9(2) proviso of the Wages Act. Thereby the necessary action to be taken by the Management by statutory operation is under the Essential Services Maintenance Act alone. "In Rohtas Industries vs. its Union AIR 1976 SC 425 : 1976 (2) SCC 82: 1976- I LLJ 274 the decision relied on by Shri Prabhakar Rao clearly supports this conclusion. In paragraph 28 it was held:

"............ The compensation claimed and awarded is a direct reparation for the loss of profits of the employer caused by the illegal strike. If so, it is contended by the respondents, the remedy for the illegal strike and its fall out has to be sought within the statute and not de hors it. If this stand of the workers is right, the remedy indicated in Section 26 of the Act viz., prosecution for starting and continuing an illegal strike, is the designated statutory remedy. No other relief outside the Act can be claimed on general principles of jurisprudence. The result is that the relief of compensation by proceedings in arbitration is contrary to law and bad."

The same ratio applies to the facts in this case. Once it is found that the remedy under proviso to Section 9(2) of the wages Act is inconsistent with penal consequences under section 4 of the Essential Services Maintenance Act, then the recourse could be had only to 2 section by operation of Section 8 thereof and not de hors it."

We are in respectful agreement with the said view. Further, the observation made by the Supreme Court in the case of Rohtas Industries (supra) extracted by the Andra Pradesh High Court also clearly indicates that it is not permissible for the Corporation to deduct any wages by way of compensation out of the wages payable to the workmen on the ground they had gone on strike. Therefore, we are of the view that the award passed by the Tribunal as well as the learned single Judge are liable to be set a side holding that it was not permissible for the Corporation to deduct additional wages payable to the workmen in addition to the deduction of wages for days of their absence. "Having said thus the court also held:

"In our view, once it is held that the workman had absented themselves from duty on account of the illegal strike resorted by them, it will not be permissible for the workmen to plead that even if the strike was illegal, still their absence was on account of reasonable

cause. It is not possible to take the view that when a strike is declared as illegal, the absence from duty in such circumstance could be held to be on account of reasonable cause. When illegal strike is made as an offence and punishable under Section 26 of the I.D Act, it is not possible to take the view that absence from duty by the workman on account of illegal strike could in certain circumstances be on account of reasonable cause. Once the strike is held to be illegal, in our view for the purpose of deciding the question whether it is a reasonable cause or not, the object or the motive of the strike cannot be gone into. The reasonable cause in the circumstances must be understood as to whether the action in question was reasonable or not." Then the court concluded:

"The only question that remain to be considered is as to whether the quantum of punishment imposed proposing to deduct four day wages for each days absence is required to be modified and reduced by this Court on the ground urged by Shri Narshimahan or it has to be enhanced as contended by Sri Rao. While the management has deducted 8 days wage for days absence, the Tribunal has modified the same and limited it to 4 days for each day absence. As noticed by us earlier, the learned single Judge has affirmed the same. We have accepted the finding recorded by the Tribunal that the strike resorted to by the workmen was illegal. It cannot be seriously disputed that on account of the strike resorted to, the members of the traveling public were put to serious hard ship and inconvenience. The services rendered by the employees of the Corporation has been treated as an essential service. We are not impressed with the submission of Sri Narsimhan that in any strike whether it is legal or illegal, some inconvenience or hardship is bound to be caused to the Corporation and also the general public and therefore, that cannot be made as the basis to impose the quantum of punishment on the workman; and even if the additional wages is required to be deducted for each days absence, it should not be more than a days wage in addition to the deduction of wages for the day of absence."

And the final order of the Court order was:

"(i) We hereby declare that the Corporation is not entitled to deduct wages for the absence of the workman from duty in addition to the deduction of wages for the dates on which they absented themselves from duty either under Section 9

of the Wages Act or taking guidance from the said provision. Accordingly, the Award dated November 25, 1997 made in ID No. 5 of 1993 by the Industrial Tribunal is hereby quashed:

(ii) *Consequently, the order dated September 11, 2000 made in Writ Petition Nos. 14636 and 15701 of 1998 by the learned single Judge is also hereby set aside in so far as it relates to deduction of wages in addition to the period of absence of the employees from their duty;*

(iii) *However, this order will not come in the way of the Corporation initiating appropriate disciplinary proceedings if it so desires, against the employees of the Corporation for their alleged unauthorized absence from duty, it is permissible in law and in accordance with law.*

(iv) *In terms stated above, Writ Appeal Nos. 1005 to 1006 of 2000 are allowed and disposed of. Writ Appeal No. 6347 of 2000 is dismissed."*

However, no order is made as to costs."[48]

In a case where consequent upon a settlement, 134 employees gave up striking of work; but 53 employees continued to strike work illegally. Enquiries were conducted and the management imposed 2 punishments viz (i) no pay for suspension period and (ii) increments varying from 1 to 4 were stopped with cumulative effect.

The labour court upheld the orders of the management. The single bench of the High court while upholding the punishment of non-payment of wages for the suspension period set aside the punishment of stoppage of increments with cumulative effect. The Division Bench held that stoppage of increment (without cumulative effect) will be proper in the case. The Supreme Court considered the matter and held that neither the single bench nor the Division Bench was justified in interfering with the order of the labour court but in the peculiar circumstances of the case did not interfere with the order of the Division Bench.[49]

The last topic is temporary stoppage of work for reasons beyond the control of a bank. Paragraph 511 of the Sastry award deals with the topic and is as follows:

" We give the following directions:

(i) In the event of fire, catastrophe, an epidemic, civil commotion or other cause beyond the control of the bank, it may at any time, without notice or compensation in lieu of notice, close down, as the event may require, the bank or any branch, department or part thereof for a reasonable period.

(ii) An employee affected by a stoppage under Clause (1) above shall be deemed to be on privilege leave to the extent such leave is admissible, and for the balance period, except where his services are dispensed with, he shall be deemed to be on leave without pay."

Appendix III hereto notes that the employee should be granted appropriate leave, including casual leave but not special leave. This would mean that if no leave is available to the credit of th employee, he will be on leave on loss of pay.

Notes

1. See S.B. Staff Union (Madras circle) vs. SBI, 1991, I LLJ, p. 163.
2. Canara Bank vs. GMV Nayak and Others, 1991, II LLJ, p. 198.
3. State Bank of India vs. Union, 1994, II LLJ 836.
4. See MPEB Diploma Engineers Assn vs. M.P. Electricity Board, 2006, IV LLJ 1021.
5. See Nellimara Jute Mills Karmik Sangam vs. State of A.P., 1995, I LLJ 507 at 516.
6. M.D. Hindustan Fastners Pvt. Ltd. vs. Nashik Workers Union, 2007, I LLJ 434.
7. Kanak Industries vs. General Labour Union, 2007, III LLJ 327 at 346.
8. See Clifton Electronix and Other vs. Lt. Governor of Delhi, 1995 II LLJ p. 894.
9. See A. S. Mills Co. Ltd. vs. Industrial Tribute, 1997, III LLJ, p. 230.
10. Muncipal Corporation for city of Kalyan and Dombivili vs. R.C. Baania, 2006, IV LLJ 94.
11. Bhag Singh vs. Punjab and Sind Bank, 2006, IV LLJ.

12. R.B.I. vs. Bhopal Singh, 1994, I LLJ p. 642.

    Note: In Anoop Kumar Srivastav vs. State of M.P. [see 2002 IV LLJ 1403] it was held that the employee is not entitled to wages from the date of his dismissal to the date of his acquittal in a criminal proceedings for he was responsible for the criminal proceedings.

13. Executives Engineers Camps & Building Division vs. Labour Court. 2007, I LLJ 413.

14. R.R. Naidu vs. ONGC, 1998, I LLJ, p. 20

15. General Manager, India Cement vs. Subramanyam N.S. 1998, I LLJ p. 584.

16. State Bank of India vs. Industrial Tribunal, 1998 III LLJ, p. 17 [If the employee is aggrieved, he must take recourse to redressal of his grievance under para 517 of Sastry Award.]

17. Mohan Singh Vikram Singh vs. Continental Textile, 1998 III LLJ p.24 [*Note*: In such an eventuality workman can claim wages under Sec 33(c)(2) of the Industrial Disputes Act, 1947] Oswal Agro Mills Ltd. vs. Union, 2001, III LLJ 503.

18. Walchandnagar Industries Ltd. vs. Association of Engineering Workers, 1998 III LLJ 564. See also Subash Silk Mills Ltd. vs. Mill Mazdoor Sabha, 2000, II LLJ 716.

19. See BKK Mahasangh vs. GKW Ltd., 2000, III LLJ, p. 367.

20. Purshtam Ganpat Bhoir vs. National Textile Corp, 2002, IV LLJ 1066.

21. See Vamen Maruty Gharat vs. M.S.Apte, 1998 III LLJ p. 603. See also Union vs. Macneil and Magor Ltd., 2004 III LLJ, 929. Doodh Kamgar Sabha vs. Zurisingh Beechusingh and Co., 2005, I LLJ 709.

22. Management of Nagammal Mills Ltd. vs. K.M.NT.M. Sangam and Another, 1999, I LLJ 505.

23. See Rajnagars Textile Mills No. 1 vs. Textile Labour Association, 1999, I LLJ 522.

24. Bharatiya Kamgar Karmachari Mahasangh vs. G.K.W. Ltd., 1999 I LLJ 719. [*Note:* In that case the High Court saw no reason or justification to deny benefit of wages by way of interim relief]. See also MFM Yusuf vs. Sri Krishna Worker Mills-n 2001 I LLJ 1363. [Wages for lock-out period cannot be claimed until legality of lock-out is adjudicated.]

25. See- Syndicate Bank vs. K.Umesh Nayak, 1994 II LLJ 836; Paluru Ram Krishnaiah & Others vs. Union of India- 1989 II LLJ 47; Bank of India vs. T.S.Kelawala- 1990 II LLJ 39 Gestatner Duplicator Pvt Ltd vs. CIT,West Bengal- 1979 II scc 354.
26. Burn Standard Co. Ltd. vs. T.K.Chakraborthy, 1999 III LLJ 41. [*Note:* "Even the plea of the appellants of hovering under a misconception and abortively approaching this Court bona fide for a clear permission cannot exhonorate them from the liability of paying the petitioner with effect from his attempted date of joining, namely October 22, 1984"].
27. See 1981 I LLJ p.64.[In that case the Court had held that full days wages could be deducted for a partial days strike.]
28. Sugunaraj vs. Syndicate Bank, 1999, III LLJ, p. 1198.
29. See Tyre Retreading Shop Committee vs. APSRTC I LLJ 438. [The concerned employees were drawing wages of over Rs. 1600 p.m & hence were outside the preview of the Payment of wages Act, 1936].
30. All India Trade Union Congress vs. Ravi Fisheries Ltd., 2000 II LLJ 745.
31. See Piece Electronics & Elelctricals Ltd., Pune vs. Union, 2000 II LLJ 823.
32. 1990, II LLJ 39 at 49 : United Commercial Bank vs. Union see also 2003 I LLJ 1046-The Bank had notified that no salary for the day would be paid to employees if they did not report for work for any part of the working hours for that day. Despite this the employees resorted to strike for part of the day. The Bank was justified in deducting wages for the whole day.
33. Reserve Bank of India vs. V. Raveendram, 2000, III LLJ 176.
34. Reserve Bank of India vs. V. Raveendram, 2000, III LLJ 176.
35. 2000, III LLJ, p. 235.
36. Ganapathy Subramanian vs. Canara Bank, 2000, III LLJ 813.
37. Modi Store Ltd vs. Union, 2001, I LLJ, p.1598 since the issue of justifiability of the lock-out could not be gone into in a proceedings under the MRTU & PULP Act, the Court did not hold whether the lock-out justified and the consequent payment of wages for the period of the lock-out.

38. Otis Elevator Co Ltd. vs. G.S. Bajaj, 2001 II LLJ, p. 298 in this case it was held that by giving appropriate notice of 14 days, the illegality can be cared.
39. GRSE Ltd Workmen s Union vs. Garder Reach Shipp Builders & Engineers Ltd., 2001, II LLJ, 1080.
40. Bank of Rajasthan Employees Union vs. Punjab National Bank 2001 II LLJ 1514.
41. See Goodlass Nerolac Paints Ltd. vs. Union, 2002, I LLJ, 605.
42. Blue Star Workers Union vs. Blue Star Ltd. 2002, III LLJ 477 [in the circumstances of the case, the court ordered the company to pay interest at 24% p.a. till such payment is made].
43. 1994 II LLJ 836.
44. Metal Rolling Works Pvt. Ltd vs. General Labour Union, 2002, IV LLJ, p. 294.
45. Pravin H. Shukla vs. Central Bank of India, 2000, IV LLJ 462.
46. The entitlement to wages for the lock-out period directly depends upon the legality and justifiability of the lock-out. [Maya Export Corp Vs. Secretary, 2002, IV LLJ 1462].
47. 2002, IV LLJ 1484.
48. See KSRTC vs. Workers Federation, 2004, II LLJ, p. 891.
49. Management of Coimbatore District Central Cooperative Bank vs. Secretary, 2007, II LLJ 724.

9

Strikes–Justifiability

The Supreme Court judgment while discussing the T. S. Kelawalas case and Charakulan Tea Estate and Crompton Greaves cases considered the issue re: justifiability of strike and said[1]: "*The question whether a strike or lock-out is legal or illegal does not present much difficulty for resolution since all that is required to be examined to answer the question is whether there has been a breach of the relevant provisions. However, whether the action is justified or unjustified has to be examined by taking into consideration various factors some which are indicated earlier. In all most all such cases, the prominent question that arises is whether the dispute was such a nature that its solution could not brook any delay and await a resolution by the mechanism provided under the law or contract of service or service rules. The strike or lock-out is not to be resorted to because the concerned party has a superior bargaining power or requisite economic muscle to compel the other party to accept its demand. Such indiscriminate use of power is nothing but assertion of the rule that "might is right". Its consequences are lawlessness, anarchy and chaos in the economic activities, which are most vital and fundamental to the survival of society. Such action, when the legal machinery is available to resolve the dispute, may be hard to justify. This will be particularly so when it is resorted to by a section of society, which can well, await the resolution of the dispute by the machinery provided for the same. The strike or lock-out as a weapon has to be used sparingly for redressal of urgent and pressing grievances when no means are available or available means have failed to resolve it. It has to be resorted to, to compel the other party to the dispute to see the justness of the demand. It is not to be utilized to work hard-ship to the society at large so as to strengthen the bargaining power. It is for this reason that industrial legislation such as the Act places additional restrictions on strikes and lock-outs in public utility service."*[2]

The various provisions, which place restrictions on the right to strike and the machineries, which provide for processing the issues of employees, are spread over the Industrial Disputes Act, 1947. A look at the relevant provisions will be of help in understanding their import.

Sections 2(q) and 2(l) deal with definitions of "strike" and "lock-out", respectively.

Section 2(q): "strike" means–

(a) A cessation of work by a body of persons employed in any industry acting in combination, or,

(b) A concerted refusal or refusal under a common understanding of any number of persons so employed to continue to work.

Section 2(1): "lock-out" means–

(a) The closing of a place of employment or suspension of work by an employer, or,

(b) The refusal by an employer to continue to employ any number of persons employed by him.

Sections 22, 23, 24(1) deal with prohibition of strikes and lock-outs in public utility services. Section 24(2) and 24(3) sets out the details regarding strikes and lockout which are not illegal. Those sections are as follows:

Section 22: Prohibition of strikes and lock-outs in public utility services.

Section 22(1): No person employed in a public utility service shall go on strike–

(a) Without giving to the employer notice of the strike within six weeks before striking in the prescribed manner; or

(b) Within 14 days of giving such notice; or after the conclusion of such proceeding.

(c) Before the expiry of the date of strike specified in such notice; or

(d) During the pendency of any conciliation proceeding before a conciliation officer and 7 days after the conclusion of such proceeding.

Section 22(2.): No employer carrying on any public utility service shall lock-out any of his workmen–

(a) Without giving them notice of the lock-out within six weeks before the locking out in the prescribed manner; or

(b) Within 14 days of giving such notice; or

(c) Before the expiry of the date of lock-out specified in such notice; or

(d) During the pendency of any conciliation proceeding before a conciliation officer and 7 days after the conclusion of such proceeding.

Section 22(3): The notice of a lock-out or strike under this section shall not be necessary when there is already in existence a strike or a lock-out in the public utility service.

Section 2(n): definition of "public utility service."

"Public utility service" means–

1. Any railway service;
2. Any section of an industrial establishment on the working of which the safety of the establishment or the workmen employed therein depends;
3. Any postal telegraph or telephone service;
4. Any industry, which supplies power, light or water to the public;
5. Any system of public conservancy or sanitation;
6. Any industry specified in the First Schedule which has been declared by the appropriate Government to be a public utility service for the purpose of the act, by notification in the official Gazette.

Industries specified in the First Schedule which may be declared to be public utility service under Section 2(n)(vi) are: (1) Transport, (2) Banking, (3) Cement, (4) Coal, (5) Cotton Textiles, (6), Food-Stuffs, (7) Iron and Steel, (8) Defense Establishments, (9) Service in Hospitals and Dispensaries, and (10) Fire Brigade Service.

Section 23: General prohibition of strikes and lock-out in all industries.

No workman employed in any industrial establishment shall go on strike, and no employer of any such workman shall declare a lock-out–

(a) during the pendency of any conciliation before a Board of Conciliation and 7 days after the conclusion of such proceeding; or

(b) during the pendency of any adjudication proceeding before a Labour Court or Industrial Tribunal and 2 months after the conclusion of such proceedings; or

(c) during the period in which a settlement or award is in operation, in respect of any of the matters covered by the settlement or award.

Section 24(1): Strikes and lock-outs which are illegal.

A strike or lock-out shall be illegal–

(a) If it is commenced or declared in contravention of section 22 or section 23; or

(b) It is continued in contravention of order under section 10(3).

Section 24(2) and 24(3): Strikes and lock-outs which are not illegal.

Section 24(2): when a strike or lock-out in connection with an industrial dispute has already commenced and is in existence at the time of the reference of that dispute under section 10(1) for settlement or adjudication, continuance of such strike or lock-out shall not be deemed to be illegal, provided that it was not at its commencement in contravention of section 22 or section 23 and continuance thereof has not been prohibited under section 10(3).

Section 24(3): A strike declared in consequence of an illegal lock-out or a lock-out declared in consequence of an illegal strike, shall not be deemed to be illegal. Now the Act also provides for penalty for illegal strikes and lockouts and for those who instigate such illegal acts. They are as follows:

Section 26,27,28: Penalties for illegal strikes and lock-outs and for their instigation and financial aid.

Section 26(1): Penalty for an illegal strike.

Any workman who commences or otherwise acts in furtherance of a strike which is illegal under the Act, shall be punishable with imprisonment for a term which may extend to one month, or with fine which may extend to fifty rupees, or with both.

Section 26(2): Penalty for an illegal lock-out.

Any employee who commences, continues or otherwise acts in furtherance of a lock-out which is illegal under the Act, shall be punishable with imprisonment for a term which may extend to one month, or with fine may extend to one thousand rupees, or with both.

Section 27 and 28: Penalty for instigation of, or for giving financial aid to, an illegal strike or illegal lock-out.

Any person who instigates or incites others to take part in or otherwise acts in furtherance of a strike or lock-out which is illegal under the Act, or who knowingly expends or applies any money in direct furtherance or support of any illegal strike or lock-out shall be punishable with imprisonment for a term which may extend to six months, or with fine which may extend to one thousand rupees, or with both.

Let us also keep in mind the definitions of conciliation officer, public utility service, and strike." 2(d) conciliation officer means a conciliation officer appointed under the Act."

"24 Public Utility Service means–

(i) ....

(ii) ....

(iii) ....

(iv) ....

(v) ....

(vi Any industry specified in the (First Schedule) which the appropriate government may, if satisfied that the public interest so requires, by notification in the official

Gazette, declare to be public utility service for the purposes of this Act,[3] for such period as may be specified in the notification:

Provided that the period so specified shall not in the first instance, exceed six months, but may, by a like notification, be extended from time to time, by any period not exceeding six months, at any one time if in the opinion of the appropriate government public emergency or public interest so require such extension. Section 2(q) defines strike. "Strike" means a cessation of work by a body of persons employed in any industry acting in combination or a concerted refusal under a common understanding, of any number of persons who are or who are or have been so employed to continue to work or accept employment.

There are other provisions which come into play once the workmen or their union(s) decide to strike work in a public utility service like a bank. The workmen concerned must give a notice of strike of at least 6 weeks and having given the notice they are prohibited from going on strike within 14 days of giving such notice and before the expiry of the date of strike specified in the notice[4] The notice of strike should be in terms of the form prescribed by under Rule 71. of the Act[5]. A copy of this notice must be sent to the conciliation officer appointed under the Act for the banking industry. For other industries or for the industry in an area, the notice should be sent to the appropriate conciliation officer appointed for the purpose. The employer immediately on receipt of the notice of strike should inform the conciliation officer of such receipt. Under Section 20 of the Act conciliation proceedings shall be deemed to have commenced on the date on which a notice of strike or lock-out under section 22 is received by the conciliation officer. From the date of receipt of such notice by the conciliation officer the workmen are prohibited from going on strike during the pendency of the proceeding before the conciliation officer.[6]

Under Section 22 (2) of the Act the conciliation proceedings shall be deemed to have concluded–

(a) Where a settlement is arrived at, when a memorandum of settlement is signed by the parties to the dispute;

(b) Where no settlement is arrived at, when the report of the conciliation officer is received by the appropriate government[7] or

(c) When a reference is made to a Court under sec.10 during the pendency of conciliation proceedings.

And what is the role of the conciliation officer? On receipt of the strike notice, the conciliation officer shall[8] -hold conciliation proceedings without any delay. His duty is mainly is to try and bring about a settlement of the dispute. For this purpose he may investigate into all matter affecting the dispute and their merits and do all such things as he thinks fit for the purpose of inducing the parties to come to a fair and amicable settlement of the dispute.[9] If a settlement is arrived at, the conciliation officer shall send a detailed report along with a copy of the settlement to the govt.[10]

If no such settlement is arrived he shall send a "Failure Report" mentioning the details of the dispute and of the efforts made by him and the reasons why a settlement could not be arrived at.[11] The conciliation officers report should be made within 14 days of the commencement of conciliation proceedings, unless the Government fixes a shorter period or unless the parties by agreement in writing extend the period.[12] Thus it will be noticed that in a public utility service where a notice of strike is given, the conciliation proceedings start compulsorily and continues till such time that the government receives the failure report and 7 days thereafter, unless of course there is a settlement or unless the government makes a reference of the dispute to a court under sec. 10(1) of the Act.[13] During such time, the Act under sec 22(1) prohibits strike. If at the end of the period, however, if the dispute remains unsettled and government has not taken any action, the employees are free to go on strike.

Now on receipt of the "Failure report" from the conciliation officer, it is incumbent on the government to normally refer the dispute for adjudication [or refer it to the conciliation board for further conciliation]. It is only in exceptional case for reasons to be recorded in writing can the government refuse to make a reference. The government can refer the matter to conciliation board as well for further conciliatory efforts. The Board is given 2 months to induce parties to arrive at a settlement unless the parties by mutual agreement extend time. In case the meeting fails at board level, the matter would go to the government for making a reference to the Court. Now once the matter is referred to adjudication, there is a prohibition on the part of the worker to go on strike under Sec. 10(3) of the Act. In this connection sec 10(3) of the Act enables the Government by an order, to prohibit the continuance of strike+. And section 23(a) and (b) provides that the strike is absolutely prohibited-

(a) during the pendency of a proceeding before a Conciliation Board and seven days after the conclusion of the proceeding; (under Section 20(2)(b). "Conclusion of the proceeding" means the date when the report of the Board is published by the Government under section 17); or

(b) during the pendency of an adjudication proceeding before a Labour Court or Industrial Tribunal, and two months after the conclusion of such proceeding.

When a settlement of the dispute has been arrived at between the employer and the workmen, or an award in respect of that dispute has been made, Section 19 provides for the period of the operation of the settlement or award. Under section 19(2), a settlement shall remain in operation initially for a period of six months, and even thereafter it will continue to be in operation until the expiry of two months from the date of the notice in writing intimating the intention to terminate the settlement. Under Section 19(3) and (6) an award shall remain in operation initially for a period of one year, and even thereafter it will continue to be in operation until the expiry of a period of two months from the date of the notice in

---

*[**Note:** +Section 10(3): Prohibition of continuance of a strike or lock-out after a reference has been made. When the Government makes a reference under section 10(1) of an industrial dispute for settlement or adjudication, if any strike or lock-out in connection with such dispute is going on, the Government may by order prohibit the continuance of such strike or lock-out after the date of the reference."*

Here no distinction is made by the Act between public utility services and non public utility industries].

writing intimating the intention to terminate the award. Section 23(c) provides that the workmen in any industrial establishment shall not go on a strike during any period in which a settlement or award is in operation, in respect of any of the matters covered by the settlement or award. Thus as legal provisions stand today, it will be safe to conclude that there is no chance of a legal strike in Public Utility Services.[14]

Section 24(1) provides that a strike commenced or continued in contravention of the prohibitions of Sections 22, 23 and 10(3) is an illegal strike, that is–

1. strike by the workmen in a public utility service without giving a notice of the strike in the prescribed manner, or before the expiry of the notice period, in contravention of section. 22(1) (a),(b),(c);
2. strike by the workmen in a public utility service during the pendency of a conciliation proceeding before a Conciliation Officer, and seven days after the conclusion of the proceeding in contravention of section 22(1)(d);
3. strike by the workmen in any industrial establishment, whether it be a public utility service or otherwise, during the pendency of a conciliation or adjudication proceeding before a Conciliation Board or Labour Court or Industrial Tribunal, and the further period after the conclusion of the proceeding specified in section 23(a) and (b), in contravention of that section, or in contravention of an order made by the Government under section 10(3).
4. strike by the workmen in any industrial establishment during the period during which a settlement or award is in operation, in respect of any matter covered by the settlement or award, in contravention of section 23(c). And section 26 and 27 provide the punishment for the commencement or continuance of an illegal strike, for acts done in furtherance thereof, and for instigation or incitement of illegal strikes, and make

these offences punishable with imprisonment or fine or both.

Now given this legal position, the Supreme Court was right in saying that determination of whether a strike is legal or illegal does not present much difficulty in resolution. It is on the issue of justifiability that considerations arise. One of the first cases on legality and justifiability in this regard that comes to mind is the case of the Indian Navigation and Railway Company limited and their workmen.[15] In that case conciliation proceedings were deemed to have commenced on 26th July, 1955 when the conciliation officer received the notice of strike. The conciliation officer sent his failure report on 8th August, 1955. The strike which commenced on 11th August 1955 was clearly illegal in view of the provisions of section 22 of the Act. The tribunal held the strike to be illegal but "perfectly justified." The Supreme Court held: *"In the first place, it is a little difficult to understand how a strike in respect of a public utility service, which is clearly illegal, could at the same time be characterized as "perfectly justified". These two conclusions cannot in law co- exist, the law has made a distinction between a strike which is illegal and one which is not, but it has not made any distinction between an illegal strike which may be said to be justifiable and one which is not justifiable. This distinction is not warranted by the Act, and is wholly misconceived, specially in the case of employee in a public utility service."*

In Charukakulam Tea Estates case the Supreme Court held: *"Therefore, the strike must be held to be neither illegal nor unjustified and in consequence it must be held that the factory workers are entitled to wages for that day."*[16]

The Punjab & Haryana High Court had an occasion to consider the issue whether Sec. 22 of the Act is directory or is it mandatory. The High Court said: *"A plain reading of the language of the above quoted Sec. 22(1) makes it evident that the requirements laid out in clauses (a), (b), (c) and (d) thereof are essential requirements of law. Confining ourselves to clauses, (a) (b) and (c), it is obvious that the requirements of notice and in the form in which they are to be given when read in conjunction with Sub. cl(4) are mandatory provisions."* Later on in the judgment the High Court held: "*It is idle to contend that the provisions of Sec. 22 are merely directory and a patent violation of these provisions would entail no legal consequences. Indeed compliance with the provisions section 22 is the core of the matter for determining whether a particular strike is legal or otherwise.*" And finally: "*It is evident from the above that the primary question was whether the strike was legal or otherwise and to brush aside this main issue on the ground of factual justifiability or otherwise of the strike was totally unwarranted.*"[17]

In A.P. State Road Transport Corporation's case also this issue was examined. "*The strike was justified and it was but, for a day, and I am therefore of the view that the workers should be paid the wages for 28.3.66 if the strike was not illegal for the reason that the settlement was not terminated. That question must be decided by the Tribunal.*"[18] It will be noticed thus far that in order to get strike day wages paid, the strike had to be both legal and justified. What is legal is easy to understand what is "justified" was never spelt out. The ordinary dictionary[19] meaning of the word "Justify" means.

(a) To prove or show to be just, right or reasonable.

(b) To show to have had a sufficient legal reason.

(c) To show a sufficient lawful reason for an act done.

The word "Justify" may warrant sufficient grounds for doing, using, saying or preferring something.

Both reason and conscience will have to be satisfied and unless this happens the act (strike) in question should be met with disapproval. There must be reasons for doing something which should be acceptable to right thinking people and sound reasons for doing so for an act to become justifiable. Thus for an act to be justifiable, not only there must be sufficient reasons to show that the act is reasonable, right and just but it must also be legal for only then can one advance lawful reason as justification.

The justifiability of a strike was considered by the Supreme Court in Crompton Greavess case.[20] The short question which the Court considered was whether the workmen are entitled to wages for the period from January 11, 1968 to 29th February, 1968. "*It is well-settled that in order to entitle the workmen to wages for the period of strike, the strike should be legal as well as justified. A strike is legal if it does not violate any provision of the statute. Again a strike cannot be said to be unjustified unless the reasons for it are entirely perverse or unreasonable. Whether a particular strike was justified or not is a question of fact which has to be judged in the light of facts and circumstances of each case. It is also well-settled that the use of force or violence or acts of sabotage resorted to by workmen during a strike disentitles them to wages for the strike period."* The Supreme Court found that the strike was not illegal. And added further: "*The strike cannot also be said to be unjustified as before the conclusion of the talks for conciliation which was going on through the instrumentality of the Asst. Labour Commissioner, the company retrenched as many as 93 of its workmen even without intimating the Asst. Labour Commissioner that it was carrying out its proposed plan of effecting retrenchment of workmen.*" The Court also found there was no proof of violence and hence confirmed the order of the Tribunal granting workmen wages for the period of strike. The issue of legality and justification of a strike briefly came on the fringes before the Supreme Court in the case of Gujarat Steel Tubes Ltd.[21] In that case, there was a long drawn strike and the management discharged all the 853 workmen and recruited fresh faces to keep the wheels of production moving. In due course of time, some of the discharged workers were taken back leaving 434 workers out in the lurch. The Supreme Court considered whether company was right in terminating the services of these workmen and in that connection had this to say with regard to legality and justifiability of strike. "*The basis of the assumption we make is that the strike was not only illegal but was also unjustified. On the latter part, a contrary view cannot be ruled out in the circumstances present but we do not reinvestigate the issue since the High Court has proceeded on what both the sides took for granted.*"[22] Referring to India General Navigation and Railways Company ltd. the conceded: "*This court did observe that if a strike is illegal, it cannot be called perfectly justified*" But went on to add, "*Between perfectly justified and unjustified strike the neighborhood is distant*".... And inferred: "..... *Mere illegality of the strike does not per se spell justifiability.*" Now this is a new proposition and does not seem to fit within the ordinary meaning of the word "Justifiable". The Calcutta High Court considered this issue elaborately in the LICs case. In that case, there was a binding settlement for payment of bonus to class III & IV employees at the rate of 15% of employees annual wages inclusive of all allowance. LIC refused to pay bonus. The employees union approached the High Court which ordered the LIC to pay the bonus due. Thereafter LIC sent a notice of termination of the settlement. This was challenged by the union and the matter went up to Supreme Court which directed[23] LIC to pay to pay bonus. LIC did not follow the Supreme Court directive and the employees initiated contempt proceedings against LIC. In the meantime the Central Government issued an ordinance under which the right to receive bonus was taken away. Again the Supreme Court directed LIC to pay the bonus due under the settlement. The union after the refusal to comply with the directions of the Court, issued a notice of strike. In the meantime the LIC moved the Supreme Court for reviewing its order which was turned down by the Supreme Court. Now as per the notice the employees struck work. LIC issued a circular for wage-cut. The High Court held that the strike is justified and that the employees are entitled to payment of wages for the strike period. There again the court noted that the employees had not resorted to any act of violence or intimidation nor violated any civilized norms during the period of strike or prior to strike.

It is thus apparent that generally the view taken by the Supreme Court was that the employees are not entitled to wages for the strike period merely because the strike is legal. For such entitlement the strike has to be legal and justified. In other words, if the strike is illegal but justified or if the strike is legal but unjustified, the employees will not be entitled to wages for the strike period. When the Supreme Court pronounced its judgment in T.S. Kelawalas case[24] it seemed as though that the Supreme Court had taken the view that whether the strike is legal or illegal, the employees are not entitled to wages for the strike period. Thus there was an apparent conflict of decisions between the judgments pronounced in Charukakulam Tea Estate and Crompton Greaves cases and T.S. Kelawalas case. This issue was considered in Syndicate Banks case[25] And the Supreme Court held that there was no such conflict.

"There is, therefore, nothing in the decisions of this Court in Churakulam Tea Estate and Crompton Greaves cases (supra) or the other earlier decisions cited above which is contrary to the view taken in T.S. Kelawala. What is held in the said decisions is that to entitle the workmen to the wages for the strike-period, the strike, has both to be legal and justified. In other words, if the strike is only legal but not justified or if the strike is illegal though justified, the workers are not entitled to the wages for the strike-period. In fact, in India General Navigation Case (supra), the Court has taken the view that a strike which is illegal cannot at the same time be justifiable. According to that view, in all cases of illegal strike, the employer is entitled to deduct wages for the period of strike and also to take disciplinary action. This is particularly so in public utility services.

We therefore hold endorsing the view taken in T.S. Kelawala that the workers are not entitled to wages for the strike-period even if the strike is legal. To be entitled to the wages for the strike period, the strike has to be both legal and justified. Whether the strike is legal or justified are questions of fact to be decided on the evidence on record. Under the Act, the question has to be decided by the industrial adjudicator, it being an industrial dispute within the meaning of the Act."

The Bombay High Court considered the issue in a 100 days strike case by the Grindlays Bank employees. Following the decision of in Syndicate Banks case, it was held that once the strike is held illegal, the question of its justifiability does not arise and the employees in public utility services are not entitled to seek wages for the strike period unless they prove that the strike is legal.[26] In that case the Industrial Tribunal had held the strike to be illegal but justified and ordered payment of 50% of wages except to employees in Calcutta to whom no wages would be payable as they had indulged in violence.

In the case between HAL employees union and the presiding officer, the Supreme Court reiterated its earlier views and that "no work no pay" is the principle applicable to public utility services and that wages would be payable only if the strike is both legal and justified. But it would not be payable if the strike is legal but not justified or is justified but not legal. The strike may be of different forms like go-slow, work to rule, refusal to work overtime, irritation strikes etc, but were bound by the ratio of the constitution bench judgment which applies to the declaration.........[27]

The judgment makes one wonder whether slowly but steadily courts are veering towards the idea that go-slow[28] and work to rule are also strikes. Then there is one more point that may be noted. The apex court held inter alia that strike day wages will not be payable if the strike is justified but illegal. All along the decisions, of the apex court inclusive, is that an illegal strike can never be justified.[29] Are the court, consciously moving towards the idea that there could be other forms of agitations like go-slow, work to-rule etc and in such instances the management would be justified in deducting wages? And the Bombay High Court made a very interesting but factual observation when it held: "*The question whether a strike or lock-out is legal or illegal does not present much difficulty for resolution since all that is required to examine to answer the question is whether there has been a breach of the relevant provisions. However, whether the action is justified or unjustified has to be examined by taking into consideration various factors some of which are indicated earlier. In almost all cases the prominent question that arises is whether the dispute was of such a nature that its solution could not brook delay and await resolution by the mechanism provided under the law or the contract or the service rules......*"[30] In the case of Glaxo Laboratories the workmen went on flash strikes several times, as also resorted to go-slow, slogan shouting etc., because a settlement had ended on 30th June,1990. The employer insisted that to enter the factory workmen should give an undertaking that they are not on strike and that they undertake that during their shift, they will not go on strike. The union claimed strike day wages. The Industrial Tribunal held that the strike was not legal or justified. The Gujarat High Court relying on Bank of India s case held that the workers were not entitled to wages for the strike period even if the strike was legal. Going further the Court observed: "......... *with a view to enforce discipline and to avoid untoward incidents within the premises, the company was justified in seeking such assurance from the employee.*[31]

In following the Supreme Court decision in Bank of India's case, the Andhra Pradesh High Court considered a situation of a strike followed by a lock-out. In that case, the Hindustan Cables Company wanted to work all 7 days in a week (which included working on the weekly day off as well). Additional hands were recruited for this purpose which would enable the workmen to enjoy their weekly day off as well. The union went on strike. The management then reverted to the old system. In the process they had to terminate the service of 48 workers who were recruited to work on weekly off days as also to revert the 7 promotees. The union again went on strike and the company declared a lock-out. This was followed by a settlement by which the 48 workmen were absorbed as and when vacancies arose and the 7 reversions were set aside by promoting the 7 employees. The dispute regarding wages for the strike and lock-out periods was referred to adjudication. The labour Court found that though the strike was not illegal as much as the company was not a Public utility service within the scope of Section 23 of the Industrial Dispute act, 1947, the strike was not justified because the workmen could have had the issue of staggered holidays referred to the Industrial Tribunal for adjudication. The Labour Court also found the demand for reinstatement of the workmen who had been recruited only for meeting the additional work load due to the introduction of the 7 day week, and the termination due to the abandonment of the 7 day week proposal and the consequent hunger strike and tool down strike as well as detention of the buses far away from the factory forcing the workmen to go on foot for a considerable distance, justified the lock-out. The Labour Court therefore, took the view that the workmen are not entitled to wages for both the periods of strike and lock-out. This decision was upset by a single bench judge and hence the company took up the matter before a division bench. The Division bench first considered the Supreme Court decision in Crompton Greaves Ltds. Case [1978 II LLJ p. 80] where it was held that the use of force or violence or acts of sabotage resorted to by workmen during a strike would disentitle them to wages for the strike period. The Supreme Court also observed that the enquiry whether the strike is justified is essentially an enquiry into the facts and has to be decided only by the authority.... Then the High Court dealt with the Syndicate Banks Case [1994 II LLJ p. 836] and held that resorting to strike without exhausting other means for conciliation could not be considered to be justifiable action. And the High Court also found the lock-out to be justifiable.[32]

A Jute mill was running into losses and hence did not pay dearness allowance to workers. The workers union gave a notice of strike for one day. The Labour Court restrained the workers from going on strike and the workers restrained themselves. The Jute mills then declared a lock-out because according to the management the workers indulged in go-slow and that caused considerable loss to the management. The Dy. Labour Commissioner issued a notice to the company for declaring a lock-out without specifying the period of lock-out and hence the managements act amounted to closing down of the undertaking without obtaining the prior permission of the state government. The management contended that they had locked-out in view of the "illegal strike" by adopting go-slow. The case of the Jute mill management was that go-slow is an illegal strike and hence the lock-out which followed the illegal strike is legal. The High Court found that there was a dispute whether there was a go-slow and it was for the industrial adjudication to come to a conclusion. The Court observed: " *The go-slow may be a form of strike but the question whether the workers in the present case adopted that course is a question of fact to be decided by the Labour Court...... The question whether the lock-out is legal or not would depend upon the decision whether there was strike and it was illegal.*" Then on payment of wages pending determination of the issue the court observed:

"In matters relating to apportionment of blame between the management and the workers, there can be no inflexible formula or rigid yardstick to determine the percentage of apportionment, and

the extent of apportionment of blame would depend upon the facts and circumstances of each case." In this case, the Tribunal had granted 50% of the wages for the lock-out period which though legal continued for an unduly long time. Where the employer could not adduce evidence to prove financial crisis and labour indiscipline, it was held that lock-out was unjustified.[33]

"The question however is whether the workers are entitled to some relief until the points relating to strike, lockout and closure are decided. The administrative authorities of the Labour department have come on the scene to assuage the plight of the workers. The decision of the Labour Court on the points referred above would take sometime. It was admitted during the course of hearing that the lockout which was declared on March 29, 1999 is continuing and the workers are not getting even subsistence wages. It is necessary that the workers must get at least two square meals a day. Their condition on account of the closure of the mill can very well be imagined. Therefore, there has to be some immediate solution of the problem. In India Marine Service Private Ltd v. Their Workmen, AIR 1963 SC 528, it has been held that in a case where a strike is unjustified and is followed by a lock-out which has, because of its long duration become unjustified, it would not be a proper course for an Industrial Tribunal to direct the payment of the whole of the wages for the period of the lock-out. In a case where the strike is unjustified and the lock-out justified the workmen would not be entitled to any wages at all. Similarly, where the strike is justified and the lock-out is unjustified the workmen would be entitled to the entire wages for the period of strike and lock-out. Where however, a strike is unjustified and is followed by a lock-out which becomes unjustified, a case for apportionment of blame arises. In that case the blame was apportioned half and half between the company and its workers and the workmen were allowed to get half of their wages. That course should be followed in the present case also at this stage as it is yet to be established that the workers were on strike and that was illegal to justify the lock-out by the petitioner."[34]

The interesting point in this case is the observation that go-slow may be a form of strike. To say that go-slow is non-fulfillment of the contract of employment is one thing- is the correct thing- and hence wages are not payable; to say that it may be a form of strike is another thing-for in go-slow there is no cessation of work. In the case of Mysore Wine Products and Allied Company Ltd. also there was a go-slow. A charter of demands was placed and the workmen resorted to illegal strike from Dec. 1983. The management claimed that office bearers and executive committee members of the union entered the administration office and instructed the administrative staff not to work. The union claimed that the management used police force and goondaism and charge-sheets were issued to the workmen. Needless to say, the workmen agitated from October 1983 and struck work on 23-12-83, which was followed by a lock-out from 24-12-1983. Ultimately though a settlement was reached on the demands, the Industrial Tribunal was called upon to decide 2 issues viz., pertaining to justification of lock-out from 24-12-83 to 8-2-1984 and wages for the period 9-2-1984 to 16-4-1984. in respect of concerted absence on the part of workmen from those sections (like still house, boiler house, water treatment, maintenance and power house departments). The Tribunal held:

(a) Declaration of lock-out from 24-12-83 to 8-2-1984 is not justified.

(b) The strike on 23-12-83 is not justified.

(c) Continuance of lock-out from 9-2-1984 to 16-4-1984 is not an issue to be considered for workmen did not report for duty in those sections where lock-out is lifted and consequently they have not been paid wages; and

(d) The workmen are not justified in remaining absent from 9-2-84 to 16-4-84 in departments where lock-out was lifted.

The Madras High Court now considered the matter. After going through the evidence the High Court set aside the findings of the Tribunal and held that the lock-out from 24-12-1983 to 8-2-1984 is justified. Regarding the strike on 23-12-1983, the High Court agreed with the Tribunal that the strike was staged with a view to withdraw the charge-sheets, "Certainly an offence is said to be committed and the charge-sheet was filed against these offenders and it is not proper for the workers to go on strike compelling the management to withdraw the charge-sheet filed against them by the police. It may even amount to prevention of prosecution of lawful cause which according to the management is lawful.........and the strike made on 23-12-1983 can certainly not be justified." On partial lifting of lock-out the High Court noted: "*The Tribunal also found that in Ex M-36, the only complaint of the union was that it was a divide tactics...... Therefore, once the management made it clear that once the workmen in those departments can keep the plant ready for work, then only the lock-out in respect of other workmen could be lifted, cannot be said to be wrong.*" Hence this issue also went against the workmen and they were not entitled to any wages for the period of the lock-out.[35]

We are therefore at a stage where it is possible to say whether a strike is legal or illegal. But on the issue whether an illegal strike is justified the answer is clear as of now. But is there a case for declaring an illegal strike as justified? After all the question of "justification" is a judge made law. Can it change? Or will it change in the times to come? Added to this are the associated issues like whether go-slows, work-to-rule etc. warrant the application of dies non? One should await future development in law to answer these questions more fully.

Notes

1. Syndicate Bank and another vs. K. Umesh Nayak, 1994, II LLJ 836.
2. "Banking" is a Public Utility Service under the Industrial Dispute Act, 1947.
3. Banking is mentioned as an item of 1th schedule.
4. Section 22(1) (a) (b) (c) of the Act. Workmen employed in non public utility industries need not give any strike notice.
5. See Form L under Rule 71 of the Industrial Dispute (Central) Rules.
6. See Sec. 22(1)(d) [*Note:* Though no notice of strike is required to be given in non public utility industries, if the conciliation officer is satisfied about existence or apprehends any dispute, he may initiate conciliation proceedings].

7. In the case of banking industry, where the bank has branches in more than one state, appropriate govt. is the Central Government.
8. There is no such legal compulsion to hold the conciliation proceedings in non-public utility services.
9. See Sec. 12(4) of the Act.
10. See 12(5) of the Act.
11. Sec 12(4)of the Act.
12. See Sec. 12(4) of the Act.
13. The provisions are the same for non-public utility industries as well
14. Same is applicable mutatis mutandis to lock-out as well.
15. See 1960 I LLJ, p. 13.
16. Mgt. of Charakakulam Tea Estate vs. Workman, 1969 II LLJ 407.
17. Muncipal Committee vs. Industrial Tribunal, 1971, II LLJ 52.
18. The Andra Pradesh State Road Transport Corporation Employees Union vs. APSRTC, Hyderabad, 1970, LIC 1225.
19. See Websters New College Dictionary.
20. Crompton Greaves Ltd vs. Workmen, 1978 II LLJ 80. [*Note:* In this case, a Joint conference was scheduled for 12.1.1968. On 10.1.1968, the company put up the notice retrenching 93 workmen in Calcutta office. The workers stuck work from 11.1.1968. Was conciliation pending? This does not seem to be clear. If so, the strike surely was illegal].
21. Gujarat Steel Tubes Ltd. vs. G.S.T. Mazdoor Sabha, 1980 II LLJ 137.
22. Amalendu Gupta vs. LIC, 1982 II LLJ 332.
23. See 1981, I LLJ, p. 1.
24. Bank of India vs. T.S. Kelawala, 1990, II LLJ, p. 39.
25. Syndicate Bank vs. K. Umesh Nayak, 1994, II LLJ, 836
26. 1995, II LLJ p. 877; See also NLC Workers Union vs. Neyveli Lignite Corporation, 2001, I LLJ 1219. [The Court after referring to Syndicate Banks case [1994 II LLJ 836] held that striking work during the pendency of conciliation proceedings is both illegal and unjustified]. See also Bharat Petroleum Corp. Ltd vs. Workmen, 2000 IV LLJ, p. 354; Bharat Petroleum Corp Ltd. vs. workmen, 2003 III LLJ, 229.

27. 1996 II LLJ 930-931; Godrej and Boyce Manufacturing Co. vs. K.H. Pathan 2000, III LLJ 204; See also PGI Employees Union vs. Director, Post graduate Institute of Medical Education, 1995, III LLJ 628 [In this case strike was held to be legal but unjustified].
28. "What is go-slow? "Go-slow methods or restrictions by workers or either in relation to some particular claim or grievance or in order to limit output for purposes of controling the labour market or same aspect of it. "In both cases out right withdrawal of labour is avoided, but the object in the first instance in more tactical and in the second more strategic. Go-slow, slow gear strikes, lazy strike, folded arms strike, stay-in-strike, working without enthusiasm or in some forms of work-to rule are expressions to describe mainly its tactical use." See Concise Encyclopedia of Industrial Relations-Arthur Marsh. See 1996, II LLJ, 930-931; Godrej and Boyce Manufacturing Co. vs. K.H. Pathan, 2000 III LLJ, 204; See also PG I Employees Union vs. Director, Post graduate Institute of Medical Education, 1995, III LLJ, p. 628. [In this case, the strike was held to be legal but unjustified].
29. Indian Navigation & Railway Co. Ltd. vs. Their Workmen, 1960, I LLJ, p. 13.
30. See Maharastra General Kamgar Union vs. Solid Containers Ltd. & Others, 1996, II LLJ 959. [*Note:* "It is not a condition of service of a workman to force his entry in the factory premises, when on strike. The workmen enter the premises because of the implied license ...." [see page 27]].
31. See Glaxo Laboratories Employees Union vs. Glaxo India Ltd. 1996, III LLJ, 266.
32. Aluminum Industries Ltd. vs. Industrial Tribunal, 2006, I LLJ, p. 16.
33. American Refrigerator Co. Ltd. vs. First Industrial Tribunal, 2006 II LLJ, 271.
34. Mohan Jute Mills Ltd. State of M.P., 2000, III LLJ, 1550.
35. Mysore Wine Products and Allied Co. Ltd. vs. Presiding Officer, 2000, I LLJ, p. 1166.

10

Effects of Strike on Contract of Employment

We have seen that the term "contract of employment" will include not only the contractual terms and conditions but also those terms which are understood and applied in practice or habitually by common consent without even being incorporated in the contract and also such legal provisions which are super-imposed and all those come into play for a consideration. This binds both the employer and the employee in terms of obligations on the part of each of them towards the other. The outcome is of the service rendered by the employee and the wages and other benefits paid by the bank. Thus the term "contact of employment" is of a wide import.

The term "strike" is often described as a "weapon" in the hands of labour. *"In the struggle between capital and labour the weapon of strike is available to labour and is often used by it, as is the weapon of lock-out available to the employer and can be used by him."*[1] In Gujarat Steel Tubes Ltd. vs. Gujarat Steel Tube Mazdoor Sabha the Supreme Court observed:[2]" *Of course, collective strike is economic pressure by cessation of work and not exchange of pleasantries. It means embarrassing business."* The important point to note is that strike is cessation of work. The Webster's new college Dictionary says that strike is a work stoppage by a body of workers to enforce compliance with demands made on an employer." The Encyclopedia Britanica says that strike is a stoppage of work by common agreement on the point of work by people for the purpose of obtaining or resisting a change in the conditions of employment.

For the purpose of the Industrial Disputes Act, 1947 strike means a cessation of work by a body of persons employed in any industry acting in combination, or a concerted refusal under a common understanding of any number of persons who are or have been so employed to continue to work or accept employment. Thus strike is cessation of work by a body of persons (working in an industry) or a concerted refusal under a common understanding to continue to work (or accept employment). Thus stoppage of work even for a short duration would amount to strike where there is concerted action on the part of workers.[3] Now, how does it effect the contract of employment. This issue was first dealt with in Cox and Kings case. "*A strike does not ipso facts terminate the relationship of master and servant between employees who have struck work... the very word strike indicates that the relationship of master and servant is subsisting although the employees have refused to work. If a strike which is lawful amounts to termination of service there cannot be any strike. The employees continue to be employees of the company during strike and the management have no right to discharge them for any reason connected with the trade dispute.*"[4]

"*A strike, legal or illegal, does not automatically put an end to that (employer-employee) relation, but it cannot now be disputed that it affects some of the rights and obligations flowing from that relationship. An illegal strike absolves the liability of the employer to pay wages during the period of absence of the striking workmen. (Mahalaxmi Cotton Mills vs. its workmen-1952 L.A.C. p. 370), but the question before us is whether his absence entitles the employer to put an end to his service? It does not when the strike is not illegal, whether justifiable or not. (Smith Strainstreat and co. vs. its workmen- Cal. Appeal no. 37/51 decided on 22nd August 1951), but the converse proposition does not necessarily follow when the strike is illegal. A strike may be illegal on account of the contravention of section 22 or 23 of the Act though it may be perfectly justified or strike though illegal by reason of those provisions may be the result of provocation on the part of the employer or such a strike may last for a very short time. Modern concept of social justice would be out-raged if in such cases the employer could dismiss a workman for his mere absence due to his participation in such a strike."*[5]

The Punjab High Court held that strike is a weapon of the workers and even if it is an illegal strike, it does not contemplate the severance of relation of the employer and employee.[6] The courts in these and the subsequent cases were merely reiterating the views expressed by Ludwig Teller in his famous book on Labour Disputes and Collective bargaining:" *Although the work ceases, the employment relation is deemed to continue albeit in a state of belligerent suspension.*"[7] The Supreme Court in 2 judgments put the final stamp on the above concept. In Express News papers Private Ltd vs. Michael Mark the Court said that where the employees absent themselves from work because they have gone on strike with the specific object of enforcing the acceptance of their demands they cannot be deemed to have abandoned their employment.[8] Elaborating on this law further, in yet another case the Supreme Court held: "While it is an accepted principle of industrial adjudication that workmen can resort to strike in order to press their demands without snapping the relationship of employer and employee; it is equally well-accepted principle that the work of the factory cannot be paralyzed and brought to a stand still by an illegal strike, in-spite of legal steps being taken by the management to resolve conflict. The management have the right in those circumstances to carry on the work of the factory in furtherance of which it could employ other workmen and justify its action on merits in any adjudication of the dispute arising therefore.[9] Right to strike has been recognized as an integral part of collective bargaining. By now it will be clear that the Sui-generis nature of striking employees or those workmen who have ceased to work under a common understanding is well recognized by law.

In U.P. Rajya Setu Nigam Sanyukt Karmachari Sangh vs. U.P. State Bridge Corporation, Lucknow the Allahabad High Court had an occasion to consider the issue of an illegal strike and its effect on the contract of employment. The court observed: "*It has not provided that because of such illegal strike, the relationship of employer and employee would cease or the contract of service would cease."* Later, in the same judgment:

"Thus, the absence may not be without leave or in excess of leave sanctioned or extended. Admittedly, in this case no leave was either asked for or sanctioned nor was there scope of any extension of the leave sanctioned. As observed earlier, the allegations of the employer was that the workmen were on illegal strike. In order to resort to strike, one is not required to apply for leave and for remaining on strike no leave is required to be sanctioned. 'Absence' means state of being away from a place or the time or duration of being away. (A New Shorter Oxford English Dictionary Edition, 1993). Thus 'absence' means to keep oneself away which is completely different from cessation of work or refusing to work. Cessation or refusing is abstention meaning abstaining from or refraining from doing. When a worker resorts to strike, he does not abandon his job nor he gives up his job. On the other hand, he very much sticks to his job but as a manner of protest he refuses or refrains from doing the work. Thus by no stretch of imagination, resorting to a strike by workmen can be termed as an absence within the meaning of the above clause nor it would mean leaving of the service and thereby terminating the contract of service. A workman does not resort to work to leave his service or to terminate his contract of service. On the other hand, it is for demanding his dues out of the contract of service, a workman resorts to strike. If resorting to strike is given the meaning of leaving of service or termination of service in that event, the most important mode of collective bargaining would perish; such an interpretation cannot be conceived of and be adhered to. The said clause cannot be applied when a workman is on strike. Though it could be applied if the workman remains absent even after the strike is over and he is permitted to join. But it cannot have any application during the period of strike whether legal or illegal.

A provision has to be interpreted in the context in which it has been used. This clause is a part of the Standing Order which deals with leave and holidays. Strike is definitely not a leave. Illegal strike may be a misconduct but cannot be a leave. The said clause in the chapter dealing with leave cannot be applied to a situation outside the scope of the said chapter dealing with leave. The question of strike cannot be brought within the scope and ambit of leave and as such its application cannot be extended to a situation when the workmen are on strike. Then again an interpretation is to be given according to the purpose and object for which it is inserted. The purpose and object is to prevent a person from misusing leave or overstaying of leave. Resorting to strike is neither misuse of leave nor overstaying of leave. Standing Order does not provide for any provision as to how the question of strike is to be dealt with."

If this is so, in banking industry as well, going on an illegal strike has not been termed as misconduct, either gross or minor. Hence it is certain that an employee from the banking industry cannot be dismissed from service for participating in an illegal strike. In Punjab National Bank Ltd vs. its workmen after holding the conduct of workmen as amounting to an illegal strike, the court[10] proceeded to consider the further question as to what was the proper punishment for that conduct, that is, whether the penalty of dismissal was justified.

"It could not be said that the entry of the striking employees in the premises of the Bank amounted to civil trespass, as employees of the Bank they had the right to enter upon the Bank premises, and as long as the relationship of master and servant continued, they could not be said to have committed civil trespass by their entry in the premises. Even assuming that their conduct amounted to civil trespass, that in itself could not justify the rejection of their claim to reinstatement.

Further, it could not be said that conduct amounted to criminal trespass. There are two essential ingredients of criminal trespass as defined in section 441 of Penal Code, namely, the physical act of entering upon or continuing upon the property of another, and the intention to intimidate, insult or annoy. The conduct of the concerned employees may have caused annoyance to their superior officers, but that is not the same as saying that they had the intention to insult or annoy. Knowledge of the likely consequence of act does not necessarily import intention, and it cannot be said that in every case where an unlawful entry causes annoyance or insult, the entry is with the requisite criminal intention. It had therefore to be held that it was not proved that the conduct of the striking employees amounted to criminal trespass under section 441 of the Code.

The question that remained was whether simple participation in a pen-down strike, by itself and without any further activity of a subversive character created a bar against a claim for reinstatement, or in other words, whether participation in a peaceful but illegal strike is called off. In support of its contention that it would, the Bank relied upon the decision of Supreme Court of America in, National Labour Relations Board v. Fansteel Metallurigical Corp, 306 U.S 238 S.C. However, the facts of that case showed that the decision was not in respect of an illegal peaceful strike, but concerned a strike which began with wrongful seizure of the employer's property and was accompanied with great violence. That being so, the decision, could be of no use in deciding the instant case.

The history of the trade union legislation, both in England and in America shows the trade union movement had to wage a long and bitter struggle to secure recognition for the workmen's right to organize themselves and to exercise their right of collective bargaining, if necessary, by resort to a strike. Fortunately, our legislature has very wisely benefited by the experience of other countries in the matter of the development of the trade union movement and has made laws which make just and fair provision for the settlement of industrial disputes. In dealing with an industrial dispute like the present, we must primarily consider the relevant statutory provisions and the material Indian decisions.

Thus considered, it must be held that the pen-down strike is a strike within the meaning of section 2(9) of the Act. The strike in the instant case was no doubt an illegal strike because it was commenced in contravention of section 23(b) of the Act which requires that the workmen shall not go on strike during the pendency of a proceeding before a Tribunal. However, though, illegal, it was a peaceful strike which was not accompanied by any act of violence. Mere participation in a peaceful strike, even when illegal, cannot necessarily involve the penalty of dismissal or the rejection of the strikers claim for reinstatement.

It is no doubt true that in the surcharged atmosphere, which generally accompanies a strike, a large-scale and continuous pen-down and continuous pen-down strike may lead to ugly incidents, and hence such strikes should be discouraged. But even so, the fear that in some cases pen-down strikes may result in disturbance or violence cannot justify the conclusion that even when the strikes have been peaceful and non-violent and have done nothing more than occupying their seats during office hours without doing work, their participation in the strike would by itself entail their dismissal and disqualify them from claiming reinstatement."

The issue was also considered in the land-mark judgment of the Supreme Court in India General Navigation & Railway Co Ltd vs. Their Workmen. For determining the quantum of punishment for illegal strikes, the first issue that should be considered is whether the workers were peaceful and passive or were defiant of prohibitory orders or violent in their conduct. Where the charges of violence or deficient behavior are not proved, the employee's conduct must be treated as peaceful. The court[11] observed:

"When determining the question of punishment for taking part in an illegal strike, a clear distinction has to be made between (a) those workmen who were merely silent participators in the strike, and (b) those workmen who not only participated in the strike, but also took an active part in obstructing the loyal workmen from carrying on their work, or instigating other workmen to join the illegal strike, or in violent demonstration, or in defiance of law and order. It is not in the interest of the industry or of the workmen themselves that there should be a wholesale dismissal of all the workmen who merely participated in a peaceful strike. In deciding the question of punishment, the Tribunals have to keep in mind the overriding consideration of the full and efficient working of the industry as a whole.

Therefore, the punishment of dismissal or termination of service has to be imposed only on such workmen as had, not only participated in the strike, but had fomented it or had been guilty of violence or of doing acts detrimental to the maintenance of law and order in the locality. Both types may have been equally guilty of participation in the illegal strike, but it is manifest that both are not liable to the same kind of punishment.

In order to determine the punishment, which must be meted out to each workman, the Tribunal has first to determine the conduct of which he was guilty, namely, whether he was only a peaceful and silent striker, or whether he was an active and violent striker. That can only be done when a regular enquiry has been held by the management into the conduct of each workman, after furnishing a charge sheet to each one of the workmen sought to be dealt with, and when the part played by each individual has been clearly established.

In a case in which it is found by the Tribunal that individual charge-sheets were not delivered to the workmen so as to give notice to each workman concerned as to what the gravamen of the charge against him was, it must be held that no regular enquiry according to the requirements of natural justice was held. In such a case, the distinction between the two categories of strikes cannot be made, and the Tribunal has to pass orders on the assumption that they were all peaceful strikers and no more. While dismissal from service a punishment for mere participation in the illegal strike would not be justified, at the same time it is not correct to order reinstatement with full back wages and allowances, because this would amount to complete condonation of the illegal act of the strikers."

In the instant case the Court came to the conclusion that the workmen had been guilty of participation in an illegal strike, for which they were liable to be dealt with by the Company, but in view of the fact that the company also was to be blamed for not having held a regular enquiry after delivering, regular charge-sheets to the workmen proceeded against, it was held that both the parties should divide the loss half and half between them. The order of reinstatement made by the Tribunal was confirmed, but is was directed that the workmen should be paid only half of their wages during the period between the date on which the strike was called off and the date when the award of the Tribunal became enforceable.

As to the 37 workmen who had been convicted under section 188 of the Penal Code for violation of the order promulgated under section 144 of the Criminal Procedure Code by District Magistrate, the Court held, after examining the record, that they were violent strikers who did not stand on the same footing as the other strikers, and that they had been guilty of defiance of the prohibitory orders passed by the public authorities for maintaining peace and order. In respect of these 37 workmen, the order of dismissal made by the Company was held to be justified and the order of reinstatement made by the Tribunal was set aside.

Going further in I.M.H. Press Delhi vs. Additional Industrial Tribunal, Delhi the Supreme Court[12] further held that punishment of dismissal is not proper for merely participating in an illegal strike unless the standing orders expressly provides for such punishment.

The charge that was given to the dismissed workmen was that they had, in addition, to taking part in an illegal strike, formented the strike and had caused other workmen to join the strike by giving them threats. However, there was no finding by the enquiry officer on the additional items in the charge, and the sole ground for the order of dismissal was that had taken part in an illegal strike.

"In the instant case, apart from the fact that the sole ground for the order of dismissal was participation in an illegal strike, it was established that the employer took it into his head to take action almost one year after the incident, only when the Tribunal had made its order dismissing the workmen's application demanding wages for the strike period. It was therefore, clear that the employer took advantage of the decision of the Tribunal in August 1956 and picked out these 17 workmen after about a year for victimization.

The decision of the Supreme Court in Model Mills Ltd v. Dharam Das, A.I.R 1958 S.C 311, has to be distinguished on facts. That was a case where there was an express Standing Order of the Company where under taking part in an illegal strike was misconduct punishable with dismissal. Where there are no such standing orders, the general rule laid down in India General Navigation case will apply, and dismissal will not be justified if it is based solely on the fact of taking part in an illegal strike."

The Model Mills Nagpur Ltd vs. Dharam Das case[13] *stood on a different footing. The Mill's Standing Orders contained an express, provision under which participation in an illegal strike was made a misconduct. The workmen refused to work on the ground that the employer made a change in the condition of service. The workmen went on an illegal strike and the Court held:*

"Since all the workmen had been guilty of misconduct amounting to an illegal strike, and the Company had acted within its powers under the Standing Orders in dismissing them from its employment, interference with the order made by the Company was not justified and the Industrial Court was wrong in setting aside that order.

The order of dismissal made by the employer was restored and the order of the Industrial Court directing the reinstatement of the workmen was set aside".

This position was reiterated with this exception that while dismissing only a few should not be picked up. To dismiss only some of the few peaceful strikers when the majority are taken back would amount to unfair labour practice.

"The dispute in the instant case related to the dismissal by the Company of its workmen for having gone on an illegal strike which continued for about a month. The finding of the Tribunal to which the dispute was referred was, (a) that the strike was begun when a bona fide settlement arrived at during a conciliation proceeding was in operation and was binding on the workmen, and was therefore illegal, and (b) that no charge of violence was proved against any of the dismissed workmen. It set aside the order of dismissal and directed the reinstatement of all the 60 workmen on the ground that the punishment of dismissal was too severe, and that in view of the fact that most of the workmen who had taken part in the strike had been taken back in service, there was no reason for the management to make any distinction between those against whom action was taken and the court held:

"In India General Navigation and Railway Co. Ltd. v. Their workmen, [A.I.R 1960 SC. 219,] it was held down that in the matter of punishment a distinction has to be made between those striking workmen who had taken part in obstructing the loyal workmen or in violent demonstrations or acted in defiance of law and order, and those workmen who were only silent participators in the strike. These observations have to be read only in the context of that case. In that case there was no standing order that an employee merely taking part in an illegal strike was liable to be punished with dismissal. In the present case, the standing orders provided that going on an illegal

strike was misconduct which merited dismissal, and there was a proper managerial enquiry. Therefore, the decision in the said case cannot be applied to the facts of this case, and merely because the workmen had not taken part in any violence, it could not be said that the order of dismissal was not justified.

It is true that if an employer makes an unreasonable discrimination in the matter of taking back employees in circumstances in which no clear distinction could be made between those who are dismissed and those who are taken back into service, there may in certain circumstances be good reason for the Tribunal to interfere with the order of dismissal. [See, Burn & Co, Ltd v. their Workmen, A.I.R 1959 SC 529]. However, the circumstances of each case have to be examined by the Tribunal before it can interfere with the order of the employer in a properly held managerial enquiry on the ground of discrimination. In the present case, the employer had not made any discrimination and he was prepared to take back all workmen, but the union which represented the large majority of the workmen was itself not agreeable that these 47 workmen should be taken back.

In these circumstances, in view of the fact that under the standing orders going on an illegal strike was misconduct punishable with dismissal, that the managerial enquiry was quite proper, and that the employer had not practiced any discrimination, it must be held that there was no justification for the Tribunal to interfere with the order passed by the employer. In a case in which the charge against the employee that he has been guilty of any unfair labour practice or victimization against the employees concerned has remained unestablished, the Tribunal is not justified in interfering with the order of dismissal made against the workmen participating in an illegal strike, in accordance with the Standing Orders.

The order of reinstatement made by the Tribunal was set aside and the order of dismissal made by the employer was restored."[14]

The Supreme Court also held that dismissal is the proper punishment for workmen who indulged in violence or is guilty of physical obstruction or intimidation of willing workmen or if they defy prohibitory orders.[15]

"Even when the strike resorted to by the workmen is justified and it is not otherwise illegal by reason of any contravention of section

22 and 23, if any of the striking workmen take part in violent activities, the employer is entitled to take action and terminate the service of such of them against whom the charge is proved. Such grave misconduct entails the consequence of dismissal, but for that purpose it is the duty of the employer to hold a proper enquiry, and each workman charged with acts of violence must be given a reasonable opportunity to show that he did not take part in the violence."

In a recent case, the Gujarat High Court had an occasion to consider matter. There was a prolonged strike by the workmen of the company which was providing public utility services. The company initiated disciplinary action against some workmen and dismissed them from service. The Labour Court reinstated the workmen without payment of back-wages. Both the management and the union approached the High Court against the award. The High Court after considering the arguments found that the powers of the Labour Court to interfere with the findings of the employer were extremely narrow. The High Court held that when the Labour Court found the workmen had proceeded on illegal strike and the concerned worker were leading participants in such a strike, it ought not to have interfered with the quantum of punishment[16].

What would be the other consequences of going on a strike in banking industry? Of course, as we have seen, wages and allowances for the strike period will not be payable unless it is a justified strike. But what about benefits like leave, leave fare concession etc, during the strike period. Now there are various kinds of leave. Privilege is calculated at the rate of 1 day for every 11 days of active service. Since during the strike period the employee cannot be said to be under active service; strike will have the effect of excluding such strike days from "active" service. However, calculation of casual leave will remain unaffected for an employee is entitled to casual leave up to a maximum of 12 days in each calendar year. Similarly, sick leave, extra-ordinary leave, maternity leave and special leave will remain unaffected. Leave fare concession is payable once in 3 years provided the employees have completed at least 11 months of active service.....etc. Since the period of strike cannot be considered as active service, it will have the effect of not having to be reckoned for calculating the 11 months of "active" service period.[17] Strike will have no effect on payment of medical aid and expenses as also the hospitalization expenses. It will have no effect on the need to give uniforms once in 2 years and one set of winter uniform once in 3 years. The age of retirement, nor the date of retirement will stand postponed by the duration of strike. However, provident fund contribution will not be payable for the duration of the strike, since wages are not payable for the period. In an interesting case, the employer contended that the employee was on illegal strike during 1979 & 1985 i.e. for 2 years. In such circumstances, payment of gratuity was made by the employer for 13 years (instead of 15 years). The issue whether the employer was justified in paying gratuity for 13 years depended on whether the employee was on strike for those 2 years. The matter was remanded to the Controlling Authority to decide.[18]

In yet another case, there was no evidence to support the contention that the employee had remained absent as a result of strike (which was attributable to the fault of the workman). In the absence of such evidence the Bombay High Court held that both Controlling Authority and Appellate Authority were wrong in treating the period 18.1.1982 to 18.10.1983 as a period for which the employee will not be entitled to gratuity.[19]

It is well established that a strike, legal or illegal, does not automatically put an end to employer-employee relation. It cannot be disputed that it affects some of the rights and obligations flowing from that relationship[20] and what are those rights? The Industrial Tribunal had an occasion to consider the issue in Patna Electric Supply Co Ltd vs. Their Workmen. The Tribunal found that the strike launched by the workmen was illegal. Now on the effect of the illegal strike the Tribunal went on to hold that the workmen are not entitled to benefits which they would have got under normal circumstances. Why?

"Thus it is well established that the strike launched by the union was illegal. It has to be considered now whether it caused break in

their service as alleged by the management. The definition of continuous service" is given in S. 2 (eee) of the Industrial Disputes Act. It is laid down therein that it means uninterrupted service and includes service which may be interrupted merely on account of sickness or authorized leave or a lockout or a cessation of work which is not due to any fault on the part of the workmen. It follows from the above that an illegal strike undoubtedly causes break in the continuity of service. This view finds support from the decisions given by the Labour Appellate Tribunal in Punjab National Bank case [1952-II LLJ 648] and by the Supreme Court in Buckingham and Carnatic Mills case [1953-I LLJ 181]. Almost a similar point came up for consideration in those cases. It was held that participation in an illegal strike caused break in the continuity of service of the workmen involved for the purposes of leave under S. 79 of the Factories Act. It is true that those cases do not deal with other benefits like gratuity, provident fund, etc, available to the workmen ordinarily but there are some observations of the Labour Appellate Tribunal in the Punjab National Bank case which are important in this connexion. It is said that participation in illegal strike disentitles the workmen to the benefits which are available to them in normal circumstances. Provident fund and gratuity benefits and other such benefits are available to the workmen in cases where there is no break in their service and though there is no express provision in those to that effect, it is obvious that such benefits cannot be extended to workmen under circumstances which are abnormal and illegal. These are benefits which flow from employer-employee relationship in normal circumstances and it could not be said that they would remain unaffected even under abnormal conditions. These rights carry certain obligation with them and unless those obligations are discharged an employee cannot be entitled to those rights. If once a break occurs in the continuity of service of an employee by his own illegal act it would be putting premium on it if he is allowed to escape the consequences of such break without any justification. There is an express provision in the factories Act about it for the purpose of leave and there is no reason why that principle should not be applicable to the employees in the matter of other benefits like gratuity, provident fund, increment, etc These advantages like the annual leave flow from the continuity of service in normal circumstances and undoubtedly where there is break in service due to the fault of the workmen themselves they cannot have the advantage of those benefits. As observed by their lordships of the Appellate Tribunal in the case D. Jha and 336 others referred to above, a worker in order to be entitled to such benefits must be actuated by the same friendly feeling as prompted the management to introduce such beneficial practice. It is further said that a strike which was neither justified nor legal could not be countenanced and the workmen were not entitled to the benefits which they are entitled to under normal circumstances. Extending that principle to the facts of the present case I am constrained to hold that the strike on the dates in question caused a break in the continuity of service of the workmen concerned for the purposes of annual increment, provident fund, gratuity, leave and other benefits depending upon the continuous service for a specified period.

On behalf of the union it was argued that provident fund rules or rules of gratuity prevailing in this company do not make any provision for such break in the continuity of the service in such circumstances and therefore the management was not justified in refusing these benefits to them. As already observed, it is apparent from the authorities quoted above that these are benefits which are available to the workers in normal circumstances but not where the workers themselves invited a break in their service by their illegal Act, they could not be allowed to claim the advantage of these beneficial provisions in spite of their conduct being illegal and adverse to the management."[21] The Madras High Court dealing with a similar issue opined that the matter is not quite an easy one to decide.

"Shri M.R. Narayanasswami, learned counsel for the management, referred to another decision of the Supreme Court, Buckingham & Carnatic Co vs. Its Workers [1953- I LLJ 181]. In that case, there was an illegal strike. The question whether by reason of that strike the workers lost their right to the benefit of the holidays they would otherwise have got under the leave rules of the mill. The question arose under S. 49B(1) of the Factories Act. The Industrial Tribunal to whom the disputes had been referred held that the continuity of service was broken by the interruption caused by the illegal strike and that as a consequences the workers who had participated in such a strike were not entitled to the annual holidays

with pay. On appeal, the labour appellate Tribunal was of the view that the strike did not cause any interruption in the workers' service and it was ordered that holidays at full rates should be given to the workers. The management appealed and contended before the Supreme Court that continuity of service was broken by the interruption caused by the illegal strike and that the workers were not entitled to annual holidays under Sec. 49B(1), in as much as they would not have completed the period of 12 months' Continuous Service in the factory and that the non-permitted absence as a result of concerted refusal to work even for two to four hours in the course of a working day amounts to an illegal strike and consequently an interruption of service of the workers. It may be mentioned that Sec. 49 of the Factories Act provided for holidays with pay if the worker had completed a period of 12 months continuous service in a factory. The explanation to that section allowed the taking into account of sickness or other leave periods, but excluded any strike which was an illegal strike. Their lord-ships took the view that this interruption by the illegal strike caused a breach in the continuity of strike or the continuous service that was required. It seems to me that the principle behind the decision must apply under the circumstances of the present case. If a strike was illegal under the law, not withstanding that a disciplinary action could be taken against the workers for that reason and that the relationship of master and servant still continued to subsist, in the context of the special enactment, I am inclined to take the view that it did break up the continuous service that was required." Thus, annual increment can be post-phoned for participation by an employee in an illegal strike.[22] What about Payment of Wages for the intervening holidays. It has been held that wages should be paid for the intervening holidays.[23]

The Madras High Court dealt with this issue as far back as 1977. In the case between Vasudevan, R M S union and LOTUS Mills Ltd. [24] the matter was considered in detail. The High Court considered Sec. 5(2) of the Tamil Nadu Industrial Establishments (National & Festival Holidays) Act, 1958.

"All that Sub-section(2) of sec. 5 does is to give the employer a right to have work done from his employees on a holiday and in case he requires them to do so he has to pay wages at an enhanced rate. The Sub-section goes no further and does not prescribe that if

an employee is unwilling to work or does not honour the requisition of the employer, he would lose his ordinary wages for the holiday. Had the legislative intended to make the wages payable only if the employee was willing to work the language used in the opening part of sub-sec. (2) of sec. 5 would have been something like this: In other words the legislature would have in that case specifically stated that the payment of wages was contingent on willingness to work and it would not have left sub-sec. 1 uncontrolled and unconditional.

The definition of "wages" as occurring in clause (g) of section 2 is also of no avail to the case of the mills. It does not lay-down the conditions when wages shall be paid. It only states what wages are. According to it wages mean a particular type of remuneration i.e. remuneration which fulfills the following conditions:

1. *it must be able of being expressed in money.*
2. *such money is to be calculated on the basis that the employee would become entitled to it if the terms of employment are fulfilled.*
3. *such money is payable in respect of his employment or of work done by him in such employment.*

The fact that the definition talks of the fulfillment of terms of employment or of work done would not make it a mandate for payment of wages only in respect of work done. The reference to fulfillment of the terms of employment and to work done are merely incidental to the definition and have really nothing to do with the contingency when wages become payable. That contingency is the subject matter of other sections of the Act including Section's. 3 and 5. In fact sub-sec. (1) of sec. 5 expressly states that wages shall be paid for holidays in spite of the contract of employment laying down a condition to the contrary. What sub-section, therefore, clearly provides is that holidays i.e. days on which an employee is given the right to stay away from work shall be paid holidays. As there is nothing incongruous in the situation created by the sub-section which appears to provide for certain paid off days to the employee by reason of the mere fact of his holding that status, i.e. the status of an employee."

This view of the matter was extended to a strike situation. The issue that arose for consideration before a division bench of the Madras High Court was whether the employer is bound to pay wages to his employees for national and festival holidays which fall within a period during which the employees were on strike? In Vasudevan vs. Lotus Mills, the High Court had earlier held that in such circumstances wages would be payable. In the present case, the division bench concurred with the decision arrived in Lotus Mills case.[25]

To sum up, Industrial Disputes Act, 1947 and the various labour legislations affecting the employer-employee relationship have been regarded as social welfare legislations. The courts generally were reluctant to interprete labour legislation which would prejudice the rights or welfare of workers. This was on 2 counts viz (1) the labour was considered weak compared with the employer in its ability to bargain and (ii) the legislature has enacted various labour laws for the purpose of redressing the balance between employers and employees. The Supreme Court in fact said "It is well settled that in construing the provisions of a welfare legislation Court should adopt what is sometimes described as beneficial rule of construction......."[26] And in the process, industrial adjudication gave freedom to industrial tribunals to vary conditions of employment and lay-down new conditions of employment, if found necessary. Justice Wanchoo in one of the cases ruled:

"It is too late in the day now to stress the absolute freedom of an employer to impose any condition which he likes on labour. It is always open to industrial adjudication to consider the conditions of employment of labour and to vary them if it is found necessary, unless the employer can justify an extra-ordinary condition."[27]

This legislative process with the lack of institutional support for collective bargaining did not encourage the collective bargaining process in India with the result that it remained an alternative method of conducting negotiations about wages and working conditions and other terms of employment between an employer or group of employers or employers association (as in banking industry) and representative of workers and their trade unions with a view to arriving at collective agreements. In this strike is it self a part of exerting pressure on the management by its timing and effect on production and marketing with a view to compelling the employer to concede to the demands of the workmen. Even a threat of a strike sometimes is sufficient to force the employer to compromise. At the other end of the spectrum is the "lock-out" which is described as anti-thesis of strike.[28] And the rules prescribe when the strike and lock-out can be said to be legal. That is important enough. Equally important is the justifiability of the strike or lock-out as the may be. In this regard the observation of the Supreme Court.[29] about the conditions of labour is not worthy'

"With the emergence of the organized labour, particularly in public undertakings and public utility services, the old balance of economic power between the management and the workmen has undergone a qualitative change in such undertakings. Today, the organized labour in these institutions has acquired even the power of holding the society at large to ransom, by with-holding labour and thereby compelling the management to give in on their demands, whether reasonable or unreasonable. What is forgotten many times, is that as against the employment and the service conditions available to the organized labour in these undertakings, there are millions who are either unemployed, underemployed or employed on less than statutory minimum remuneration. The employment that workmen get and the profits that the employers earn are both generated by the utilization of the resources of the society in one form or the other whether it is land, water, electricity or money which flows either as share capital, loans from financial institutions or subsidies and exemptions from the Governments. The resources are to be used for the well-being of all by generating more employment and production and ensuring equitable distribution. They are not meant to be used for providing employment, better service conditions and profits only for some. In this task, both the capital and the labour are to act as the trustees of the said resources on behalf of the society and use them as such. They are not to be wasted or frittered away by strikes and lock-outs. Every dispute between the employer and the employee has, therefore, to take into consideration the third dimension, viz., the interests of the society as a whole, particularly the interest of those who are deprived of their legitimate basic economic rights and are more unfortunate than those in employment and management. The justness or otherwise of the action of the employer or the employee has, therefore, to be examined also on the anvil of the interests of the society which such actions tends to affect. This is true of the action in

both public and private sector. But more imperatively so in the public sector. The management in the public sector is not a capitalist and the labour an exploited lot. Both are paid employees and owe their existence to the direct investment of public funds. Both are expected to represent public interests directly and have to promote them."

This is not a sole decision, standing by itself. There has been considerable feelings amongst the employers as a class that over 25 years since the 1965 that there has been an over emphasis on the right of the workers in court rulings. They had watched the judicial pendulum swing towards labour. In Shembunath Goyal vs. Bank of Baroda the employer who wanted to amend his pleadings was not permitted to do so. Normally, such amendments are permitted provided the party concerned explains the delay to the satisfaction of the Court. And in our own subject issue the judiciary tried to enter into the thin wedge that an illegal strike "cannot be unjustified."[30] Then in one of the judgment the employment contract was characterized as a contract between Lion (employer) and the lamb(employee). The employer's cup of woe was full with several other pronouncements going against him. And out the blue came the observation of the Supreme Court in Syndicate Bank's case. With privatization, globalization and liberalization going on a firm footing, there is surely a measure of support for those processes in several directions. Over the last decode, things seem to be changing in the employment contract front and the harbinger of this change is perhaps the above observation of the Supreme Court about organized labour in public under takings.

Notes

1. Kairbetta Estate vs. Rajamanickam, 1960, II LLJ, 275(278); Gwalior Rayons Silk Mfg. (Wng) Co. Ltd. vs. District Collector, Alleppey-1982, LIC (370).
2. 1980, I LLJ, 137.
3. See AIR 1958 Pat 51(56); AIR 1953 SC, page. 47(48, 49).
4. Cox and King's (Agents) Ltd. vs. Their Employees, 1949 LLJ, 796.
5. Punjab National Bank vs. Their Workmen, 1952, II LLJ, 648 at 658-659.
6. Vol. I, p. 237, S. 78.

7. AIR 1963, SC 1141.
8. 1965 cur L J, 251 (Punj).
9. Oriental Textile Finishing Mills Ltd vs. Labour Court 1971 II LLJ 505 SC; See also B.R. Singh and others vs. Union of India, 1989, II LLJ 591(SC) "The Right to Demonstrate and Therefore the Right to Strike is an Important Weapon in the Armory of Workers."
10. 1960, I SCR 806.
11. 1960, II SCR, page 1.
12. 1961, I LLJ 499.
13. 1961, I LLJ 499.
14. Bata Shoe Co. (Pvt.) Ltd. vs. D.N. Ganguly, 1961, 3 SCR 308.
15. Swadeshi Industries Ltd. vs. Workmen, 1960, II LLJ 78, also see Bengal Batdee Coal Co. vs. Ram Prakesh Singh, 1963, I LLJ 291.
16. Gujarat Ambuja Cement Pvt. Ltd. vs. U.B. Gadha, 2006, IV LLJ NOC 897.
17. Buckingham & Carnatic Co. Ltd. vs. Their Workers, 1953, I LLJ p. 181 [The Supreme Court held that consequent upon the illegal strike, the workers who participated in the illegal strike were not entitled to annual holidays with pay under Factories Act].
18. General Manager, Sarada Mills vs. Asst. Labour Commissioner, 2002, I LLJ, p. 261.
19. R. A. Manjerekar vs. N.T.C. (M.N.) Ltd. 2005, I LLJ, 311.
20. Punjab National Bank vs. Workmen, 1952, II LLJ, 648.
21. Patna Electric Supply Co. Ltd. vs. Workmen, 1957, II LLJ, 575
22. See Patna Electric Supply Co. Ltd. vs. Workmen, 1957, II LLJ, 575.
23. Vasudevan vs. Lotus Mills, 1977, II LLJ 483.
24. Vasudevan vs. Lotus Mills, 1977, II LLJ 483.
25. See Madura Coats Ltd vs. Inspector of Factories, 1980, I LLN, p. 221; See also Kailas Rubber Co. vs. Inspector of Plantation & Others, 2000, III LLJ, p. 205.
26. Alembic Chemical Works & Ltd vs. Its Workmen, 1961, I LLJ 328.
27. Bombay Labour Union vs. International Franchised Ltd., 1966, I LLJ 417.
28. Kairbetta Estate vs. Rajamanikam, 1960, II LLJ, 275.
29. Syndicate Bank vs. K. Umesh Nayak, 1994 II LLJ, 836.
30. See Gujarat Steel Tubes Ltd. vs. Workmen, 1980, I LLJ, 230.

References

Bills of Exchange Act, 1882-s.92; Banking and Financial Dealings Act,1971-Sections 3(1),4(3),(4).

All India Central Health Scheme. Employee Association vs Union of India 2006 I LLJ 798.

Bangalore Water Supply vs A.Rajappa. AIR 1978 s.c. p.549 = 1978 LIC 467.

Coir Board, Eruakulam vs. Indira Devi, 1999 I LLJ 1109.

Federal Bank Ltd Vs Sagar Thomas 2004 I.L.L.J 161.

Dhar Jilla Sahakari Bhoomi Vikas Bank Maryadit, Dhar Vs. Labour Court 1996 И LLJ 1065.

Workmen of Hinustan Lever vs. Hindustan Lever Ltd. 1984 LIC p. 1573 at 1576.

Bank of India Vs Presiding Officer 2002 I LLJ 232.

South Indian Bank Vs. A.R.Chacko 1964 I LLJ 19.

J.G.Vakharia vs. Regional Provident Fund Commissioner- 1957 I LLJ 448 at 451.

Prakash Cotton Mills Ltd vs. State of Bombay, 1957 II LLJ p.490 at 494.

State of Mysore vs. workers of gold mines- AIR 1958 S.C 923.

J.K. Cotton and Weaving Mills co Ltd vs. Labour Appellate Tribunal 1963- И LLJ 436.

Principles of Administrative Law by Griffity and Streat 4th Edition at pp.98-99.

Avon Services (Production Agencies) Pvt.Ltd as Industrial Tribunal. 1979 I LLJ p. 1.

Gujarat Steel Tubes vs. Workmen 1980, I LLJ, p. 131.

1994- II L L J, p. 836.

Per Cleasly B, Hall Vs Nothingham-I Ex.D 3.

Salmond's Jurisprudence.

State Bank staff union vs. union of India, 2001-ILLJ 846.

H.R.Adyanthaya vs. Sandoz (I) Ltd. 1995 I LLJ 303.

Dowlatram Lekhraj Rupchandani Vs Western Railway 1958 I LLJ 456

Gangadhar Mishra vs. Director-2006 IV LLJ 92.

Jawahar Mills Vs. Rajamanikam-1954 II LLJ 733.

North Arcot Dist Motor Workers Union Vs. Angalamman Transport. Fort St. George Gazette 27.5 1959 Part-I, suppl. 1 page 1[Madras Labour Court].

ANZ Grindlays Bank Vs. Union 1985 I LLJ, p. 392.

Karnataka Bank Ltd. Vs. Sunita B. Vatsaraj, 2007 III LLJ 714.

Thakur P. Mahrota Vs. Central Bank of India. Gazette of India dt. 19.8.1950 part 2 and 3 p. 436.

Clause 14.2 of Bipartite settlement dated 19.10.1966.

Clause 14.3(c) of Bipartite settlement dated 19.10.1966.

Punjab National Bank vs. Workmen-Gazette of India, part-II, Sec. 3(11) dated 5.6.1976, p. 1960.

Bank of Baroda vs. Workmen-Gazette of India, part-11, Sec. 3(11) dated 17.5.1972 p. 2282.

Gurudas Chatterjee and another vs. State Bank of India and others, 1983 II LLN 822 Publishing Co. Vs Harkins, 9 ont. L.R.504 at 508

Fillient Vs. Armstrong- (1837) 7.A.D and E.L 557.

Thomas Vs. Vivian (1872) 37 J.P. 228.

Clause 14.3 of the Bipartite Settlement dated 19.10.1966.

Clause 14.4 of Bipartite Settlement dated 19.10.1966.

Clause 14.5 of Bipartite Settlement dated 19.10.1966 as amended by Bipartite Settlement dated 17.9.1984.

Clause 14.5 of the Bipartite Settlement dated 19.10.1966.

Clause 14.6 of the Bipartite Settlement dated 19.10.1966.

Jaihind Motor Service Vs Workmen- 1958 II LLJ 530.

Employees of BCB Ind Vs BCB Ind and printers Ltd-1954 LAC 254.

Babcok and Wilcox of India Ltd Vs Their Workmen, 1956 II FJR 82 at p. 90. See also Sridharan Motor Service, Attur V/s Ind. Tribunal-1959 I LLJ 381.

Paragraphs 299 and 300 of Sastry Award.

Paragraph 10.33 of Desai Award.

Clause 14.7 of Bipartite Settlement dated 19.10.1966.

Refer Decision of C.G.I.T.. Calcutta. In Allahabad Bank's case in Ref. No. 92 of 1967.

Sridharan Motor Servicee Vs Ind. Tribunal- 1959 I LLJ 380.

Para 14.9 - 1st Bipartite Settlement.

Clause 14.10 of Bipartite Settlement dated 19.10.1966.

Caltex Ltd. Vs their employees-1952 II LLJ 183 at 189 and associated Cement Cos. Ltd. Vs Their Workmen-1951 II LLJ 387 at pages 399 and 400.

T. Ramanujam Vs Corporation of Madras AIR 1955 Mad. 366.

Express News Paper Ltd Vs Industrial Tribunal, 1960 I MLJ 96.

Bank of India vs. Tapan Kumar Sil, 2007 III LLJ 934

Kushilal Vs Hukamchand Mills 1960-II LLJ 626.

Bradan Dunne Ltd Vs Fitzpatrick, 1958 I R. 29(37).

British Broadcasting Corporation Vs. Hearb 1978, A.E.R (118) (C.A)

Andra Bank Vs P.Balkrishna. 2005 III LLJ 892.

Patna Electric Supply Co Ltd Vs Workmen, 1957 II LLJ 575 at 578.

Shanti Kusum Das Gupta Vs Natural Gas Commission U.P., 1970 AIR (Guj) 149 at 155 [see For e.g. clause 19.5 (m) inserted by Settlement dated 17.9.1984.

Chesire and Fifoot's Law of Contract, 9th ,pp, 132.

Cronin and Crime's introduction to Industrial Law, 1974 Ed., p. 21.

Vikram Tamaskar Vs Steel Authority of India Ltd. 1982 II LLJ page 84.

V.K.Verma Vs. Hindustan Machine Tools Ltd. 1994, I LLJ page 621.

Union of India Vs Chhaganlal, 1974 LIC 497: Project Manager Vs Authority under Payment of wages Act 2000 III LLJ 1199.

Taichar Coal Mines Employees Union Vs Taicher Colliery, 1994 III LLJ 747.

Taichar coal Mines Employees Union Vs Taicher Colliery, 1994 III LLJ 747.

State of Rajasthan Vs Mohammed Ayub Naz 2006 I LLJ 742.36.

1988 II LLN p. 132.

Taichar Coal Mine Employees Union Vs Taichar Colliery, 1994 III LLJ, p. 747.

Chandeswar Mestar Vs. Vice Chancellor, 2003 IV LLJ 830 [NOC].

2005 IV LLJ p. 45 at 48.

Industrial Tubes Manufacturing Co Ltd. Vs. S.R. Sawant, 1980 II LLJ 444.

Engineering Mazdoor Sabha Vs. S. Taki Belgrom's AIR 1970 (Bombay) 402; Workmen of Motipur Sugar Factory Vs. Motipur Sugar Factory, 1965 II LLJ 162.

Maharashtra Labour Union Vs. Pride Hotels Ltd., 2003 IV LLJ page 285.

The decision in ANZ Graidlays Banks case was delivered.

Bombay Dying and manufacturing Co Vs. Mumbai Majdoor Sabha 1987, I LLJ 50.

A.M. Khan and Others Vs. State 1992 II LLJ p.140 at 146. See also Union of India Vs. Raijada------ 2004 II LLJ 953 at 961.

Vinod Kumar Malik Vs. State Bank of India 2005 II LLJ 968.

Brahma Chandra Gupta Vs. Union of India, 1984 SCC p. 268.

Union of India Vs. Jaipal Singh, 2004 I LLJ 431.

Krishnakant Raghunath Bibhavekar Vs. State of Maharastra and Other, 1997 I LLJ 1190 at 1191.

Vinod Kumar Malik Vs State Bank of India 2005 II LLJ 968.

Krishi Utpandan Mandi Samiti Vs Industrial Tribunal, 2004, IV LLJ 116.

Clifton Electronix Vs Lt. Governor, Delhi 1995 II LLJ 894; S.C. Banwari Vs M.P.Rajya Bhumi Vikas Nigam-2004 II LLJ 252.

Clifton Electronix Vs Lt. Governor 1996 II LLJ 1110.

2001 I LLJ 381.

Pest Control (India) Ltd. Vs C.D.Konale- 2000 III LLJ 588.

Para 471 of the Sastry Award.

Pandian Roadways, Corp, Ltd. vs. Principle District Judge 1996 II LLJ 1229; See also Rajasthan vs. Mohamed Ayub Nag-2006 I LLJ 742.

D. Jayabalakrishnan Vs. Tamilnadu Water Service and Drainage Board-1996 I LLJ 877; see also Bhagwan Shukla Vs. Union of India and Others. 1995 II LLJ 726.

2001 I LLJ page 957.

Clause 13.35 of Bipartite Settlement dated 19.10.1966 Shrikant S Sheldekar Vs Central Bank of India-2000 II LLJ 580.

See Bhagawan Singh Vs. Canara Bank 2001- II LLJ 636; Vidya Bhusan Prasad Vs Canara Bank-CWJC No-11923 of 1995, (Judgment dated 16.1.1997); Amiruddin Vs State Bank of India, 1995(i) AK PLR 164.

Manohar Burde Vs Union of India.2003 II LLJ 304; State of Mysore Vs. C. R. Seshadri C.A. No. 875 of 1968.

Pravina Solanki Vs State of U.P 2003 II LLJ 507; R.K. Khare Vs U.P. Coop. Sugar Factories Federation Ltd 2003 II LLJ, p. 725 par 729; 2003 IV LLJ 102.

Union of India Vs. K.V. Janakiraman-1991 II LLJ 570.

India Perfumary Co. Vs. Presiding Officer, 2004 II LLJ 413; (102) A.I.R 1957 SC, 82.

University Granth Nirman Board Vs. Ude Singh Togaji Solanki, 2003 IV LLJ 950.

Dena Bank vs. Ghanshyam, 2001 II LLJ 252, 2001 ILLJ 1411.

Secretary General, Family Planning Association Member of Others Vs. Sunil Kumar Srivatsava, 2007 II LLJ 350.

Rajgariha Vishram Sadan Vs. Vijay Kate, 2007 II LLJ 555.

1998 I LLJ 1.

Rajgariha Vishram Sadan Vs. Vijay Kate, 2007 II LLJ 555 at 560.

UPSRT Corporation Vs. Surendra Singh, 2007 III LLJ 155

Ranipur Colliery Vs. Bhuban Singh, AIR 1959 SC 833.

Hotel Imperial Vs. Hotel Workers Union, 1959 II LLJ 544 at 551.

Fakirbhai Fulabhai Solanki Vs. Presiding Officer-1986 II LLJ 124.

Ram LakhanVs. Presiding Officer- 2000 I LLJ 1067.

Standard Chartered Grindlays Bank Ltd Vs. Govind Phople, 2002 III LLJ 1036.

Air India Ltd. Vs. Libio Fransisco Colaco, 2004 I LLJ 850.

Vikram Tamaskar Vs. Steel Authority of India, 1982 II LLJ at p. 86.

See 4th Edition. Vol. 16, Halsbury's Laws of England.

Ralli Bros. Vs. Ambika, ILR 35 All 131.

Dhuma Behara Vs. Seven Daks, 1886 ILR 13 Cal. 80.

A.M. Chokkalinga Muddaliar vs. G.Mohmmad Sharif Sahab, 23 ILJ 680.

Arjun Vs. Hormusjoe Shapurji Seervai, 1921 ILR 46. BOM. 44.

Manoj Kanti Bose Vs. Bank of India, 1977 II LLJ, p. 285.

Algemene Bank Vs. Labour Court.

V. Ramachandran Vs. Indian Bank, 1979 I LLJ, p. 122.

Dharam Singh Vs. Bank of India, 1979 LIC 1079

V. Ganesan Vs. State Bank of India, 1981 I LLJ, p. 64.

R. Rajamanickam Vs. Indian Bank, 1981, II LLJ, p. 367.

1982 II LLJ, p. 86

1986 II LLN, p. 222.

State Bank of India Vs. Sudharshan 1986 II LLN, P. 278.

1980 II LLJ 344

Bank of India Vs. T.S. Kelavala, 1988 I CLR 382 at 384.

Sengamalam Vs. Indian Bank, 1988 I LLN 878.

U.P. Bank Employees Union Vs. New Bank of India, 1986 LIC 754.

Bank of India Vs. T.S. Kelawala 1990, II LLJ 39.

Bharat Sugar Mills Ltd. Vs. Jai Singh & Ors. 1961 II LLJ, 664.

Firestone Tyre & Rubber Co. of India Ltd. Vs their workmen, 1951 II LLJ 125 at 131.

Somasunderam Vs. State of Mysore & Ors., 1969 II LLJ, 334 also see Rashtriya Mill Mazdoor Sangh Vs Jam Mfg. Co. Ltd. Mill No. 1-1952, I LLJ, 388.

Zarikh Vs. Firestone Tyre and Rubber Co. Ltd., 1954 I: LLJ 281 at 283.

Vasant Govind Madhav Rao Vs. Gujarat Rubber Works Ltd., 1956 I LLJ 731.

Ashok Motors Ltd. Vs. Their Workmen, 1953 II LLJ 793.

Chandra Ball & Ors. Vs. Munir Mills, 1953, II LLJ, 864.

Zarikh Vs. Firestone Tyre and Rubber Co. Limited, 1954 I LLJ 281 at 282-284, also see J.M. Isreal and Ors. Vs. Saxby and Farmer (India) Ltd., 1956 I LLJ 72.

Apar (Pvt.) Ltd. vs. S.R. Samant, 1980 II LLJ p. 344 at 350 & 351.

Bank of India vs. T.S. Kelawala, 1990 II LLJ, p. 39.

U.P. Bank Employees Union Vs. New Bank of India 1986 LIC 754.

S.B. Staff Union (Madras circle) vs. SBI, 1991 I LLJ, p. 163.

Canara Bank V. GMV Nayak & Others, 1991 II LLJ, p. 198.

State Bank of India vs. Union-1994 II LLJ 836.

MPEB Diploma Engineers Assn vs. M.P. Electricity Board, 2006 IV LLJ 1021.

Nellimara Jute Mills Karmik Sangam vs. State of A.P., 1995 I LLJ, 507 at 516.

M.D. Hindustan Fastners Pvt. Ltd. vs. Nashik Workers Union, 2007 I LLJ 434.

Kanak Industries Vs. General Labour Union, 2007 III LLJ 327.

Clifton Electronix and Other vs. Ltd. Governor of Delhi, 1995, II LLJ p. 894.

A.S. Mills Co. Ltd. vs. Industrial Tribunal, 1997, III LLJ p. 230.

Muncipal Corporation for city of Kalyan & Dombivili vs. R.C. Baania-2006, IV LLJ, 94.

Bhag Singh vs. Punjab and Sind Bank-2006, IV, LLJ

R.B.I vs. Bhopal Singh 1994, I LLJ p. 642.

Executives Engineers camps & Building Division vs. Labour Court. 2007-I LLJ, 413.

R.R. Naidu vs. ONGC, 1998 I LLJ, p . 20.

General Manager, India Cement vs. Subramanyam N.S., 1998 I LLJ p. 584.

State Bank of India vs. Industrial Tribunal 1998, III LLJ, p. 17.

Mohan Singh Vikram Singh vs. Continental Textile, 1998 III LLJ, p. 24.

Walchandnagar Industries Ltd vs. Association of Engineering workers, 1998 III LLJ 564. See also Subash Silk Mills Ltd. vs. Mill Mazdoor Sabha 2000 II LLJ 716.

BKK Mahasangh vs. GKW Ltd. 2000 III LLJ, p. 367.

Purshtam Ganpat Bhoir vs. National Textile Corp 2002 IV, LLJ 1066. 74 .

Vaman Maruty Gharat vs. M.S.Apte 1998 III LLJ p. 603. See also Union vs. Macneil and Magor Ltd 2004 III LLJ, 929. Doodh Kamgar Sabha vs. Zurisingh Beechusingh and Co., 2005 I LLJ 709.

Mgt. of Nagamnal Mills vs. KMNTM Sangam, 1999 I LLJ 505

Rajnagars Textile Mills No. 1 vs. Textile Labour Association, 1999 I LLJ 522.

Bharatiya Kamgar Karmachari Mahasangh vs. G.K.W. Ltd. 1999 I LLJ 719.

Syndicate Bank vs. K. Umesh Nayak, 1994 II LLJ 836; Paluru Ram Krishnaiah & Others vs. Union of India, 1989 II LLJ, 47, Burn Standard Co Ltd vs. T.K. Chakraborthy, 1999 III LLJ, 41.

Barn Standard Co. Ltd. vs. T. K. Chakraborthy, 1999 III LLJ 41.

1981, I LLJ p. 64.

Sungunaraj vs. Syndicate Bank, 1999 III LLJ, p. 1198.

Tyre Retreading Shop Committee vs. APSRTC I LLJ 438.

All India Trade Union Congress vs. Ravi Fisheries Ltd., 2000 II LLJ 745.

Piece Electronics and Elelctricals Ltd, Pune vs. Union, 2000 II LLJ 823.

1990 II LLJ 39 at 49: Union Commercial Bank vs. Union. See also 2003 I LLJ, 1046.

Reserve Bank of India vs. V. Raveendran, 2000 III LLJ, 176.

2000 III LLJ, p. 235.

Ganapathy Subramanian vs. Canara Bank, 2000 III LLJ, 813.

Modi Store Ltd vs. Union, 2001 I LLJ, p. 1598.

Otis Elevator Co Ltd vs. G.S. Bajaj, 2001 II LLJ p. 298.

GRSE Ltd. Workmens Union Vs. GR Shipp Builders of Engineers 2001 II LLJ 298

Bank of Rajasthan Employees Union vs. Punjab National Bank, 2001 II LLJ, 1514.

Godlass Nerolac Paints Ltd vs. Union, 2002 I LLJ, 605.

Blue Star Workers Union vs. Blue Star Ltd. 2002, III LLJ, 477.

1994 II LLJ 836.

Metal Rolling Works Pvt. Ltd vs. General Labour Union, 2002, IV LLJ, p. 294.

Pravin H Shukla v. Central Bank of India, 2000, IV LLJ 462.

2002, IV LLJ, 1484.

KSRTC vs. Workers Federation, 2004 II LLJ, p. 891.

Coimbatore Dist. Central Coo. Bank Vs. Secretary 2007 II LLJ 724.

Syndicate Bank and another vs. K. Umesh Nayak, 1994 II LLJ, 836.

1960, I LLJ, p. 13.

Mgt of Charakakulam Tea Estate vs. Workman, 1969 II LLJ 407.

Muncipal Committee vs. Industrial Tribunal, 1971, II LLJ, 52.

The Andra Pradesh State Road Transport Corporation Employees Union vs. APSRTC, Hyderabad, 1970, LIC, 1225.

Crompton Greaves Ltd. vs. Workmen, 1978, II LLJ, 80.

Gujarat Steel Tubes Ltd. vs. G.S.T. Mazdoor Sabha, 1980 II LLJ, 137.

Amalendu Gupta vs. LIC, 1982, II LLJ, 332.

1981 I LLJ, p. 1.

Bank of India vs. T.S. Kelawala, 1990, II LLJ, p. 39.

Syndicate Bank vs. K.Umesh Nayak, 1994 II LLJ, 836.

1995 II LLJ p. 877; See also NLC workers union vs. Neyveli Lignite Corporation, 2001 I LLJ,. 1219.

1996 II LLJ 930

Indian Navigation & Railway Co Ltd vs Their workmen, 1960 I LLJ p. 13.

Maharastra General Kamgar Union vs. Solid Containers Ltd. & Others, 1996, II LLJ, 959.

Glaxo Laboratories Employees Union vs. Glaxo India Ltd., 1996 III LLJ, 266.

Aluminum Industries Ltd vs. Industrial Tribunal, 2006, I LLJ, p. 16.

American Refrigerator Co. Ltd. vs. First Industrial Tribunal, 2006 II LLJ, 271.

Mohan Jute Mills Ltd. State of M.P. 2000 III LLJ, 1550.

Mysore Wine Products and Allied co Ltd vs. Presiding officer, 2000, I LLJ, p. 1166.

Kairbetta Estate vs. Rajamanickam, 1960 II LLJ 275(278); Gwalior Rayons Silk Mfg(Wng) Co Ltd vs District Collector, Alleppey, 1982 LIC (370).

1980 I LLJ 137.

Punjab National Bank Vs. Workmen 1952 II LLJ 648

1965 cur L J 251 (Punj.).

Vol. I, p. 237 S. 78.

AIR 1963, SC 1141.

Oriental Textile Finishing Mills Ltd vs. Labour Court, 1971 II LLJ 505 SC.

1960 I SCR 806.

1960, II SCR, page 1.

1961, I LLJ 499.

Bata Shoe Co (Pvt.) Ltd. vs. D.N. Ganguly, 1961-3, SCR, 308.

Swadeshi Industries Ltd vs. Workmen, 1960-II LLJ 78. Also see Bengal Batdee Coal Co vs. Ram Prahesh Singh, 1963 I LLJ 291.

Gujarat Ambuja Cement Pvt. Ltd vs. U.B. Gadha, 2006 IV, LLJ NOC 897.

R.A. Manjerekar vs. N.T.C. (M.N) Ltd. 2005, I LLJ, 311.

Punjab National Bank vs. Workmen, 1952, II LLJ, 648.

Patna Electric Supply Co. Ltd. vs. Workmen, 1957, II LLJ, 575

Vasudevan vs. Lotus Mills, 1977, II LLJ, 483.

Madura Coats Ltd. vs. Inspector of Factories, 1980 I LLN p. 221; See also Kailas Rubber Co. vs. Inspector of Plantation & Others, 2000 III LLJ, p. 205.

Alembic Chemical Works & Ltd vs. Its Workmen, 1961, I LLJ, 328.

Bombay Labour Union vs. International Franchised Ltd., 1966, I LLJ 417.

Khairbhetta Estate vs. Rajamanikam, 1960 II LLJ 275.

Syndicate Bank vs. K.Umesh Nayak, 1994, II LLJ 836.

Appendix-I

Duties of Special Pay Carrying Positions in Clerical Cadre

Posts	*Duties*
Telephone Operators	Their work involves operating a Telephone PBX/EAPBX Board with a minimum of three external lines on regular assignment.
Audit Clerks Category 'A'	Clerks in the Internal Audit Department whose work involves audit checking of completed vouchers, entries, statements, balances, books of accounts, etc, with a view to confirming their correctness and ascertaining whether office procedures and rules are correctly followed. The irregularities detected by them are reported to the head of the Audit Department and/or his immediate superior, who is responsible for taking necessary action. (*Note:* checking of returns and statements from branches by other than Internal Audit Department clerks would not be covered by 'audit checking').
Audit Clerks-Category 'B'	Audit clerks category 'B' would be audit clerks attached to inspectors on tours and will perform all routine checking functions and generally assist the inspector in the functions including preparation and typing of reports. Their duties include: 1. Assisting in the counting of cash balances, securities, etc. in the presence of the inspecting officials;

2. Assisting the inspecting officers in checking the quantities and values of the securities charged to the bank;
3. Checking the balancing of various deposit account ledgers and verifying the out-standings in inter-branch/sub-office(s) items-in-transit, suspense sundry deposits, drafts payable, term deposits and deposits at call accounts;
4. Checking items of stationery and marking off vouchers and acknowledge-ments and assisting in the examination of vouchers other than those of inter-branch/sub-office(s) items-in-transit, suspense charges, sundry deposits and stationery accounts;
5. Assisting in preparing the audit returns/ reports and typing and generally assisting the inspecting officer in his functions as may be required.

Tellers	Passing and cash payment of all cheques/ withdrawal forms/ traveler's cheques/gift cheques/demand drafts/pay orders/bank orders etc. up to and including Rs. 10,000/- Receipt of cash and issuance of pre-signed drafts/gift cheques/travellers' cheques/pay orders/bank orders, etc both against cash and transfer up to and inclusive of Rs. 15,000/-.
Stenographers	Employees required to take dictation in shorthand and/or type letters, statements, documents, etc. and attend to secretarial work.
Assistant Head Cashiers	Their job is to assist the head cashier in looking after and checking the work of clerks in the cash department.
Head Cashier-I	Their duties involve:

1. Holding the bank's cash, key and/or other valuables in safe custody jointly with an officer and being accountable for them and being responsible for the running of the cash department;

2. Opinion compilation;
3. Verification of vernacular signatures/ endorsements;
4. Countersigning cheques and/or drafts (on selves or correspondents), payment orders, deposit receipts, etc.
5. Attending to Government Treasury work.
6. In banks where the practice of discharging bills/ hundies, for payment received only, is in existence, it may be continued to be done by this category.

Head Cashier-II — Their duties involve:

1. Holding the bank's cash, key and/or other valuables in safe custody jointly with an officer and being accountable for them and being responsible for the running of the cash department;
2. Opinion compilation;
3. Verification of vernacular signatures/ endorsements;
4. Countersigning cheques and/or drafts (on selves or correspondents), payment orders, deposit receipts, etc.
5. Attending to Government Treasury work;
6. Discharging/endorsing bills, cheques, etc;
7. Being in charge of clearing and Godown departments, etc.;
8. Passing independently clearing and transfer cheques, vouchers, etc. (whether credits or debits) upto and including Rs. 50,000/- and cash vouchers upto Rs. 50,000/- jointly with an authorised person.

Special Assistants — Special Assistants will be accountable and responsible for running of the department/ section under them and their duties will involve looking after and checking the work of other clerk or clerks and substaff and will include:

1. Passing independently, manually or online, cash instruments upto Rs.35,000/- and clearing and transfer cheques vouchers etc., (whether credits or debits) upto and including Rs.1,50,000/- Passing will include verification of signatures and scrutiny as to the correctness of endorsements on and other particulars of such instruments. There shall be no limits for verification of signatures, passing of authenticated credit vouchers/ entries and for verifying authenticated credit vouchers/entries and for verifying authenticated vouchers in the ledgers, books, computer print-outs etc.
2. Accept, verify and post cash/transfer/ clearing cheques and other instruments, as the case may be, in appropriate books of accounts / ledgers, either manually or online, and give the acknowledgements.
3. Signing vouchers, cheques, drafts, mail transfers, pay orders, advices such as non payment advices, inter branch fate calling advices, bill schedules, demand notices, statements, certificates etc.
4. Checking all vouchers, advices, statements, cheques, drafts etc., bills and books of accounts including current savings and other ledgers, cash, postal and revenue stamps, franking machine balances, exchange, discount, brokerage calculations and initialing by way of authenticating them for accuracy/correctness;
5. Checking, manually or online, current, savings and other accounts;
6. Checking the coding and decoding of telegrams (excluding check symbols or ciphers).
7. Discharging, endorsing cheques, bills, etc.,
8. Perform, when required in a computerized set up, system control functions either jointly

with an officer or independently, upon specific authorization in this regard;

9. Briefly explain, the features of Bank's various products and services to customers, to reply their queries and to refer interested customers to appropriate personnel;
10. Inspecting Godown (only in banks where such work is already being done by workmen).

For the purpose of efficient and effective functioning of the section or department the special assistant shall ensure that all acts, things and steps necessary therefore are taken by himself or by the clerks placed under him and shall ensure that, wherever necessary;

a. Reminders are sent on time and followed up.
b. Pass sheets/books are filled up and issued promptly.
c. Deposits are renewed on due dates or reminders sent to the parties.
d. Standing instructions are complied with.
e. Bills are accepted and due dates diarised /advised and followed up
f. Interest, commissions and service charges are collected.
g. Proceeds of bills are received or remitted promptly.
h. Confirmation of balance of accounts of the customers and its follow up.
i. All securities relating to the department/ section of which the special assistant is in charge are secured and/or kept in proper custody and properly handed to the authorized person at the close of the day.
j. Balances promptly taken, tallied and reported and followed up and also returns submitted.

k. Advices and/or duplicate advices summaries are issued/responded promptly, whether called for.

l. Checking the proper recording of entries and all relevant particulars in regard to accounts opened under due authorization.

Agricultural Assistant

1. Assist in the bank's lending and/or operations for agricultural development and/or financial assistance to small enterprises (other than small scale industries) such as vegetables/fruit vendors, artisans, self employed persons including beneficiaries under the differential rate of interest scheme.
2. To distribute and collect application forms and assist the farmers/small borrowers in filling up the forms.
3. To scrutinize application forms, title deeds, farm plans etc., to ensure that applications are complete in all respects and the particulars furnished in the forms are prima facie in order and for this purpose he may be required to visit the farms for verification and for collection of relevant data.
4. To take necessary steps to ensure that the periodical details, as called for are received from the farmers/small borrowers in time.
5. To keep in constant touch with farmers and to bring any adverse features to the management's notice.
6. To verify farms/all farms machinery/ equipments/livestock/tractors etc.
7. To verify proper utilization of the bank's loans or the progress in work in respect of which loans are granted and to furnish reports on such verification.
8. To make efforts and effect recoveries upto amounts not exceeding Rs. 15,000/- from farmers/small borrowers from their place of work/residence, subject to the necessary arrangements being made with regard to

fidelity and transit insurance and personal risk insurance by the bank.

Note: Banks will evolve appropriate procedure about issuance of provisional receipts etc. of the cash not exceeding Rs.15,000/- collected on a day by an agricultural assistant from the agricultural/small borrowers/depositors.

9. To assist in the deposit mobilization efforts by encouraging farmers/small borrowers to deposit their savings in the bank.
10. To collect information about the conditions of crops in the villages.
11. To collect necessary data for determination of village, adoption of financing of agriculture like farmers' land holdings, availability of infrastructure facilities, source of irrigation, use of tractors, pump sets etc., credit facilities available in village, recovery performance and the like.
12. To maintain liaison with Land Record and Registration Officers and other Governmental/ Developmental agencies for expeditious handling of the bank's work.

Note: With a view to making optimum use of the technical skill of the agricultural/ development assistant, normally he may not be entrusted with usual clerical work, but where necessary he may be asked to do the clerical work.

Computer Operator 'A' (without passing powers): Computer Operator will perform all duties and functions of clerical cadre, either online or manually, which does not involve any passing or supervisory function of an officer of the bank. He will, wherever and whenever required, function as a single window operator where he will also receive and pay cash.

Computer Operator 'B' (with passing powers): In addition to the duties of Computer Operator 'A', their duties will include:

a. Passing and cash payment of all cheques etc., upto and including Rs. 20,000/-

b. Passing independently clearing and transfer cheques, vouchers, etc, (whether credits or debits) upto and including Rs. 25,000/-

c. Receipts of cash and issuance of pre-signed drafts/ gift cheques/ travellers cheques/ pay orders/ bank orders etc, upto and including Rs.25,000/-

Notes

1. In respect of the above special pay carrying posts in clerical cadre:-
   - Countersigning would mean signing in a manner whereby the primary responsibility for ensuring that all the formalities are complete rests with the other signatory.
   - Checking/verifying would mean verifying that the instrument/material checked is in order in all respects and also includes verification of signature irrespective of the amount of the instrument and authenticating the same on the instrument/material, initialing the relative entries in the respective books of accounts, manually and/or online.
   - Passing includes verification of signatures and scrutiny as to the correctness of endorsement on and other particulars of such instruments. It will also include checking and authenticating the relative entries in the respective books of accounts/ ledgers/computer sheets and/or online.

2. Henceforth, selection of staff for being entrusted with special pay carrying posts shall be on the basis of their suitability for the specialized function, norms for which shall be decided at the bank level.

Special Pay Carrying Positions in Subordinate Cadre

Liftman	Persons required to operate the lifts on regular assignment
Cash Peon	Persons required 1. To take money orders, to buy stamps etc., which involves carrying of cash not exceeding Rs.5,000/- and to carry insured letters., etc to post office 2. To stitch currency note bundles. 3. To stitch and seal parcels and packets containing currency notes; 4. To transit cash from the bank to an office outside or vice versa, if unaccompanied by a watchman/ Armed Guard.
Watchman	Persons other than "Armed Guards" who are required to perform watch and ward duties i.e to watch or look after the premises or a department, for the purposes of its safety, security and guard against infiltration and against removal of the bank's property by any unauthorized person and/or to watch and guard as above, the movement of cash from one place to another inside the bank premises or outside where an Armed Guard is not employed at the Branch/ Office.
Armed Guard	Persons required to perform watch and ward duties i.e. to watch or look after the premises or department for the purposes of its safety, security and guard against attack or assault or infiltration and against removal of the bank's property by any unauthorized persons and/or to watch and guard as above the movement of cash from one place to another whether inside or outside the bank, for which purpose they are required by the bank to carry any of the following weapons: 1. Gun, Pistol or any other fire arms; or 2. Dagger, sword, khukri or spear; or 3. Any other licensed weapon

Note: "Retainers" Peons (other than watchmen) whose names are registered in the bank's license as Retainers will, when they perform "Armed Guard" duties, be entitled to special pay for "Armed Guards" pro rata.

Daftary

Their work involves:

1. Obtaining acceptance of bills of exchange, hundies etc., drawn on local parties or banks and/or collecting payments thereof.
2. Collecting payments for cheques or postal order etc., from banks or post office counters. They may also be required to collect cash not exceeding Rs. 5,000/- at a time against various instruments.
3. Simple binding of books and registers;
4. Press copying;
5. Filling independently letters and other papers in respective files as per indications marked thereon;
6. Assisting in issuing stationery;
7. Stacking under guidance old records in orderly manner and assisting in giving them out when required and
8. Undertaking the whole process of sorting, arranging, numbering, tallying and total number or stitching the vouchers.

Head Peon

Persons required to assist in supervision of various matters pertaining to subordinate staff like;

1. Cleanliness of the office premises;
2. Cleanliness of uniforms;
3. Leave arrangements;
4. Arrangements for safekeeping of keys; and
5. Distribution of duties amongst the subordinate staff.

Air-Conditioning Plant Helper

Semi skilled persons who under the supervision of the technician attend to routine maintenance of and minor repairs to air conditioning plants.

Electrician	Their work involves carrying out semi-skilled electrical work like routine maintenance of electrical equipments, effecting minor repairs to electrical fixtures and appliances.
Drivers	Persons required to drive, maintain and effect minor repairs (not requiring a technician's skill) to motor cars, motor vans, station, wagons, scooters, motor cycles or other motor vehicles,
Head Messenger	
In IOB	

Appendix-II

Restrictive Practices

The parties agree to adopting a joint declaration as per Annexure I given herein below:

PREAMBLE- The IBA, AIBEA and NCBE are in full agreement that no efforts should be spared by them to ensure efficient, courteous and speedy customer service in the banking industry. With this common objective in view, some 'restrictive practices' were gone into jointly. The unions do not accept that there are any such practices. It is admitted by both sides that the details of situations or circumstances in which certain incidents might have taken place are not available and hence they cannot be gone into in detail. The unions, however, make it clear that it has never been the intention of the unions to indulge in any restrictive practices. The IBA concedes that in view of the size of the industry, there are difficulties in attaining perfection in the matter of control of the large work force and also of regulations and distribution of work at all the offices in the country. Both IBA and the Unions agree that much depends on the climate that develops and the relations that are built at the various offices by mutual understanding and respect for each other's difficulties.

Accordingly, the IBA, AIBEA and NCBE jointly express themselves on the issues as under:

(1) It is for the management to distribute the work equitably amongst the employees with a view to ensuring that every one has a full day's work. Adjustments would, however, become necessary in the day-to-day working of the offices and, in the interest of smooth working, the workmen should carry out all reasonable orders of the local management. The workmen would, however, be free to take up with the management any genuine difficulty in this

behalf. The question of fixing any arbitrary ceiling on quantum of work by the employees themselves does not, however, arise.

(2) While the services of senior employees would generally be utilized on desks requiring experience and knowledge, no one should refuse to work on any desk in exigencies that may arise.

(3) Allotment of ledger/s to ledger keepers would depend on the number of transactions and the volume of work and not on the number of transactions and the volume of work and not on the number of ledgers. Accordingly, it may be justifiable and necessary to allot more than one ledger whether in current Account, Cash Credit, Demand Loan etc.

(4) Employees with double designations such as Clerk-Typist, Cash-Cum-Clerk. Etc., may be asked to perform both the duties on the same day. It would, however, be ensured that they are not subjected to frequent changes of work on the same day. Where an employee who is handling cash is asked to work outside cash section he should be given time to tally and hand over his cash.

(5) Where volume of cash work is not heavy, a cashier may be required to work both as a Paying and Receiving Cashier.

(6) Go-down-keepers attached to branches may be required to perform clerical duties whenever they are free from go-down work.

(7) The system of checking payment made by an employee by another employee and of entrusting the job of issuing tokens exclusively to an employee, are prevailing only in certain banks at certain centers The Managements may decide on their own about the necessity of continuance or otherwise of these systems.

(8) On special occasions it might be necessary to attend to cash transactions outside business hours. However, due care and caution should be exercised by managements in entertaining such late transactions, such later transactions should be duly authorized by a competent official.

(9) Normally cash should be accepted/paid at the cash counter. But the employees should accept/make payment of cash other than at cash counters under instructions from a competent official in special circumstances and in such cases the concerned employees would be granted immunity from attendant risks.

(10) The work of clerks posted in administrative offices includes drafting of letters, dealing with correspondence, etc. Similar work

of a routine nature should be performed by clerks posted in branches/departments and offices other than administrative offices.

(11) The balancing of ledgers/registers and calculations of monthly products/interest, etc., should not be claimed as work to be necessarily and essentially performed only outside normal working hours.

(12) Improvement in working in bank's branches/offices, etc.

1. Having regard to the vital role of the banking industry in the national economy and the various social and economic responsibilities including implementation of national programmes they have been entrusted with from time to time, parties agree that there is need to improve housekeeping in the offices/branches of banks throughout the country, to ensure efficient, cordial and speedy customer service at all times in the banking industry and to promote harmonious industrial relations and better discipline at all levels.

2. (a) Every workman shall take all possible steps to ensure and protect the interest of the bank and discharge his duties with utmost integrity, honesty, devotion and diligence.

(b) Every workman shall be at his place of work, commence the allotted work at the time fixed and notified, work for the full prescribed hours of work and give maximum output.

3. Unions agree that the authority of the branch manager/officer-in-charge in matters like deployment of staff from time to time and enforcement of rules of the bank in the matter of discipline, customer service and the like, shall be respected by all workmen so as to ensure that the day-to-day smooth and efficient functioning of the branch/office/department is not adversely affected. If, however, there be any grievances or dissatisfaction in regard to the handling of such matters by the branch manager or any other authority, the matter shall be resolved amicably through mutual discussions with the branch manager or the authority concerned either by the aggrieved workman himself or by the office bearer (s) of the concerned union or its unit avoiding dislocation of customer service.

Managements discourage abuse of authority on the part of any branch manager or other authority concerned.

Unions deprecate use of any violence or abusive language or vulgar slogans by name against individual officers or their family members.

Appendix-III

Unauthorized Absence from Duty–Consolidation of IBA's Guidelines

It is not unusual for bank managements to deal with cause of employees on unauthorized absence from duty. Normally unauthorized absence from duty should attract wage-out and appropriate disciplinary action. At times the management may condone unauthorized absence to the extent of no disciplinary action and may effect only wage-out for the day(s) of absence. There could also be occasions when an employee is compelled to abstain from work for reasons beyond his control. The management may in some of such circumstances, as an exception, agree not to effect wage-cut and regularize the absence by grant of appropriate leave, and on very rare occasions even by grant of special leave.

How to treat the involuntary absence from duty is a matter which has been discussed on a number of occasions at the industry level and the out-come is consolidate here below under different headings of eventualities so that there is no difficulty in observing the principles involved uniformly.[1]

(1)	Bundhs	(i)	No.PD/76/Q/1882 dated 22.10.1983
		(ii)	No.PD/CIR/76/Q/H/787 dated 15.4.1986
(2)	Strikes/agitations etc.	(i)	No.PD/CIR/76/H(i)/2442 dated 4.11.1985
		(ii)	No.PD/CIR/76/Q/4783 dated 24.11.1986
(3)	Curfew	(i)	No.PD/MISC/33 dated 18-11-1981

	(ii)	No. PD/CIR/76/Q/H(iv)/4016 dated 12.9.1986
(4)	Floods	(i) No. PD/MISC/10 dated 10.1.1983
(5)	Breakdown o public transport system or any other control of the bank.	(i) No. PD/76?H/2392 dated 21.7.1981
(6)	Absence of employees for part of the day	(i) No.PD/CE/6 dated 2.12.1982 (ii) No.1BA/Bolc/93/6988 dated 15.2.1993.

Guidelines

(A) Absence of employees on account of curfew:

(i) Where a bank office is kept closed for the day

If a bank office remains closed on account of a curfew order imposed during the entire working hours, the employees should be given special casual leave for the day

(ii) Where a bank office is kept closed for part of the day

If curfew is imposed only for part of the day and therefore the bank office is kept closed for part of the working hours, the employees who attend office during the hours the office is kept open should be treated as having attended the office for the full day. The absence of employees who do not attend office during the time it is open should be adjusted against their appropriate leave account.

(iii) Where the bank office remains open

Where an employee is unable to attend office on account of imposition of curfew at the place of residence or at the place which falls on way to the bank office, his absence could be treated as a special casual leave. Special casual leave in such cases would be permissible only if it is physically impossible for the employee to report for duty. No special casual leave should be given if it is possible for him to reach the office by a circuitous route avoiding curfew bound area or if special permission has been given by the Government authorities to move through the curfew bound areas for to and fro journeys to the bank/office, on production of identity cards etc.

(B) Absence of bank employees due to natural calamities or civil commotion or any other cause beyond the control of the Bank

If the closure of the bank is necessitated for reasons of natural calamities such as fire, rains, deluge or civil disturbance such as riots or any other cause beyond the control of the Bank, only appropriate leave including casual leave, but not special leave, should be granted to bank employees in terms of Paragraph 511 of the Sastry Award.

(C) Absence of employees due to Bundh, Morcha, Strike, Rail/Rasta Roko, etc. organized by various Political/religious and other parties, unconnected with the banking industry.

(i) In all cases where the Bundh etc, is supported/co-sponsored or actively assisted by bank employees or their affiliated Union/Association action should be taken against employees who absent themselves from duty by effecting 'Wage-Cut' on the basis of the principle 'No Work No Pay', in addition to any action the management may like to take as per the service rules.

(ii) In all cases where the Bundh etc, is not supported/co-sponsored or actively assisted by bank employees or their affiliated Union/Association, if an absenting employee gives a letter stating that he was not a member of any Union/Organization which gave a call for the Bundh etc., and he did not participate in the Bundh etc., but was prevented from attending office due to non-availability/disruption of transport facilities, physical obstruction or other ilegimate reasons, his appropriate leave account may be debited.

(D) Absence of employees during strike/agitation, etc.,

If there is a call for strike given by any union of bank employees and an employee remains absent on the strike day he should be deemed to be on strike and his wages for the day should not be paid on the principle of 'no work no pay', in addition to any action the management may like to take as per the Service Rules.

If on the day of the strike, a particular office of a bank remains locked, the absence of the employees who were not on strike should be regularized as special casual leave by an authority not lower than the Deputy General Manager subject to fulfillment of the following conditions:

(a) If the employee is a member of the union which has given a call for strike, he should advise the bank in writing before the strike day that although he is a member of the union which has given a call for strike, he has no intention to go on strike.

(b) A letter by the employee, even if he is covered by (a) above stating that he was not on strike and he had come to attend the office in the usual manner but could not do so as all the doors were locked.

(c) If it is established that even one or two employees were able to enter the office and the doors were opened any time before the close of business hours, special leave should not be given to those who did not enter the office.

(E) Absence of employees for part of the day

Wherever employees without prior permission of the management go on agitation of any form during office hours, they will have to be treated as having committed breach of contract of service and the principle of 'no work no pay' should uniformly apply subject to the decisions of the Court if any. Even where an employee is in breach of his contract for part of the day, he will not earn wages for the full day subject to the condition that the bank does not acquiesce in the breach by taking work from such employee for the rest of the way. In such a in such a care should be taken to give an intimation to the employees sufficiently in advance, through a notice which may be displayed or circulated, that no further work is expected of them for the rest of the day. In a 'no work no pay' situation, the question of deduction of wages does not arise as the employees have not earned wages, as normal work in the normal manner in accordance with the contract of employment which is a condition precedent for earning wages has not been satisfied. Banks should also ensure that appropriate adjustments are made at the time of disbursing the salary for that month.

Clearing house is considered as an extension of the Bank, the non-participation of employees in clearing (whether on account of picketing or for other reasons) may be dealt as follows:

(1) Where the employees could not participate in the clearing since the doors of the clearing house were not opened by the Management any time during the day and a letter is given by the employees that they did not disrupt the clearing house functioning and they had come to attend the clearing house in the usual manner but could not do so as all the doors were locked, the absence may be treated as special leave.

(2) In all other case the non-participation of employees in clearing house operation may be treated as unauthorized and full day's wage cut may be effected.

Note

1. See IBA circular.